Private Lives, Public Conflicts

DATE DUE

SEP

Private Lives, Public Conflicts

Battles over Gay Rights in American Communities

James W. Button
University of Florida

Barbara A. Rienzo
University of Florida

Kenneth D. Wald
University of Florida

Foreword by Representative Barney Frank

A Division of Congressional Quarterly Inc.
Washington, D.C.

Printed and bound in the United States of America

Cover design: Paula Anderson

Photo credits—Front cover: Black Starr/Martin A. Levick *(top);* Michael Jenkins,
Congressional Quarterly *(middle);* Lenny Gonzalez *(bottom).* Back cover: Ricardo Ferro and
Fred Victorin, *St. Petersburg Times* and *Evening Independent.*

The paper used in this publication meets the minimum requirements of the American
National Standard for Information Science—Permanence of Paper for Printed Library
Materials, ANSI Z39.48-1984.

Library of Congress Cataloging-in-Publication Data

Button, James W., 1942–
    Private lives, public conflicts : battles over gay rights in
  American communities / James W. Button, Barbara A. Rienzo, Kenneth
  D. Wald; foreword by Barney Frank.
      p.   cm.
    Includes bibliographical references and index.
    ISBN 1-56802-279-4 (cloth). -- ISBN 1-56802-278-6 (pbk.)
    1. Gay rights--United States. 2. Gay men--Legal status, laws,
  etc.--United States. 3. Lesbians--Legal status, laws, etc.--United
  States. 4. Homosexuality--Government policy--United States.
  5. United States--Politics and government--1989- 6. United States-
  -Social conditions--1980- I. Rienzo, Barbara Ann. II. Wald, Kenneth D. III. Title.
  HQ76.8.U5B87   1997
  323.3'264--DC21   96-53442

To our parents, Frederick, Frank and Alberta, and our sons, Matt and Adam,
whose love and support are continual and invaluable
—JWB and BAR

To Curt and Regina Schönwald, of blessed memory
—KDW

CONTENTS

FOREWORD

This book is useful in several ways. First, by analyzing the varying degrees of success met by people seeking to persuade local governments to adopt policies protective of the rights of lesbians and gay men, it provides a useful look at how democracy actually functions. Often, critics of the way in which the political process functions in America argue not simply that the outcomes of that process are disappointing but that the process itself is so flawed that even trying to influence it through democratic participation is a waste of time.

This is, of course, a sad example of a self-fulfilling prophecy. Tell the people most interested in influencing government that democracy is a sham, that public policy decisions are controlled by an unapproachable, uninfluenceable elite, and that money and not votes dictates the outcomes and you help persuade them that participation in the political process is useless.

This book documents that determined, thoughtful citizens who care about particular issues can and do make a real difference—that democracy works, for those who understand its workings and are prepared to commit themselves to the effort necessary. The authors show that in substantial part local policies opposing discrimination against gay people have resulted when lesbians, gay men, and our allies use our rights as citizens in a democracy—when we out-organize, outargue, and outvote the opposition. Notable by its absence here is a controlling role for money. Campaign contributions have obviously played a part, but the authors conclude that political participation and, particularly, the numbers and political skills of the various actors have been the major determinants of these outcomes.

Second, that lesbians and gay men have been able to use the political process to advance the fight against homophobia is an important lesson in itself. Democracy, the authors show, not only works much of the time but it works in many cases for those who have been victimized by antihomosexual prejudice.

Although this may seem an obvious conclusion to many, for a long time it was not at all obvious within the gay community. Indeed, the argument that gay men and lesbians would profit from engaging in the sort of conventional political activity documented here has been a controversial one. This is not surprising. For most of American history—indeed for much of the history of the entire world—the political process has not only not been welcoming to homosexuals, it has been quite hostile.

Public policy at the national and state levels was until fairly recently explicitly antihomosexual in many respects. And the earliest efforts to change this state of affairs were complicated by the response most lesbians and gay men made to this hostility for most of our history—we hid. We avoided the penalty of antigay prejudice by concealing from most people—often including each other—that we were who we were.

Consequently, when a combination of America's increased sensitivity to the issues of unfair discrimination and the determination of many lesbians and gay men to challenge antigay prejudice led to the gay activism of the early 1970s, there was no consensus as to what form that activism should take. Several factors made conventional political activity—registering voters, voting, supporting friendly candidates, lobbying elected officials, and the like—the distinctly unfavored method of choice. Not only was it the experience of the overwhelming majority of gay men and lesbians that mainstream America was hostile and that electoral majorities would be therefore very hard to muster, there existed, especially for the earliest activists, an obvious alternative: what can best be described as cultural politics.

The very fact that lesbians and gay men had hidden their sexual orientation from most other people was correctly seen as part of the problem we faced in confronting homophobia. Thus, for gay men and lesbians, unlike other minorities, simply announcing the fact of our existence, both as a group and as individuals, became political activity in the broadest sense. This explains the role of "gay pride" celebrations in the earliest days of gay organizing. Simply announcing our presence by marching through the streets identifying ourselves was an obvious, dramatic challenge to a homophobic status quo.

This demonstrative, cultural phase of gay and lesbian activity was an important one. There was a very real role to be played in efforts to end the silence by and about us that had long existed. But this sort of announcement of our presence was never a substitute for the kind of sustained political activity that is described in this book. By now it is clear that significant gains will come only when the latter form of activity becomes dominant.

Unfortunately, cultural self-expression is more fun than conventional political work. Defying prejudice in colorful and expressive ways brings a good deal more immediate satisfaction than registering voters, lobbying public officials, educating people who may genuinely be ignorant about the realities of the prejudice facing gay men and lesbians, and campaigning for candidates who, while significantly better than their opponents on the issues of sexual orientation discrimination, are far from perfect.

As a result, many gay men and lesbians remained committed to cultural self-expression as the primary form of political activity far longer than made strategic sense. Once again it is significant what the studies in this book do not report—in no case do the authors attribute the successful adoption of policies supportive of the rights of gay men or lesbians to marches, demonstrations, or other cultural activities. In every case it was ultimately the willingness and ability of committed opponents of homophobia to use the political process that brought about victory.

This does not mean that the expressive activities have no value. Some excesses in public acting out have done damage, but on the whole cultural self-expression has been an indispensable part of the organizing within the gay and lesbian community that is a prerequisite for effective political action. Rather, the problem has been that too many people have seen the cultural activity as a substitute for democratic political participation. In too many cases over the past decades we have left the political arena to our most dedicated opponents, whose letter writing, phone calling, and lobbying have easily triumphed over our marching, demonstrating, and dancing. The most important lesson of this book for people who want to make America a fairer place is that politics—conventional, boring, but essential politics—will ultimately have a major impact on the extent to which we can rid our lives of prejudice.

Third, the authors convincingly demonstrate the fallacy of the argument that laws, ordinances, and rules are of no avail in protecting the victims of prejudice. Their conclusion that gay rights laws and school policies that protect students against homophobia play a real role in diminishing discrimination is an important one. Again, this may seem an obvious conclusion to some, but those who have participated in political efforts to win passage of antidiscrimination legislation know that the argument that prejudice is invulnerable to law often becomes one of the obstacles that must be overcome. The conclusion of these authors about the effect of the policies they have documented will help us do that.

And finally, as in each of the other cases, there is importance in what the authors did not find, as well as what they did find. In every debate in which I have been involved where some of us have sought to adopt policies banning discrimination of a particular kind, our opponents have predicted chaos and upheaval if we were successful. Opponents of antidiscrimination laws have consistently argued that the cost of compliance will be enormous, that legitimate social mores will be undermined, that children will be assailed by various illegitimate forces. As the authors show, none of the ill effects conjured up by opponents of gay rights laws appear ever to have come to pass in any of the communities they studied. Morality was no worse off after than before; children in these communities were in no more jeopardy of being mistreated after the laws were passed or the school policies enacted than before; businesses were in no case burdened by any significant economic cost; and the general demeanor of the people living in the communities appears to have undergone no significant change. It is not only gay rights laws that have been opposed by people making widely exaggerated predictions of social disorder—in my experience similar arguments have been made against laws seeking to protect racial minorities, women, and people with disabilities. In no case have ill effects remotely approaching those predicted come true, but it is rare that analysts have taken the trouble to document that. By including a study of the effects of the passage of these policies in their work, and by finding none of the negative effects that opponents had claimed would occur, the authors have contributed to our understanding here as well.

Given the total domination of our society by homophobic prejudice until fairly recently, this book would not have been possible twenty-five years ago, since there would have been virtually no activity to write about. Given the progress I believe we are making now in combating homophobia, twenty-five years from now no such activity is likely to be necessary. But in this particular time, understanding how in a democracy one best deals with antigay and lesbian prejudice is extremely important, which is why this book is such a welcome one.

Representative Barney Frank

PREFACE

The issue of basic rights for gays and lesbians has generated one of the most volatile conflicts in recent American politics. Although the literature on sexual politics is extensive and growing, few authors have explored the battle over gay rights laws or the impact of such struggles on public schools. As a rule, these local conflicts do not attract the same level of media attention as the debate over gays in the military, the possibility of same-sex marriages, or other highly charged national controversies involving sexual orientation. Yet the local conflicts may well affect the daily lives of gays and lesbians more than the events that draw national headlines. This book is an attempt to fill this gap.

Apart from its subject matter, the book has several distinguishing features. First, it combines data from a broad survey of public officials throughout the country with the results of intensive study of five representative cities. This combination of quantitative data from a national survey and information gleaned from lengthy personal interviews permits us to offer broad generalizations and to explore the meaning of those grand hypotheses in more intimate detail. Second, unlike studies that concentrate solely on community conflict, policy adoption, or program implementation, the book includes an examination of all phases of local antidiscrimination laws that cover sexual orientation. We are interested in why communities consider and choose to adopt such policies, how such laws are written and enforced, and, equally important, how and why they are resisted with such vehemence. We also want to know how such laws affect public schools, key battlegrounds in the struggle over homosexuality. To understand the gay rights conflict requires paying attention to each of these facets. Third, this book approaches the subject from the theoretical perspectives of social science. The politics of gay rights undoubtedly differ in many ways from most other political conflicts, implying perhaps that they stand outside the theoretical models employed by political scientists. But rather than concede that claim, we think it important to recognize that community battles over sexual orientation also resemble other types of political conflict. Accordingly, to make sense of the phenomenon under investigation, we have followed relevant approaches suggested by scholars in urban studies, social movements, public policy, minority politics, religion and politics, and the politics of education. These approaches have helped us better understand the local gay rights battles, and in turn, studying the gay rights campaign has suggested some ways to improve theories of the political process.

Another unique feature of the book is its interdisciplinary nature. The book is a collaborative effort of three scholars with expertise in the areas of minority group and urban politics (Button), sexuality education and school health programs (Rienzo), and religion and politics (Wald). These scholarly interests attracted us to this project and account for particular features of the study. None of us had prior experience studying gay politics or was gay affiliated. That does not mean we lacked opinions, of course, but it meant those opinions were not sustained by first-hand observation. Although our outsider status may have blinded us to certain distinctions, we suspect that it has also given us some freshness of insight. As our goal has not been advocacy but understanding, we have tried to empathize with both the advocates and opponents of gay rights legislation. At the least we hope we have brought greater clarity to a complex and emotionally charged issue.

In a sense that Tennessee Williams could surely never have intended, this study depended on the kindness of strangers. Our research design assumed the willingness of local informants to speak frankly to a team of outside scholars, and our confidence was vindicated. Altogether almost five hundred busy officials took the time to reply thoughtfully to our mail survey of municipal governments and school districts. They were joined by dozens of local experts—public officials, gay activists, religious leaders, members of the business community, party activists, school personnel—who granted us lengthy and informative interviews in Cincinnati, Iowa City, Philadelphia, Raleigh, and Santa Cruz. Some also responded to follow-up telephone inquiries. The cooperation of local news reporters and newspapers that made their files available to us supplemented these efforts.

In the course of this study, we received advice and counsel from a wide array of scholars and advocates. Without in any way associating them with our interpretations, we want to thank Robert Bailey, John D'Emilio, David Leege, Kenneth Meier, Morgan Pigg, Kenneth Sherrill, and the anonymous reviewers who read our proposal and complete manuscript. The International City/County Management Association generously provided its database of municipalities and counties. This study was made possible by a research grant from the Division of Sponsored Research at the University of Florida. We are grateful to both the review committee and the appropriate administrators for judging the proposal on its scholarly merit rather than on the political controversy surrounding the subject. Precisely because the subject is so controversial, we must emphasize that the opinions, arguments, and claims in this book are those of the authors and do not represent the institution that employs and funds us.

We were fortunate to have the help of a dedicated and talented crew of graduate research assistants. The work of John Auman, Holly Brasher, Rika Canin, Sean McKenzie, Michele Johnson Moore, Scott Richards, Peter

Von Doepp, and Lori Wirth enabled us to conduct the research for this book.

We especially want to thank the staff of CQ Books. Working with Brenda Carter has been a wonderful pleasure for us. Likewise, we have been pleased and grateful for the professional service of a superb copy editor, Joanne S. Ainsworth.

Finally, the fieldwork for and writing of this book have provided us with a wonderful journey, one filled with excitement and learning that comes with the exploration of new areas and concepts. We would like to express our deepest gratitude to our friends in Gainesville and to our families, who no doubt grew weary of listening to our latest ideas but were always helpful, loving, and supportive.

CHAPTER 1

Identity Politics, Law, and Policy Innovation

No issue seems to divide Western society more passionately and more deeply than homosexuality.
—Andrew Sullivan, *Virtually Normal: An Argument about Homosexuality*

The Reverend Fred Phelps, pastor of a small Baptist church in Topeka, Kansas, is on a mission. He is challenging homosexuals who want to "force their unnatural, God-defying lifestyle down our throats." As part of this mission, he organizes a daily protest outside a downtown restaurant managed by a prominent Topeka lesbian. Greeting her with shouts, threats, and signs proclaiming "God Hates Fags" and "No Tears for Queers," Pastor Phelps accuses the manager and "fag cooks" of deliberately planting the HIV virus in the restaurant's meat dishes. The target of this effort, the restaurant manager, reports that she has been stalked and her home and property vandalized. Phelps also picketed the funeral of a male AIDS victim he described as a "filthy dead sodomite." Before the funeral, Phelps accused the parents of the dead man of killing their son by raising him to be a homosexual.[1]

Every few years, advocates for gay and lesbian rights stage a march on Washington, a mass protest demanding that the federal government expand legal protection for homosexuality. At the 1993 gathering, the marchers included bearded men dressed as nuns, assorted drag queens, bare-breasted women walking arm in arm, and leather-clad sadomasochists armed with whips, chains, and cattle prods. Under banners reading "Fags 4 Ever" and "Queer Nation," demonstrators threatened to throw bombs if their demands went unmet and chanted in unison, "F—k the church, F—k the state, Hormones will decide our fate!" Others cheered enthusiastically for a speaker who had previously suggested the need for an AIDS army to terrorize the government into spending more on medical research. In public parks along the parade route, some participants sprawled on the ground, groping and writhing in simulated and real sex acts, while others attended "marriage" ceremonies for threesomes of men and women.[2]

In wildly exaggerated form, these two portraits illustrate the extreme emotions and vivid images that suffuse the issue of homosexuality in America. Both images are caricatures, selected by each side to portray the other as repulsive and beyond the pale. The antics of one marginal and unbalanced minister do not even represent the position of his own denomination, which has pointedly condemned Rev. Phelps's words and actions. By the same token, the fringe groups depicted in the Washington march no more represent the mainstream of the gay and lesbian community than do similar exotic groups among heterosexuals. To more objective observers, the hundreds of thousands of people at the 1993 march for equality appeared mainly middle class and thoroughly conventional. Distorting more than they enlighten, such polarizing images prove useful in times of war when the objective is to inflame the public and deny the very humanity of the opponent. Not by coincidence, both Rev. Phelps and speakers at the 1993 March on Washington likened their efforts to a war.

Even though our book focuses on somewhat less dramatic efforts to amend local government laws and policies, it is important not to lose sight of the deep moral concern that churns beneath public debates about sexuality in the United States. For all of Fred Phelps's excesses, his hostility to homosexuality represents a widely shared point of view. At various times, homosexuality has been treated by experts as a sin, an illness, a crime, a genetic defect, a mental disorder, and a learning disability.[3] To judge by public opinion surveys, ordinary citizens have shared the same pronounced distaste for gay people.[4] To summarize a vast array of polling material, gays are perceived as people who have chosen to pursue an unhealthy and immoral lifestyle, whose code of behavior makes them unfit to occupy many important positions in society. For example, homosexual conduct is regarded as "always wrong" by two-thirds to three-fourths of the adult population, and the prospect of contact with gays inspires discomfort among many heterosexuals. Believing that gays are likely to "recruit" or molest children, the public is decidedly hostile to the notion of putting gays in positions of direct contact with children as teachers or as adoptive parents. This produces ferocious opposition to proposals to provide education about homosexuality in the public school curriculum. Short of "welfare queens," it is hard to find another group that is so unpopular in the American mind.[5]

Despite public antagonism to gays, many Americans nonetheless recognize that "there is a difference between telling people that an active homosexual life is sinful and telling them that they should support criminal sanctions for that behavior."[6] This distinction grows out of a strong commitment to human rights and individual freedom in the American political culture. Therefore, most Americans do not favor criminal penalties for homosexual conduct and have increasingly adopted a live-and-let-live mentality toward gays and lesbians. Without abandoning the view that homosexuality represents deviant behavior, most Americans now perceive gay people as a minority group that needs legal protection from discrimination. During the 1992 presidential campaign, large majorities of adult Americans reported that they favored laws forbidding job discrimination against homosexuals and permitting gays and lesbians to serve in the armed forces.[7] Thus, the hostility to gays as practitioners of deviant behavior is mitigated somewhat by the widespread belief that discrimination is generally wrong.

For the past quarter of a century, gays, lesbians, and bisexuals have sought to draw on the American belief in equality, forging a legal shield against the hostility reflected in Pastor Phelps's words. In some instances, the goal of this movement has been literal protection—to be achieved by including verbal and physical assaults on gays and lesbians among those actions known as hate crimes. Gays have also sought to remove the threat of legal persecution by persuading states to repeal antisodomy laws and to disregard sexual orientation in child-custody proceedings. The effort to eliminate the military's ban on gay service represents a less defensive posture and a greater emphasis on opening up opportunities to the gay community. These activities at the state and national levels have at times received more publicity than the simultaneous crusade to prohibit antigay discrimination at the local level. We often associate local government with basic services like garbage collection, road paving, sewer maintenance, police protection, and the running of elementary schools. Although not without controversy, these services rarely induce much public outrage. But increasingly, these same local governments have been forced to confront the rancorous politics of "gay rights" by considering local laws and regulations designed to fight discrimination based on sexual orientation. Because of the public's hostility to gays and lesbians, however, efforts to combat such discrimination have often unleashed firestorms of local conflict.

When, for example, the commissioners of Alachua County (located in rural north Florida) considered an ordinance that prohibited discrimination against gays in housing or employment, they received an avalanche of telephone calls, faxes, and letters. The public hearing on the ordinance drew the largest crowd of any local issue in living memory, forcing the County Commission to broadcast the proceedings to an overflow crowd packed into a nearby auditorium. Immediately upon passage of the bill by a narrow 3–2 vote, the opponents announced their intention to put the issue to a public referendum and easily obtained the 6,000 signatures needed to force a vote. During the campaign, the community was blanketed with leaflets, barraged with full-page newspaper ads and letters to the editor, confronted by energetic canvassers walking door to door, and exposed to a seemingly endless array of press conferences. To support their efforts, the two sides raised and spent the kind of money normally reserved for congressional elections. The opponents of the new law warned that the legislation would force day care centers to hire homosexuals and lead to citizens being fined or imprisoned for refusing to hire or rent to homosexuals. The supporters countered with strong statements of support from Jesse Jackson and Coretta Scott King, the widow of Martin Luther King. Even in a community with a rich history of citizen activism, this degree of popular mobilization was not politics as normal. In the end, a county known for its political liberalism rejected decisively the antidiscrimination protection for gays and lesbians.

Hundreds of American communities have similarly grappled with questions about the degree that local laws and policies should provide civil rights protection on the basis of sexual orientation. In some places, such laws have been passed and sustained with virtually no public comment. Elsewhere, as in the Alachua County story, laws have been passed by local government officials and quickly overturned in heated public referendums. Many communities have decided against taking action, and some cities and towns, not content to refrain from action, have gone on record with ordinances condemning homosexuality as behavior contrary to the standards of the community. Whatever the outcome, the drive for legalized protection against discrimination on the basis of sexual orientation has challenged politics as normal.

Precisely because it is so unusual, the politics of gay rights provides a basis to examine the nature of political life and social change in American local politics. Through both a series of community case studies and a national survey of government officials, this book offers an opportunity to explore three larger themes in American politics: the rise of what has been called "identity" politics, the relationship between law and social change, and models of public policy innovation.

Identity Politics

When we think and talk about "politics as usual," what images come to mind? For most people, *politics* probably evokes institutions like government agencies, political parties and interest groups, processes such as elections and lobbying, or controversies involving taxation, government spending, or regulation. Most of what political scientists study easily fits into these categories. But since the late 1960s and 1970s, this conception of politics has been challenged by another model of political action. Social movements devoted to the interests of women, blacks, and ethnic minorities spawned a type of political conflict known today as identity politics. This style of political conflict is "concerned with the political meanings of everyday life and interpersonal relations, sexuality and subjective experience, lifestyle and popular culture."[8] For all their differences from one another, the new social movements that practice this type of political action have certain common traits. At the risk of considerable oversimplification, the traits that distinguish identity movements from more conventional political efforts can be reduced to three essential qualities.

First, identity politics represents *new lines of political cleavage*. Identity politics is rooted in groups based on "race, ethnicity, gender and sexuality" rather than the traditional group divisions associated with politics—economic classes, interest groups, industries, labor unions, and the like.[9] In organizing on the basis of age, gender, sexual orientation, race, and ethnicity, the advocates of identity politics assert that these group identities are relevant to politics and should not be ignored or denied. We easily recognize that consumers, entrepreneurs, parents of school-age children, taxpayers, labor union members, investors, and highway drivers have distinct interests in certain public policies. Nobody finds it strange or illegitimate for people to band together on the basis of such issues. But when women or racial minorities sought power, many people wondered what common interests could possibly unite such large and diverse categories. According to the theory of identity politics, people may band together on the basis of some seemingly personal or private trait when that quality becomes the basis for the way they are treated by the larger society. Belonging to groups defined by qualities such as gender or race may confer social status or disadvantage, promote common conditions of life, or involve patterns of social behavior that are affected by public policy. These personal traits may prove more compelling as a basis of political identity than the more familiar group identities and economic interests accepted in political debate.

Second, identity politics encompasses *broad goals*—not simply to secure additional economic resources for groups like women, blacks, and Latinos but to ensure that they are accorded a full measure of equality and social respect. Politics is not just about money or regulation or power. Groups may enter political combat to attain recognition and honor or secure the prestige that comes from a place on the public agenda. When social movements develop political programs, the specific elements may be less important than the underlying concern with attaining a place at the table. What is at stake in such conflicts, Kenneth Karst recognizes, is the very meaning of citizenship:

Although the social issues often do implicate interests in the classical sense—the distribution of money or of jobs—their emotional centers lie in cultural symbols. To the extent that law and government officially endorse the values of a cultural group as the "true" American values, the members of that group can feel justified in claiming the status of "true" Americans.[10]

To achieve this end, the groups promote formal representation by making certain that minorities serve on agencies and boards that deal with their concerns. More broadly, the concern for public acceptance may take the form of a contest over the moral authority of different cultural models. In the civil rights movement, blacks sought equality both for its own sake—to enable them to live fuller and more satisfying lives—and as a means of enhancing the dignity and self-respect that come with full citizenship. The movement's aims clashed directly with a more traditional moral code that proclaimed the supremacy of whites and consigned blacks to second-class citizenship. The drive for equality by women similarly entailed a drastic change in public image. Women were no longer to be defined solely as wives and mothers but as people who could choose from a variety of social roles. These efforts were challenged by people—men and women alike—whose moral code allowed women a narrower range of choices.[11]

Finally, the social movements that pursue identity politics typically embrace a *wide array of political tactics.* In addition to the tried and true measures that are the staple of conventional politics—voting, lobbying public officials, passing laws, sponsoring referendums, filing lawsuits—new social movements pick from a broad repertoire of political mobilization techniques that include public demonstrations, sit-ins, boycotts, and various other forms of unconventional protest. Such tactics are appealing to movements that may lack resources like money and expertise but can capitalize on the passions of group members and the empathy of others. Movement activists may turn to unconventional political action because they have been shut out of avenues for traditional forms of political activity. For example, neither blacks nor the young protestors against the Vietnam War could use the electoral process to obtain redress of grievances because access to the ballot was precisely what they lacked. But more than lack of opportunity may account for the decision of many social movements to keep their distance from established advocacy institutions. The movements that emerged in the late 1960s rejected organizational models that stressed hierarchy and centralization in favor of patterns of decentralization that ensured the autonomy of local movements and individuals. Through participation in these groups, many people who had not previously been active underwent something of a political baptism by fire. In the process, they gained power that was eventually used on new issues and controversies, permanently altering the balance of political forces in communities.

Although it is not one of the essential characteristics of identity-based politics, such activity often produces an expanded role for government.[12] The demands of social movements can often be met only if public agencies take on a wider range of responsibilities. To enforce laws against racial discrimination in employment requires the government to monitor and assess the hiring and firing practices of private businesses. When feminists call for action against the sexual and physical abuse of married women by their husbands, this prompts the police and social service agencies to intervene in what had been regarded as the private sphere of married life. Similarly, abortion opponents have called on the government to participate in decisions that have been the province of the pregnant woman and her doctor. In all these cases, achieving a policy aim associated with social identity meant that government would absorb new responsibilities and play an active role in areas once deemed outside the range of public authority.

In describing identity politics as a new type of political action, we should not overstate its departure from older models and methods of analysis. In the first place, the style of politics associated with identity movements is not altogether new. According to some scholars, the most intense political conflicts throughout American history have engaged questions of social identity. That may be obvious for early twentieth-century debates over prohibition and immigration, which represented veiled attacks on Roman Catholics and the foreign-born, but cultural tensions also affected a wide range of issues conventionally thought to involve primarily economic interests. For example, the subject of slavery was deeply salient to many people with no economic stake in the "peculiar institution" because it touched on fundamental values and national identity. In that sense, slavery was as much a cultural conflict as an economic debate. More generally, as we learn from social historians of the nineteenth century, "The matters that touched the voter's daily life and affected his values and life-style were much more likely than others to arouse his concern and evoke a voting response." [13] This sounds a great deal like the style of conflict connected with identity politics.

If it is not new, neither is identity politics wholly different in emphasis from conventional politics. New social movements may crave respect for their constituents, but that goal does not blind them to more tangible objectives. Nor does the allure of unconventional protest mean that such movements refrain from using conventional political methods when those tactics promise success. The mass movements in behalf of African Americans and women, the prototype of identity-based campaigns, sought to give women and blacks better access to economic resources and sought to achieve these goals by passing legislation. The laws that resulted were both remedies for specific grievances and means to the larger goal of achieving full citizenship for blacks and women. All in all, then, it is best to consider identity politics as the result of social movements that give relatively greater emphasis to certain kinds of group division, include social respect as an objective, and are not wedded to any single style of political mobilization.

Does this model of political conflict apply equally well to the local battles over gay rights? The struggle for gay rights chronicled in this book partakes both of identity politics and more conventional forms of political action. On the surface, the campaigns for antidiscrimination laws based on sexual orientation resembled ordinary political movements: individuals united to force passage of laws and regulations by local government agencies. These individuals used a variety of political tactics—influencing election results, lobbying public officials, swaying public opinion—and sought to use the law to make material improvements in their condition. The end product envisioned by the gay rights movement was concrete government activity, ordinances and policies that enjoined public officials and private citizens from discriminatory acts. But we also recognize the hallmarks of identity politics in the movement for gay rights. Those involved in the campaigns asserted that a social identity long regarded as illegitimate was in fact deserving of protection by the state. The core of that identity was "a worldview out of which alternatives to the nuclear family have been forged and which regards sexuality as not only a key aspect of both personal and group identity but as existing more for pleasure than for procreation." [14] The claim for public action rested on the belief that lesbians and gays faced a common threat of discrimination by virtue of their identity as gay people. The threats to the security of gays ranged from scattered incidents of verbal harassment to murderous physical assaults. While sexual orientation was on one level a private matter, it became grist for public action when gay people asserted a need for legal protection from harassment and discrimination.

The campaigns for gay rights also exemplified the concern for public respect that signifies identity politics. The movement in behalf of these ordinances and policies, although it focused on specific acts of discrimination in employment, housing, and other domains, was also fueled by a desire to attain public recognition of the legitimacy of gays and lesbians and their right to the same privileges and protections enjoyed by other Americans. For a group that faced enormous social pressure to keep its identity secret, the campaigns for civil rights were not simply a drive to challenge legal barriers but part of a broader movement to achieve social respect. In the final sign that they were a form of identity politics, the campaigns for gay rights used a wider range of political strategies than are customarily deployed in local political conflict.

The distinctive political qualities surrounding the issue of gay rights were also revealed by the nature of the opposition to the antidiscrimination ordinances and policies. The proponents of the issue were unusual by virtue of using *sexual orientation* as a basis for political mobilization in local politics. By the same token, the leading opponents of including sexual orientation as a category in antidiscrimination law were also defined by a trait seldom seen as relevant to local politics—religious identity. These opponents claimed to speak for the large majority of the community, a population they described with adjectives such as *pro-family* or *traditional* or *old-fashioned.*

On both sides, then, the conflict over gay rights conferred political relevance on social identities that are not normally invoked in local politics. The opponents also recognized that the stakes of the conflict went far beyond the specific laws and regulations under discussion. Rather, they portrayed the proposed ordinances and policies as the thin edge of the wedge, with the ultimate objective being society's endorsement of homosexual conduct as fully equivalent to heterosexuality. The conflict was often framed as a battle for cultural superiority in which the community could choose between "a lifestyle that is unhealthy, unnatural and unworthy" or a social order based on "the sanctity of marriage." [15] Critics of gay rights believe "that the values that form the core of who they are, their beliefs, their visions of goodness and truth, and their very modes of living are being threatened to an extent not unlike that which brought about the demise of the biblical Sodom and Gomorrah." [16] The details of the proposals might well be lost in this larger debate over cultural authority. In the same way that proponents of gay rights adopted a range of tactics to prosecute their claims, the opponents also brought new techniques of mobilization to the battle. In the controversy over gays in the military, for example, the opponents flooded the White House and Congress with thousands of messages mobilized by call-ins to television and radio evangelists, "900" telephone numbers, fax machines, messages in church bulletins, and other communication networks. [17]

As with many conflicts rooted in social identity and contested by social movements, the gay rights struggle also raised the question of the proper role of government in society. Some of the most modest state and local laws dealing with gay rights, issued mostly by executive orders and some formal legislation, restricted only the actions of government itself. But more commonly, the proposed legislation empowered government to prohibit discrimination in a wide variety of social practices and private agencies. These laws provided the government with an extended set of responsibilities and, in some communities, appeared to equip public agencies with strong enforcement capacity. The debate over gay rights was not simply a dispute over the rights of gays, lesbians, and bisexuals but also a broader referendum on the role that government should play. Many critics of gay rights ordinances, particularly from local business communities, argued that they did not oppose gay rights on principle but objected to expanding the scope of government authority to yet another area. Although gay rights advocates called on government to broaden efforts to restrict discrimination, they also wanted public officials to cease attempting to regulate intimate behavior and invading their privacy.

Whatever its resemblance to other political debates, then, the conflict over gay rights is not politics as usual. When he commented that "some issues are intrinsically harder to be reasonable about than others," one scholar might have been thinking about the battles surrounding the gay rights campaign. [18] The passion that animates the competing sides in a moral struggle sometimes threatens to overwhelm the capacity of government to maintain social order.

The issue of gay rights, like community conflicts over abortion, pornography, hate speech, book burning, rape, and sexual battery law, has also challenged the explanatory capacity of the theories that dominate the study of urban politics. As Elaine B. Sharp has noted, issues rooted in cultural differences "do not fit existing urban theory very well" because contemporary urban theory, rooted in a political economy perspective, "takes material interests, not moral values, as the fundamental elements of political conflict."[19] With such a framework, scholars have treated these culture wars "as irrational flashes of political insanity on the fringes of the normal life of the community."[20] Like Sharp, we believe that these cultural conflicts are worthy of sustained investigation both because of their intrinsic importance and because such unusual struggles provide a fuller understanding of the political process in American communities. We also believe that the movement for and against gay rights can be explored with many of the same tools and perspectives commonly deployed by social scientists who examine more conventional political movements.

Law and Social Change

The drive to secure antidiscrimination protection for gays and lesbians provides an example of the attempt to use law as an instrument of social change. Americans generally hold an optimistic view of the influence of law on social change. The successes of the black civil rights movement of the 1950s and 1960s created a widespread feeling that a combination of legislative enactments and judicial rulings would "breach the barricades of traditional discrimination."[21] This recent history and the legacy of English common law have infused Americans with an unusual faith in the ability of government statutes and policies both to regulate behavior and to affect the hearts and minds of citizens. As the legal historian Roscoe Pound claimed, "Laws may not only set standards but may also help to create habits of conformity to them."[22]

Thus, law is often an agent of social change. Most citizens believe that the law defines what is morally right and proper. As the psychologist Gordon Allport observed: "Laws in line with one's conscience are likely to be obeyed; when not obeyed they still establish an ethical norm that holds before the individual an image of what his conduct should be."[23] Given the coercive powers of the state, considerable compliance with the law is normally achieved. Moreover, "in establishing the boundaries of acceptable behavior, law creates new behavior patterns which frequently produce new attitudes."[24] In this manner, law changes the values of society.

The supreme test of this theory of law and social transformation was the case of oppressive white attitudes toward black Americans in the South prior to the civil rights era. There is the belief that one of the most important functions of law is to provide equality of opportunity.[25] In an important study of the impact of federal laws and policies in the Deep South area of Panola County, Mississippi, the political scientist Fred Wirt reported that even with considerable resistance to laws meant to change the racial culture, change did take place in time. Wirt concluded that "law when enforced can change reality, which can change perceptions, which can alter behavior which, in time, can alter attitudes."[26] While well-enforced law was able to shape individuals in Panola County, it also ultimately affected institutions such as politics, schools, and the economy. Other studies of race relations elsewhere have shown that changes required by law have reduced prejudice in the armed forces, housing projects, and employment.[27] Moreover, the ability of legal codes to influence deep-rooted attitudes in areas other than race has been demonstrated as well.[28]

Although there has been a good deal of popular and scholarly interest in the relationship between law and social reform, relatively little is known about the exact connection between the two. Those who claim that law is an instrument of change state that behavior is the foremost focus. According to this view, behavioral changes produce changes in attitudes, not vice versa as is commonly believed. Implicit here is the notion that law can educate people, or in some cases restrain their behavior, in such a way as to create new beliefs or attitudes.[29] Not all persons, however, are equally amenable to instruction or restraint. As Allport has reminded us, "Laws do not prevent violations altogether. . . . They will deter whoever is deterable. They will not deter the compulsive bigot or demagogue."[30] Even after thirty years of civil rights laws, Wirt reported that Panola County still had some recalcitrants who retained their old behaviors and attitudes. Nonetheless the number of recalcitrants had been much reduced over time.

The focus on law is clearly the paramount emphasis of mainstream attempts to create greater equality for gays and lesbians in the United States. Viewing the gay issue through the prism of blacks and the civil rights movement, proponents of this approach seek to extend to gays the same rights and protections granted to African Americans and certain other minorities. The primary instrument for accomplishing this is the inclusion of lesbians and gays in existing civil rights laws, thus offering state protection against discrimination in employment, housing, and other basic institutions.

According to advocates, the emphasis on a legalistic, rights-based approach provides several advantages for the gay movement. First, and most important, legal recognition of gays helps to increase social acceptance of homosexuality. Representing gays as a political minority within the civil rights framework has granted them greater legitimacy. As the lesbian activist Urvashi Vaid puts it, "We defined ourselves as a distinct minority group, not people with a medical condition. We came to understand and represent ourselves as a people, not a perversion or a behavior."[31]

Second, advocates contend that the increased acceptance and legitimacy brought about by inclusion in the law encourages more gays to become visible, or come out of the closet, and increases the confidence and security of those already claiming lesbian and gay identity. Armed with protection against discrimination, more gays may enter the mainstream openly and with self-respect. This "liberation" of gays will release in them new energy formally used in systematically disguising their identity. The increasing acceptance of homosexuality will also tend to liberate the larger society from its reliance on rigidly defined gender roles, and society will in many ways be "richer for acknowledging another aspect of human diversity."[32]

Finally, a strategy focusing on law and civil rights is politically propitious and expedient given the present status of gays in America. The emphasis on basic human rights to which all Americans are entitled has broad appeal within our society. Linking this cause, moreover, to that of African Americans and other minorities who are commonly viewed as unjustifiably oppressed helps to defuse the emotion and criticism that is raised by the subject of homosexuality. In addition, employing the rhetoric that human rights laws, in reality, make little difference in most peoples' daily lives, while only partly true, tends to quiet the opposition. All these approaches enhance the probability of passage of gay rights laws at a time that homosexuals are still looked upon with much scorn and fear. The greater likelihood of passage serves in turn to politicize lesbians and gay men, drawing them into political battle, educating them, and facilitating local organization.[33] Ultimately, the achievement of civil rights protections may well provide a necessary and important step in gays' political challenges to restrictive laws and policies, such as denial of child custody, sodomy laws, limitation of domestic partner benefits, and the plethora of laws predicated on marriage that exclude lesbian and gay couples.

Although advocates of this legalistic approach to social change present a convincing case, this strategy has been increasingly criticized not only by conservative opponents of gay rights but by several influential gay and lesbian activists as well. Many critics contend that the linkage of gay rights with blacks and civil rights is a badly flawed comparison. The primary liberal argument is that race and sexual orientation are analogous in the basis for discrimination and the need for protective legislation. While there are similarities here, there are also distinct differences that profoundly challenge this analogy. First of all, race is clearly and always visible, but sexual orientation can be and often is hidden. In this vein, some contend that the more appropriate analogy is to antisemitism because religious belief need not be visible. Second, race is not normally viewed as a behavioral characteristic. Sexual orientation, however, though increasingly believed to be a cultural and biological condition, is commonly linked to a consistent pattern of sexual behavior.[34]

These differences from the racial issue have significant consequences for perceptions of gay rights legislation. Since most gays remain in the closet hiding their identity, relatively few public allegations of antigay discrimination are made, even in communities with civil rights laws that include lesbians and gay men. As a result, many heterosexuals do not believe that gays suffer nearly the discrimination that blacks and some other minorities do, and therefore perceive no dire need for gay rights laws. More important, gay and lesbian sexual behavior is the major obstacle to their full acceptance as human beings deserving of basic rights. As Vaid states it, "We are hated because of how, with whom, and how much (mythic or real) we do it."[35] Most heterosexuals find same-gender sex to be both abhorrent and threatening. Such sex is considered by many to be the most glaring indicator of moral and social decay. While heterosexuals may be content to leave gay persons alone, they resist being told that they cannot avoid their company in the workplace or when renting housing. Thus, antidiscrimination statutes are seen as extremely coercive, dictating the behavior of heterosexuals against their will in an area that is emotionally charged.[36] As a result, the increased emphasis on legal protection for homosexuals often produces extreme reactions, typically in the form of antigay initiatives and attempts to repeal gay civil rights.

Critics of the emphasis on human rights also express more general concerns about the role of law in fostering social change. Some contend that law has commonly been employed as an instrument of *oppression*, not liberation, for many minorities. From Jim Crow laws for blacks to sodomy laws directed at homosexuals, legal codes have frequently been used to reinforce social norms and maintain the status quo. Other critics argue that even when civil rights legislation is adopted, it is very limited in both its intent and impact. They charge that such laws, even many of those designed to protect the civil rights of blacks, are primarily symbolic gestures used politically to appease minorities. Politicians are not interested in resolving deep-seated problems that would require significant action and thus increase the risk of political retribution. Most are content with limited responses that at best deal with only the peripheral aspects of a problem.[37] Thus, much civil rights legislation, especially for unpopular groups like gays, is seriously circumscribed in nature and scope. It is, for example, often filled with exemptions for religious, educational, and other institutions in order to make it politically acceptable.

Such laws, moreover, are almost always poorly implemented and enforced. The emphasis on an individual-level, case-by-case bureaucratic response is time consuming and expensive. As with other civil rights legislation, only the most brave and economically secure individuals take full advantage of the law. Such legislation rarely touches those who need it most, especially those whose jobs or social situations are most vulnerable or who live in communities where antigay prejudice remains most virulent. Andrew Sullivan, a gay author, goes even further, arguing that antidiscrimination laws in general often have a pernicious effect on the very minorities they are designed to protect. In his words, "By legislating homosexuals as victims, it sets up a psychological dynamic of supplication that too often only perpetuates cycles of inadequacy and self-doubt."[38] Such an effect may reinforce a passivity among gays that makes them even more vulnerable to oppression and discrimination.

Ultimately, the civil rights strategy fails, these critics maintain, because it does not lead to significant institutional and societal change. This approach typically results in some legal reform, greater lesbian and gay visibility, and somewhat fairer treatment generally. This enables many gays to enter the mainstream, coopted into acceptance of the status quo, but it does not grant them full equality. The liberal, legalistic path yields only "virtual equality," according to Vaid, and this is merely a simulation of genuine equality. What is lacking is a strategy that challenges "the moral and antisexual underpinnings of homophobia," thereby effecting real change in social attitudes and institutions.[39] Instead, says Vaid, gays "possess some of the trappings of full equality but are denied all of its benefits. . . . We are at once marginal and mainstream, at once assimilated and irreconcilably queer."[40] Although the civil rights strategy has been traditionally promoted as a pragmatic, wise, and expedient course of action, its critics contend that it is a short-term palliative that is doomed to fail in the long run as a source of widespread societal change.

One of the main purposes of this book is to provide a way of entering the debate concerning the politics and impact of gay rights laws. Clearly, opinions differ significantly, even within the lesbian and gay movement itself, about the goals of the movement and how they might be best achieved. To date, little systematic research of this issue has been carried out. We hope to make up for this lack, providing new and important information about the politics of gay rights in American communities. We hope also to shed light on the larger issue of the role of law in social change.

Models of Policy Adoption

In portraying the politics of gay rights in American communities, we draw on the scholarly literature about public policy adoption and innovation. Broadly speaking, this research attempts to determine why certain communities adopt government programs and school policies that other localities do not. The various forces that impinge on the decision to embrace a particular practice can be organized into factors that increase the demand for a given policy, factors that add to the resources of advocates or opponents and constraints or limits on policy adoption.[41] We use four models of policy adoption to illuminate the factors that determine whether communities provide legal protection based on sexual orientation.

The demand for innovative policies is usually highest in large, densely populated communities marked by social and economic diversity, what we call the *urbanism/social diversity model*. Research on both domestic and comparative public policy has usually linked the adoption of innovative social programs to the process of modernization most apparent in large cities.[42] Critics of urbanism once viewed cities as dangerous, overpowering environments that condemned their inhabitants to alienation and social isolation. These critics, who saw cities as the breeding ground for rootlessness and antisocial behavior, appear to have overlooked the capacity of city residents to adapt to the challenge of urbanism. As subsequent research has indicated, the urban setting is often conducive to the development of strong social networks. In such environments, groups often congregate in densely populated neighborhoods in sufficient numbers both to form durable subcultures and to develop a strong sense of political commonality.[43] The result, decidedly not a melting pot, is instead a cauldron of distinctive subcommunities marked by religion, race, ethnic identity, class, or other common markers.

This pattern clearly holds for the politics of gay rights, a movement that first emerged in large urban centers and has attained fullest expression in such diverse metropolitan centers as New York; Washington, D.C.; Chicago; San Francisco; and Boston.[44] Such cities were among the first places to develop recognizably gay neighborhoods, which acted as magnets, drawing in gay migrants who felt isolated and threatened in smaller towns and rural areas. Capitalizing on the tolerant milieu associated with advanced modernization, gays—like other minorities—found in large cities the physical and psychological space to develop communities that were somewhat insulated from the larger culture and that provided, in time, a critical mass for political mobilization. In addition to promoting the development of homosexual subcultures, urbanism also encouraged gay mobilization by promoting an ethic of permissiveness among city residents, prompting them to accept unconventional behavior even if they did not themselves practice it.[45] As we shall see, the adoption of gay rights legislation and school policies recognizing sexual orientation is strongly associated with city size.

The second of the four policy models refers to some of the resources that may be employed by those who want to promote political change. Among the key resources available to advocates of new public policies, the *political opportunity structure* refers to the presence of political institutions and actors who are open to innovation. Groups that have been excluded from power and decision making often find their interests dependent on resources from outside their own immediate circle.[46] The success of the national movement in behalf of women's equality was not just the product of enhanced political consciousness among feminists, as crucial as that was, but also depended heavily on the responsiveness of the political system to new claimants for power. As Anne Costain argued, progress was achieved because advocates for gender equality exploited the "openness of government to new interests, the stability or instability of political alignments, [and] the availability of allies and supporters."[47] In the same manner, communities are most ripe for policy change favorable to such outsiders when government agencies can be accessed or captured by outside forces, local elites are sympathetic to the demands of social movements, and the population includes large numbers of supporters who are not themselves members of the group seeking changes. The political opportunity structure is likely to be crucial in explaining the adoption of gay rights policies. Because they belong to a minority that often incites considerable public hostility, gay rights advocates have to enlist the support of influential allies and press their demands in communities with institutions that are open to pressures from below. We expect to find that the progress of local campaigns for gay rights will depend on the political environment of the community.

In *resource mobilization theory,* the third policy framework we use in this study, the success of a group in persuading the larger community to adopt a policy depends on the tools that the group can wield on its own behalf.[48] Scholarly explanations of mass movements once painted them as largely irrational crusades, capitalizing on chaos and driven by societal misfits and malcontents. This approach, emphasizing the crucial role of the poor and deprived, may have been useful to account for short-term outbursts of social disorder such as riots and lynchings. It was wholly inadequate to explain the success of other protest movements—such as the black civil rights campaign or the struggle against the Vietnam War—which were durable, conducted in a rational manner, and often led by people with middle-class credentials. These movements inspired scholars to develop new models of social movements, which emphasize the crucial role of political and organizational resources.

Unlike political opportunity structure, a term that identifies resources drawn from outside the social group seeking change, the concept of resource mobilization refers to characteristics internal to the group. Apart from sheer size and intense grievances, the ability of any social movement to achieve its goals depends on such vital resources as wealth, organizational capacity, and leadership. As a rule, these qualities are most accessible to groups that have developed a pattern of extensive social ties marked by high levels of social interaction and internal communication. Armed with such resources, groups that possess these qualities in abundance have a better chance of persuading local governments to adopt policies on their behalf. The pertinent resources, in the campaign to adopt gay rights legislation and school policies sympathetic to gay and lesbian concerns include the level of social and political organization, the skills of gay leaders, the financial condition of the gay community, and similar traits.

The fourth and final policy model emphasizes the constraints that limit the capacity of movements to change public policy. This perspective recognizes that a full accounting of policy adoption and innovation does not depend solely on the demands for and resources available to promote change. Advocates of change face potential resistance from groups and organizations that do not welcome policy innovation. Indeed, the very same processes of modernization that have generated demands for political and social change have long encountered fierce resistance from some sectors of the population. During the Industrial Revolution, when technological innovation threatened traditional ways of life, bands of "reactionary radicals" challenged the new forms of social and economic organization that threatened community-based values and identities.[49] The *communal protest model* emphasizes the groups that deploy "tradition and the yearning for security, status and community" to challenge threatening social practices.[50] On questions that have to do with social identity, proposals for a more inclusive society will attract resistance from groups that stand to lose their privileged position. If those opponents are sufficiently concentrated and energized, they can block policy adoptions that threaten to change the moral, economic, and social order of a community. Because the campaign for gay rights does involve challenges to dominant social identity—particularly the notion that heterosexuality is the only legitimate basis of social relationships—it often draws resistance from groups wedded to the existing social order. If these changes also involve shifts in the distribution of tangible resources, the new policies may also inspire opposition from groups with an interest in the prevailing system of rewards.

In explaining the adoption, resistance, and implementation of gay rights policies by local governments and school boards, we repeatedly encounter these theoretical models and highlight the social forces associated with each perspective.

The Nature and Scope of This Study

As we have suggested, this book does much more than simply chronicle the gay rights movement and the resulting political battles in American communities, as important and interesting as this story is. Instead, we analyze the quest for human rights for lesbians and gays (including gay youth); the politics of adoption of gay rights policies; the implementation of this legislation and its effect on various institutions within the community, including the schools, police, and businesses; and the new politics of identity, including the political opposition so intrinsic to this movement. In this manner, we hope to make sense out of one of the most intense political struggles in recent American history.

The sources of data for this study are unique in that they are not only rich and varied but consist of a blend of quantitative and qualitative information. They include a comprehensive national survey of all U.S. cities and counties with laws or policies prohibiting discrimination on the basis of sexual orientation. Such communities numbered 126 in mid-1993 when we began our survey, and we received responses from at least one public official in each of these communities. Similar data were collected for a comparison sample of 125 cities and counties without such legislation, selected randomly from a comprehensive list of local jurisdictions in the United States. These data are unusual in their breadth, covering all communities with legal safeguards for gays and lesbians as well as a "control group" of comparison cities and counties. In the same manner we surveyed school districts both in communities with and in those without protective laws or policies. These surveys provided us with a good deal of general information about the status of gay rights measures in the nation as a whole. For more details about the sampling procedures and surveys, see the Appendix.

Our other, and equally important, source of information comes from in-depth case studies of five representative, geographically diverse cities that have enacted gay rights laws: Cincinnati, Ohio; Iowa City, Iowa; Philadelphia, Pennsylvania; Raleigh, North Carolina; and Santa Cruz, California. We chose these communities after conducting a cluster analysis of all cities with antidiscrimination laws or policies. This analysis, using a variety of discriminating variables such as social structure, demographic qualities, and political history, divided the cities into four distinct, homogeneous clusters. One cluster clearly depicts communities with a dominant college or university. Not surprisingly, the cities in this group are characterized by a high proportion of nonfamily households, a low median age, and high levels of education among the population. Iowa City is a typical such community. Another grouping is characterized by large, industrial cities, found predominantly in the Northeast and industrial Midwest. These communities shared a propensity to an "unreformed," more traditional, political system, large populations, and relatively large concentrations of liberal Protestants. Disproportionately found in states with gay rights policies, the localities in this second cluster tended to have extensive ordinances and some openly gay officials. Philadelphia was chosen as the representative city of this group.

The third cluster comprised mostly older southern cities or communities in border states. These cities were distinctive in that they had a sizable

African-American population, a high concentration of predominantly black churches, and substantial support for Bill Clinton in the 1992 presidential election. We selected Raleigh to represent this group. The final cluster, the largest and in some ways the most intriguing, consisted of smaller and medium-sized communities marked by relative affluence, an older population, a high proportion of households with unmarried partners, and neighboring communities with similar gay rights ordinances. Because a very large number of communities in this cluster are found on the West Coast or eastern seaboard, we tended to describe this as the "bicoastal" cluster. Santa Cruz is our prototypical coastal community.

Finally, we decided to study a fifth city that was selected as quite different from any of the others. This city is one that adopted but then repealed its gay rights law and is therefore representative of those locales where the opponents of protective legislation for lesbians and gay men have been most visible and successful. Such a community provides us with a greater range of settings in which to study the dynamics of gay rights politics. Cincinnati was selected as typical of this kind of city.

In each of the communities we interviewed a variety of individuals who were considered knowledgeable about the passage and impact of gay rights legislation. These individuals typically included elected city officials and administrators, gay and lesbian activists, religious and other leaders of opposition groups, members of the business community, minority group leaders, and school personnel such as administrators, teachers, and school board members. In all, we interviewed sixty-five respondents, divided almost equally among the communities in accordance with city size. All interviewees were guaranteed anonymity because of the controversial nature of the topic.[51] We also perused local newspapers and available public records. These multiple modes of analysis offered a wide range of sometimes rich sources of information; they also often provided a cross-check on the reliability of any single source.

In Chapter 2 we describe in general terms the modern gay and lesbian political movement in the United States. We also present an overview of each of our case study communities, including the nature of the gay movement and the quest for gay and lesbian rights in each city. Chapter 3 contains an examination of civil rights legislation inclusive of gays and lesbians, including the rationale for such laws, when and where they were first passed, and most important, the politics of their passage with specific consideration given to gay and lesbian mobilization, the role of universities and colleges, and other supportive forces. In Chapter 4 we discuss the antidiscrimination ordinances in regard to their institutional coverage, the nature and degree of their enforcement, their influence on police behavior toward gays, their impact on local businesses, and the more general effects of the laws on community values. Chapter 5 includes an exploration of the gay movement and public schools, often referred to as the most intense battleground in this cultural war, and issues related to educational curriculum, services, and policies. An analysis of the political opposition to the gay movement and human rights laws, with particular emphasis on the religious right, its ideology and tactics, is the focus of Chapter 6. Finally, our book concludes in Chapter 7 with a consideration of the implications for identity politics, theories of policy innovation, and the impact of law on the process of social change in American communities. We also take a brief look at more current needs and political issues confronting many lesbians and gay men.

NOTES

1. Chris Bull, "Us vs. Them: Fred Phelps," *Advocate*, November 2, 1993, 42–45. The *Advocate* is a leading gay political periodical based in San Francisco.
2. Traditional Values Coalition, "Gay Rights/Special Rights: Inside the Homosexual Agenda," Jeremiah Films, Anaheim, Calif., 1993, videotape.
3. Karen M. Harbeck, introduction to *Coming Out of the Classroom Closet: Gay and Lesbian Students, Teachers, and Curricula*, ed. Karen M. Harbeck (Binghamton, N.Y.: Harrington Park Press, 1992), 1.
4. In the interest of brevity, we will use the term *gay* or *lesbians and gay men* (or vice versa) inclusively to refer to male homosexuals, female homosexuals, and bisexuals without intending disrespect to any particular group.
5. The American National Election Study uses a "feeling thermometer" that asks respondents to rate their warmth of feeling toward various groups on a scale from 0 to 100. The American public has consistently ranked homosexuals *below* virtually all other groups. In 1992 the average rating for gays and lesbians was 15–30 points below such controversial groups as blacks, Jews, Hispanics, Asians, Christian fundamentalists, big business, feminists, and people on welfare. Measured by the percentage of respondents who assigned them the lowest possible rating of zero, gays and lesbians were even less popular than illegal immigrants. These data were calculated from National Election Studies, *American National Election Studies 1948–1994* (Ann Arbor, Mich.: Institute for Social Research, 1995), machine-readable data on CD-ROM. For further analysis of these data and more evidence about the political status of gays and lesbians, see Kenneth Sherrill, "The Political Power of Lesbians, Gays, and Bisexuals," *PS: Political Science and Politics* 29 (September 1996): 469–473.
6. Kent Greenawalt, "The Participation of Religious Groups in Political Advocacy," *Journal of Church and State* 36 (winter 1994): 155. Here again, terminology is important. Critics of homosexuality usually describe it as a *preference* or chosen way of life—an impulse that can be controlled or allowed to run free. Advocates for the gay community regard it as a *sexual orientation* that is relatively fixed and immutable, possibly rooted in biology. In this view, individuals may repress latent homosexuality or bisexuality but at a considerable psychological cost. Analytically, we recognize the distinction between sexual orientation and sexual behavior but do not accept that such a distinction means that homosexuality is a matter of choice.
7. Specifically, 60 percent of adults favored "laws to protect homosexuals against job discrimination" and 58.5 percent thought that "homosexuals should be allowed to serve in the United States Armed Forces." By contrast, public opinion was split 3 to 1 against permitting gays to adopt children. See note 5 for the source of these data.
8. Marcy Darnovsky, Barbara Epstein, and Richard Flacks, eds., *Cultural Politics and Social Movements* (Philadelphia, Pa.: Temple University Press, 1995), xiii.
9. Ibid.
10. Kenneth L. Karst, *Law's Promise, Law's Expression: Visions of Power in the Politics of Race, Gender, and Religion* (New Haven, Conn.: Yale University Press, 1993), 13.

11. Kristin Luker, *Abortion and the Politics of Motherhood* (Berkeley: University of California Press, 1984); Donald G. Mathews and Jane S. De Hart, *Sex, Gender, and the Politics of ERA* (New York: Oxford University Press, 1990).
12. David Plotke, "Two Questions about Social Movements," *The Good Society* 6 (winter 1996): 10–13.
13. Paul Kleppner, *The Third Electoral System* (Chapel Hill: University of North Carolina Press, 1979), 305.
14. Debra Burrington, "Competing Visions of Community: The Religious Right and Gay Rights" (paper presented at the annual meeting of the American Political Science Association, Washington, D.C., 1993), 7.
15. This language is from a letter by fifteen members of the Florida legislature, criticizing the decision of the Walt Disney Company to provide health benefits to the domestic partners of Disney employees. See "Disney Blasted for Giving Benefits to Gay Partners," *Gainesville Sun,* October 19, 1995.
16. Burrington, "Competing Visions of Community," 7.
17. Jeffrey Schmalz, "Homosexuals Wake to See a Referendum: It's on Them," *New York Times,* January 31, 1993.
18. Peter McDonough, "On Hierarchies of Conflict and the Possibility of Civil Discourse: Variations on a Theme by John Courtney Murray," *Journal of Church and State* 36 (winter 1994): 124.
19. Elaine B. Sharp, "Culture Wars and the Study of Urban Politics," *Urban News* 10 (spring 1996): 2. For attempts to develop a theoretical framework of local government behavior that incorporates cultural conflicts, see Sharp, "Culture Wars and City Politics: Local Government's Role in Social Conflict," *Urban Affairs Review* 31 (July 1996): 738–758, and "A Comparative Anatomy of Urban Social Conflict" (paper presented at the annual meeting of the American Political Science Association, Chicago, 1995).
20. Sharp, "Culture Wars and City Politics," 742.
21. Charles S. Bullock III and Charles M. Lamb, eds., *Implementation of Civil Rights Policy* (Monterey, Calif.: Brooks/Cole, 1984), 1.
22. As quoted in Jack Greenberg, *Race Relations and American Law* (New York: Columbia University Press, 1959), 2.
23. As quoted in ibid., 26.
24. Harrell R. Rodgers Jr. and Charles S. Bullock III, *Law and Social Change: Civil Rights Laws and Their Consequences* (New York: McGraw-Hill, 1972), 204.
25. Frederick M. Wirt, *Politics of Southern Equality: Law and Social Change in a Mississippi County* (Chicago: Aldine, 1970), 6.
26. Frederick M. Wirt, *"I Ain't What I Was": Civil Rights in the New South* (Durham, N.C.: Duke University Press, forthcoming), 4.
27. Greenberg, *Race Relations and American Law,* 2–3; Duane Lockard, *Toward Equal Opportunity: A Study of State and Local Antidiscrimination Laws* (New York: Macmillan, 1968), 10–11; Rodgers and Bullock, *Law and Social Change,* 181–204.
28. Wirt, *Politics of Southern Equality,* 10.
29. Ibid., 8–9.
30. Gordon W. Allport, *The Nature of Prejudice* (Garden City, N.Y.: Doubleday, Anchor, 1958), 439.
31. Urvashi Vaid, *Virtual Equality: The Mainstreaming of Gay and Lesbian Liberation* (New York: Doubleday, Anchor, 1995), 181.
32. Richard D. Mohr, *A More Perfect Union: Why Straight America Must Stand Up for Gay Rights* (Boston: Beacon, 1994), 17.
33. Didi Herman, *Rights of Passage: Struggles for Lesbian and Gay Legal Equality* (Toronto: University of Toronto Press, 1994), 48–49.
34. Andrew Sullivan, "The Politics of Homosexuality," *New Republic,* May 10, 1993, 34–35.
35. Vaid, *Virtual Equality,* 192.
36. Andrew Sullivan, *Virtually Normal: An Argument about Homosexuality* (New York: Knopf, 1995), 160–161.
37. Lockard, *Toward Equal Opportunity,* 142–143.
38. Sullivan, "Politics of Homosexuality," 36.
39. Vaid, *Virtual Equality,* 183.
40. Ibid., 4.

41. Christopher Z. Mooney and Mei-Hsien Lee, "Legislating Morality in the American States: The Case of Pre-*Roe* Abortion Restrictions," *American Journal of Political Science* 39 (August 1995): 611.

42. Theda Skocpol, Marjorie Abend-Wein, Christopher Howard, and Susan Goodrich Lehmann, "Women's Associations and the Enactment of Mothers' Pensions in the United States," *American Political Science Review* 87 (September 1993): 686–701.

43. Herbert Gans, *Urban Villagers* (New York: Free Press, 1962); Gerald D. Suttles, *The Social Construction of Communities* (Chicago: University of Chicago Press, 1972).

44. For a definitive account of the urban basis of gay political activism, see the forthcoming book by Robert W. Bailey, *Gay Politics, Urban Politics* (New York: Columbia University Press).

45. Thomas C. Wilson, "Urbanism and Unconventionality: The Case of Sexual Behavior," *Social Science Quarterly* 76 (June 1995): 346–363.

46. Sidney Tarrow, *Power in Movement: Social Movements, Collective Action, and Politics* (New York: Cambridge University Press, 1994), chap. 5.

47. Anne H. Costain, *Inviting Women's Rebellion: A Political Process Interpretation of the Women's Movement* (Baltimore: Johns Hopkins University Press, 1992), 14–15.

48. Mayer N. Zald and John D. McCarthy, eds., *The Dynamics of Social Movements: Resource Mobilization, Social Control, and Tactics* (Cambridge, Mass.: Winthrop, 1979).

49. Craig Calhoun, *The Question of Class Struggle* (Chicago: University of Chicago Press, 1982).

50. Clarence Y. H. Lo, "Communities of Challengers in Social Movement Theory," in *Frontiers of Social Movement Theory*, ed. Aldon D. Morris and Carol McClurge Mueller (New Haven: Yale University Press, 1992), 224–247.

51. Although a few respondents refused to be interviewed or were unavailable at the time of our visit, somewhat more opponents of gay rights denied us interviews than did either advocates or those holding more neutral views on such legislation. Nonetheless, we were able to interview a variety of persons opposed to protective legislation in each community.

CHAPTER 2

The Contemporary Gay
Political Movement

*The movement's history cannot be understood merely as a chronicle of how
activists worked to mobilize masses of gay men and lesbians. . . . Instead, the
movement constitutes a phase, albeit a decisive one, of a much longer process
through which a group of men and women came into existence as a self-conscious,
cohesive minority.*

— John D'Emilio, *Sexual Politics, Sexual Communities: The Making of a
Homosexual Minority in the United States, 1940–1970*

Throughout American history gay identity has remained hidden because
of an atmosphere of pervasive hostility to homosexual expression. In
the dominant Judeo-Christian tradition, "homosexual behavior was
excoriated as a heinous sin, the law branded it a serious crime, and the medical profession diagnosed homosexuals and lesbians as diseased."[1] Fearful of
exposure, lesbians and gay men were a furtive minority, tightly closeted and
isolated. This environment made it extremely difficult to formulate a gay identity or to locate a homosexual subculture. Such an ideology also created a
degree of self-hate within many gays.[2] Under these oppressive conditions, it is
surprising that a major gay political movement was ultimately able to emerge.

By the late 1800s and early 1900s, lesbians and gay men in the United
States began to experience a sense of community. In the past the burdens of
subsistence farming and the primacy of the family in the economic process
had precluded the emergence of a gay subculture. Industrialization and
urbanization, however, brought a division of labor and large concentrations
of individuals relatively free to pursue pleasure.[3] The early organized networks of gays, all secretive and underground, were social in nature, consist-
ing of clubs, baths, restaurants, bars, and music halls. They appeared only in
major cities such as Boston, Chicago, New York, San Francisco, and Washington. World War I and the 1920s, moreover, created a greater freedom that
encouraged these nascent gay communities to grow in number and diversity.[4] The small, evolving subcultures of gays and lesbians provided the early
seeds in the eventual development of a sense of identity and political consciousness among these individuals.

World War II played a major role in the formulation of the modern lesbian
and gay community. As a result of the war, millions of American men and

women were uprooted from their families and neighborhoods in which they had grown up and placed in nonfamilial, often sex-segregated, environments. Men left home to serve in the armed forces, and many women entered the depleted civilian labor force in order to support both their families and the country's production of goods. So great were the demands of war, numerous women also took their places in the military. The war served to bring previously isolated gays and lesbians into contact with each other. These unusual conditions not only afforded a greater opportunity to express homosexual desire but also raised the expectations of many gays and lesbians.[5] No longer would homosexuals remain so closeted and secretive. According to D'Emilio, World War II represented "something of a nationwide coming out experience" for American homosexuals.[6]

The war and its aftermath left many gays and lesbians who had served in the military or civilian defense industries in large port cities or other urban areas. Others began to migrate to major cities, seeking greater freedom to express their sexual identity. Lesbian and gay bars and social clubs multiplied dramatically in these urban settings. In such an environment, gay and lesbian subcultures began to expand.[7]

Nonetheless, the increased visibility of gays, plus the escalation of the cold war, intensified the oppression of homosexuals beginning in the late 1940s. The anticommunist witch hunts, led by Sen. Joseph McCarthy, soon spread to other unpopular groups. Homosexuals were a particular target of persecution because they were viewed as deviant and subversive, and campaigns to purge lesbians and gay men from government agencies and the military increased significantly. Local police forces as well began to crack down brutally on homosexuals. Police raids on gay and lesbian bars and clubs multiplied in most large cities, and even the homes of gays were unprotected from the intrusion of local vice squads.[8] The legal status of gays reinforced this oppression. Homosexual acts were illegal in most states under existing anti-sodomy statutes. In New York, for example, homosexual behavior was a felony punishable by as much as twenty years in jail. Furthermore, gays and lesbians were specifically excluded from laws and policies regulating fair employment practices, housing discrimination, rights of child custody, immigration, inheritance, security clearances, public accommodations, and police protection.[9]

Despite the antigay hysteria of the McCarthy era, a nascent but fragile gay political movement began to develop. The first modern gay rights organization, the Mattachine Society, was founded in Los Angeles in 1951. Organized as a secret society in order to protect its members, Mattachine provided support, camaraderie, and a sense of pride in belonging to an oppressed minority.[10] In 1955, the first notable lesbian organization, the Daughters of Bilitis, was begun in San Francisco. Although the initial purpose of the organization was social, it soon took on a political bent by demanding lesbian rights.[11] By the early 1960s both the Mattachine Society and the Daughters of Bilitis had developed chapters in other major cities. These organizations as well as other groups of homosexuals became more politically active in the mid-1960s, protesting police harassment, defending legally their right to congregate, playing a role in several big-city political races, and demonstrating against antigay employment discrimination by the federal government.[12]

Although the number of gay and lesbian activists remained small and their political influence limited, these first political groups, especially the Mattachine Society, had a profound impact on the gay movement. By defining homosexuals as a sexual minority, similar to other ethnic and cultural minorities and entitled to the same rights and benefits granted other groups, these early activists aided the movement greatly. The characterization of gays as a minority was particularly important politically.[13] In the words of Urvashi Vaid, it "moved homosexuality from the domain of illness and sociopathic deviance and into the public domain of civil rights."[14] The minority group framework provided lesbians and gays with a political legitimacy they had not previously enjoyed, and this helped the movement to grow. This conception also gave focus to gay political activity by directing it toward the pursuit of civil rights. In turn, the emphasis on civil rights for homosexuals gained moral and political support from other groups involved in the 1960s mass movements, including blacks, women, and the more radical students.

The Stonewall riots in New York City in 1969 proved to be a crucial catalyst to the mass political mobilization of lesbians and gay men. The riots or rebellions, wherein gay men openly and violently resisted police harassment in a Greenwich Village gay bar, sparked demonstrations of homosexual pride across the country. The politics of protest practiced by other minorities in the late 1960s encouraged lesbians and gay men to voice their own complaints. As Lillian Faderman states it, "The gay liberation movement was an idea whose time had come. The Stonewall Rebellion was crucial because it sounded the rally for that movement. It became an emblem of gay and lesbian power."[15]

Almost immediately following Stonewall, countless new lesbian and gay liberation organizations came into being. Mobilized by the women's movement, lesbians became a greater force in the new gay movement. More radical in tone and tactics than previous homosexual organizations, these new political groups not only challenged antigay policies but focused on sexual oppression more generally. The increased emphasis on coming out gave the movement "an army of permanent enlistees" who were propelled into political activity.[16] By 1973, there were more than eight hundred gay political groups across the country; prior to Stonewall less than fifty such groups had existed. Gay and lesbian migration to large cities increased, and organizations for homosexuals, such as community centers, health clinics, professional associations, and coffeehouses, flourished as never before.[17]

Within a few years of the Stonewall riots, the gay movement achieved many significant political successes. The American Psychiatric Association removed homosexuality from its classification as a mental disorder, a position it had held for almost a century. Numerous states repealed their sodomy laws, the U.S. Civil Service Commission eliminated its ban on the employment of gays, and the National Education Association amended its nondiscrimination statement to include protection for "sexual preference." In addition, several nationally prominent politicians came out in favor of gay rights, and in 1980 the Democratic Party included gay rights in its national platform.[18]

A primary political goal of the 1970s movement, however, was the introduction of sexual orientation into human rights laws. This was one of the few goals upon which both moderate and more liberal groups of lesbians and gay men agreed. Such civil rights legislation typically prohibited discrimination on the basis of race, sex, religion, ethnicity, and sometimes other characteristics, and provided legal recourse for protected minorities when denied employment or shelter. Beginning in 1974, Congress attempted to amend the 1964 Civil Rights Act to include gays and lesbians in the federal ban on discrimination, but it repeatedly failed to do so. This failure at the national level fueled attempts to pass such measures at the state and local level, and by the latter part of the 1970s several dozen communities had adopted gay rights ordinances or policies.[19]

No doubt the initial success of these legislative enactments was due to the increased mobilization of lesbians and gays, and often their allies. It could also be attributed to the lack of organized opposition. But in 1977 a significant right-wing political backlash emerged, best symbolized by the fundamentalist Anita Bryant and her antigay Save Our Children organization, which resulted in the overwhelming vote to repeal a recently passed gay rights law in Dade County, Florida, of which Miami is the county seat. The increasingly reactionary climate culminated in the additional repeals in 1978 of gay rights laws in Eugene, Oregon; St. Paul, Minnesota; and Wichita, Kansas. Similar campaigns that emerged at the same time, California's Proposition Six Initiative and Oklahoma's proposed state law, focused on children and education. Although the California initiative failed, Oklahoma enacted a law (modeled on California's Proposition Six) prohibiting homosexual conduct, activity, or advocacy by school employees. Police and street violence against gays escalated and, in the most visible demonstration of hate and fear, Harvey Milk—the best-known openly gay public official in the country— was assassinated in San Francisco in November 1978.[20]

Opposition to gay rights continued through the 1980s and early 1990s. Indeed, the antigay theme proved to be one of the most potent themes deployed by conservatives in their efforts to mobilize religious traditionalists on behalf of "family values." The gay movement also suffered a significant legal setback when the U.S. Supreme Court ruled in the *Bowers v. Hardwick* case (1986) to uphold Georgia's antisodomy law. This landmark decision allowed states to continue to criminalize homosexual behavior. Despite this setback and continued opposition, gay men and lesbians in general felt more safe and confident by the 1980s, and were not about to retreat to the closets of the past. Gays increased their politically vocal numbers as more came out to join the movement. Clearly the AIDS epidemic pushed many individuals (some prominent, like the movie star Rock Hudson) out of the closet, helped to mobilize others, and served to revitalize sexuality education as a school and community issue. In addition, a Department of Health and Human Services Report (1989), which estimated that gay and lesbian youth were two to three times more likely to attempt suicide than their heterosexual peers, became a powerful "call for action" for schools.[21]

The collective power of homosexuals was clearly demonstrated in the massive 1987 National March on Washington for Lesbian and Gay Rights. The number of participants exceeded half a million, making it one of the largest civil rights marches in U.S. history. The march (along with a similar national parade in Washington in 1993) boosted gay and lesbian political activism at both the national and local levels. Small but militant groups such as ACT-UP (AIDS Coalition to Unleash Power) and Queer Nation formed in the late 1980s and early 1990s, inspired in part by the slow response to the AIDS crisis. Openly gay and lesbian politicians began to compete for and win election to office, particularly at the state and local level.[22] By 1993 some 120 openly gay and lesbian officials held local office, and eight states and more than one hundred cities and counties had passed gay rights laws or policies.[23] In addition, gaining greater recognition of their personal relationships became increasingly important for many gay men and lesbians, and in response several larger cities and some businesses adopted domestic partnership policies extending health and other benefits to gay and lesbian couples. Gays also exercised political influence nationally by having sexual orientation included in the 1990 federal hate crimes law (and in its renewal in 1995) and by their considerable contribution to Bill Clinton's successful bid for the presidency in 1992.

The increased visibility and mobilization of lesbians and gay men led to further countermobilization of the political right. The focus of much of the opposition was on state and local gay rights laws or policies that seemed to legitimate the homosexual subculture. A number of communities faced well-organized attempts to deny or abolish equal rights for gays and lesbians. Many of these initiatives were successful, including the much-publicized Colorado state-wide referendum in 1992 that banned civil rights protection on the basis of sexual orientation, thereby overturning local laws in Denver, Boulder, and Aspen. This action, however, was ruled unconstitutional in 1996 by the U.S. Supreme Court in the case of *Romer v. Evans*. This important decision suggested for the first time that the nation's highest court may be sympathetic to the constitutional claims of gays.

Furthermore, the schools increasingly became a prime target of antigay activists, who attempted to ban books and educational materials that discuss homosexuality and opposed any school programs and policies that would benefit gay youth. At the national level attempts to remove the longtime ban on gays and lesbians in the military were effectively thwarted, despite the Clinton administration's stated support of a policy to allow homosexuals to serve openly in the armed forces. More recently, the question of the legalization of same-sex marriage has been a significant issue in many states and in Congress. Clearly the political debate surrounding lesbian and gay issues has become increasingly hostile and conflictual as gay advocates assert their demands and right-wing forces counterattack in what has become a cultural war.

Over the last several decades lesbian and gay mobilization has become a significant social movement. Much of its political focus, however, remains at the community level. Whether in response to police harassment or the AIDS crisis, or as an attempt to pass an antidiscrimination ordinance, gays and lesbians are increasingly organized politically in many American cities. In the remainder of this chapter we take a look at the emergence of the gay movement in each of our case study communities. As will be seen, the movement varies somewhat from one city to another as the social and political contexts differ. Nevertheless, one of the primary goals of the lesbian and gay movement in each community has been the passage and implementation of gay rights legislation. Since this is the major focus of our book, we emphasize political developments that affected the achievement of this goal.

Iowa City: A University Town

Tucked away in the rolling farmlands of eastern Iowa, Iowa City is the quintessential college town. It is built around the University of Iowa, whose 27,000 students make up almost half the city's population. Like many other college-dominated towns, the residents of Iowa City are relatively young and well educated. They are also quite liberal and largely Democratic in a state dominated by Republicans. Indeed, Iowa City is one of the few places in the state where Clinton won a majority of the presidential vote in 1992. In the words of one city official, "The city is an island of liberalism in a sea of conservatism."

Because of its university atmosphere and reputation for tolerance, Iowa City has long been considered by gays as a good place to live. "It's probably right between Chicago and Minneapolis as being the gay center of the Midwest," claimed a gay University of Iowa student.[24] Since the early 1980s the city has officially celebrated Gay and Lesbian Pride Week, which is typically capped by a rally and parade through the downtown area. Even the police are relatively sensitive to the concerns of gays, and they willingly provide security for the Gay Pride Parade. The city is perceived to be a safe haven for gays and lesbians, and many feel accepted enough to be fairly open about their sexual orientation.[25]

Despite this atmosphere of tolerance, Iowa City's gays have not been totally immune to discrimination and harassment. In 1984 the community was shaken by openly antigay graffiti and vandalism at a downtown bar and at two buildings on the university campus. The spray-painted epithets included "Kill Gays," "Homosexuals Equal Satan," "Death to All Gays," and "Nuclear Arms to Kill All Gays."[26] Local and university officials only belatedly condemned the graffiti, but the incident helped to persuade the university to add sexual orientation as a protected classification to its human rights policy.[27] A second well-publicized instance of gay harassment occurred in 1990 when the *Campus Review,* a right-wing student publication, displayed a Bart Simpson poster showing the cartoon character poised with a loaded slingshot and the caption, "Back off, Faggot!" Under the Bart character were the words, "AIDS activists: another lost opportunity." The poster display ignited a storm of controversy while prompting debate on homophobia and free speech. In response to the poster, a graduate student filed a complaint with the university's Human Rights Committee, claiming the display incited violence against homosexuals. Two members of the committee resigned due to conflicts over what action should be taken, but the committee ultimately ruled in favor of the student and the poster was banned for violating the university's human rights policy.[28]

While such antigay incidents have not been common in Iowa City, they do suggest a latent degree of homophobia. For some gays, particularly those who are open about their sexual orientation and politically active, blatant discrimination has been an issue. One gay leader and longtime resident claimed that he had received violent threats and that baseballs had even been thrown through his windows. Another gay student activist said he knew of people who had been physically attacked because of their sexual orientation and that verbal harassment of gays was common.[29] In addition, the AIDS crisis had "given people reason to be homophobic," according to a gay leader, and had served to increase discrimination against homosexuals.[30]

Against this paradox of tolerance and diversity yet lingering homophobic and antigay discrimination, the gays and lesbians of Iowa City first mobilized politically in the late 1960s, beginning at the University of Iowa. Motivated by the Stonewall rebellion, gays and other student activists created the Gay

Liberation Front, later known as the Gay People's Union. The organization functioned as an advocate on gay issues, with the ultimate goal of eliminating homophobia. Early on it played a key role in initiating discussions of gay rights legislation for the city.[31]

The city's Human Relations Commission, prompted by gay students and others, first proposed adding homosexuals to the Human Rights ordinance in 1976 after two years of discussion. The recommendation also included age, marital status, and disability as protected classifications. Most controversial, however, was the proposed ban on discrimination against gays. In 1977 in the lengthy hearing before the city council on the issue, twenty-one persons spoke in support of legal protection for gays. No one spoke against the proposal, but several council members and others in the community held deep sentiments against it. Several opponents, including some clergymen, wrote letters to the council. The most basic fear was that adding sexual orientation to the ordinance would, in effect, condone homosexuality and promiscuous sex. One city council member also expressed concern that such legislation would force employers to hire gays regardless of qualifications.[32] Still, there was no organized opposition to the measure.

Advocates for amending the law won the day by representing themselves as a cross-section of the community and by emphasizing the need to protect the basic rights of lesbians and gays. "Being gay means that no matter how hard we work, how well we do in our jobs, we can be fired, not for incompetence, not for having broken any law, but merely for who we are," claimed Neil O'Farrell, chairman of the Gay People's Union.[33] He asked the council to recognize that homosexuals are an important part of the community. "We are your doctors, lawyers, dentists, accountants, clergymen, secretaries, teachers, and reporters," he said.[34] In addition, several members of the clergy, including two Catholic priests, spoke at the city hearing in support of legal protection for gays. Fifteen members of the Association of Campus Ministers also submitted a statement favoring the amendment. Even a few businesspersons and apartment owners, whose conduct would be controlled by the changed ordinance, advocated the protection of homosexuals against discrimination in employment and housing.[35]

Gay rights legislation was adopted in April 1977, by a 4–3 council vote, but only after housing was deleted from its coverage. Landlords and rental property owners objected most vehemently to the legislation, arguing it would bring more costly liability suits and would force them to condone sexual activity they considered immoral. With local elections approaching, council members decided to drop this controversial provision.[36] Later in the year, several landlord organizations, fueled by the national backlash on gay rights and by Anita Bryant's visit to nearby Des Moines, attempted to petition the council to reconsider the legislation. The petition drive failed to secure the necessary 2,500 signatures, however.[37] In 1984, after a compromise to exempt owner-occupied complexes of four units or less, rental housing was added to the legislation protecting gays. According to a city official, after seven years of experience with the gay rights measure, most citizens and policymakers were convinced that it "worked" and was "not the basis for hundreds of complaints."[38] As a result, the extension to housing was less controversial and easier to pass than the original gay rights measure.

Having achieved human rights legislation, gays and lesbians began to push for the fulfillment of other political goals. As always, the focal point of organization was the university. In response to the crisis created by the Bart Simpson AIDS poster in 1990, eight lesbian and gay rights groups, most of which were based or supported on campus, appealed to the university president for greater support. They also decided to form the Lesbian, Gay and Bisexual Staff and Faculty Association to promote homosexual interests. With support from the university president, the association quickly grew to approximately 150 members. It worked to develop classes and a program in gay and lesbian studies, to conduct workshops in order to educate people about gay issues, and to help process complaints by homosexuals.[39] Perhaps the most important achievement of the association was to plan and carry out a gay and lesbian statewide assembly in 1991. Drawing more than three hundred people, the assembly proposed and later lobbied for a state gay rights bill. The bill passed the Iowa Senate but failed in the lower house in 1992. The assembly also developed a domestic partner benefits plan that was adopted by the state regents to cover all university employees.[40]

Gays continued to be active in city politics as well. Although not well organized as an interest group or party, gays and lesbians have nonetheless been an influential part of the liberal coalition that has dominated local politics recently. The gay vote is seen as critical for any progressive candidate for local office, and candidates often show up at gay events. The annual Gay Pride Parade, which normally draws several hundred marchers, typically includes a few public officials. Moreover, gays and lesbians were the main thrust in the political push that persuaded the city council and school district to provide health insurance for same-sex couples in 1994. This domestic partner policy was similar to the one adopted by the university two years earlier, and marked the city as a forerunner in gay legislation.[41] In 1995 the progressive city council voted unanimously to amend the Human Rights law to include transgendered persons, and added a half-time staff person to the Human Relations Commission to help investigate discrimination complaints. In addition, Iowa City schools expanded educational and support services on behalf of gay and lesbian youth.[42]

While gays have shown themselves to be an important political force in Iowa City, openly gay and lesbian political candidates have been few in number and notably unsuccessful. Two recent candidates for the city council who were open about their homosexuality both lost the election partly because of their announced sexual orientation. One of the candidates, a lesbian employed at the university, claimed that "running openly as a lesbian hurt her." She said her opponent made it clear that he was running against a "lesbian," provoking homophobic fears. During the campaign, she experienced antigay remarks and several threatening phone calls. Without an effective political organization, she lost by a wide margin in the 1993 primary election. Afterward she stated, "What they learn from races like mine is that people aren't ready to elect an openly gay or lesbian candidate yet, even in Iowa City."[43] Thus while the city is a liberal college town that is much more supportive of gay rights than most communities, the gay movement here has not fully achieved the political power and acceptance one might expect.

Philadelphia: Brotherly Love?

Philadelphia was founded in the late seventeenth century by William Penn, who attempted to create a haven for those seeking religious and political freedom. Known as the City of Brotherly Love, Philadelphia's reputation was enhanced a century later when the city became the site of the Continental Congress, the Liberty Bell, and the Declaration of Independence. Near the eastern seaboard, Philadelphia attracted immigrants from many nations. By the mid-1950s, the city's population had swelled to more than two million, and its diverse neighborhoods included sizable numbers of blacks, Hispanics, Asians, and ethnic whites.

Such a setting proved to be relatively fertile ground for the development of a lesbian and gay political movement. Just prior to the 1950s, Philadelphia was controlled by suburban, mainline Republicans and was, according to a local gay activist, "famed for the blue laws, mediocrity and industry."[44] Political corruption led to the election of Democratic "reformers" in the 1950s. The protest movements of the 1960s, focusing first on black civil rights and then the youthful antiwar sentiment, created a more pluralistic politics in the city.[45] During this period of tension and change, the local gay movement first began to blossom.

A Philadelphia chapter of the Mattachine Society, known as the Janus Society, was organized in 1961. Greatly influenced by the larger and more active Mattachine organizations in New York and Washington, the Janus Society joined these other groups in 1963 to form a loosely structured coalition, the East Coast Homophile Organization (ECHO), to share information and ideas.[46] Although the Janus Society attracted only a small number of gay activists, the more militant members dominated the organization. In the spring of 1965, for instance, the society staged sit-ins at a local restaurant after the manager refused service to several persons he suspected of being gay. Several gay activists were arrested, but the distribution of flyers and local television coverage gained valuable publicity for the movement.[47] The Janus Society was also active in the ECHO-sponsored picket line held on July 4 at Independence Hall in 1965 and on the same date for several years thereafter. Contending that gays were denied rights granted to all Americans in the Declaration of Independence, the protesters carried signs with such slogans as "Homosexual American citizens, our last oppressed national minority."[48] Philadelphia lesbians were less active politically than gay men during this period, but they had organized a Daughters of Bilitis chapter that also challenged abuses suffered by homosexuals. Foremost among the abuses were the antigay harassment and violence by the police, who, under the "law and order" police commissioner Frank Rizzo, routinely raided gay bars and coffeehouses.[49]

By the early 1970s the Philadelphia gay movement was larger and more diverse. A Gay Liberation Day march through downtown in June 1972 attracted "thousands of homosexuals," according to the *New York Times*.[50] Lesbian and gay liberation organizations developed rapidly in the aftermath of the Stonewall rebellion. Although the goals of these groups varied somewhat, most agreed on the need for local gay rights legislation. In the spring of 1974, after several years of quiet lobbying and sometimes vocal demonstrations by gays, the Philadelphia city council began to consider protective legislation that would include sexual orientation.[51] The proposed measure would amend the city's Fair Practices Ordinance, established in 1952, which barred discrimination in employment, housing, and public accommodations for reasons of race, religion, national origin, sex, and physical disability (employment, however, was not covered for the disabled). The Philadelphia Commission on Human Relations (PCHR) recommended the legislation to the city council after two days of public hearings. A large majority of the fifty-nine persons who gave testimony supported the antidiscrimination amendment and provided evidence of how discrimination had limited the potential, and sometimes ruined the lives, of gay people. The various gay and lesbian organizations represented among the speakers included the Gay Activists Alliance, the Gay Nurses Alliance, the Gay Switchboard, the Lesbian Hotline, and the Homophile Action League. Many other traditionally liberal groups in the areas of health, religion, law, labor, civil rights, and women's rights also supported the legislation.[52]

The police and fire departments and the Catholic archdiocese strongly opposed the gay rights bill, but surprisingly, no spokespersons from these organizations appeared at the 1974 hearings. Of the half-dozen speakers against the legislation, the most outspoken were ministers who raised biblical admonitions against homosexuality and expressed fears of gays threatening young children.[53] Despite the strong support in public hearings and the endorsement of the PCHR, the bill remained bottled up in city council committee until late 1975. In the city elections of November 1975, the conservative Mayor Rizzo (the former police commissioner) won reelection by a large margin, and the new council was considered more conservative than the previous body.[54] In a desperate attempt to get the bill released from committee for a floor vote before the new council took office, seventy-five gay and lesbian activists disrupted a city council meeting in protest. Some of the protesters clashed with security guards and were forcibly ejected from the chambers. The protests were to no avail, however, and the bill failed to emerge from committee.[55]

The general political mood in the state was not conducive to gay rights. No other city in Pennsylvania had yet adopted, or even strongly considered, such legislation. Moreover, when Gov. Milton Shapp issued an executive order in April 1975 barring discrimination in state employment because of sexual orientation, the state legislature quickly responded by overwhelmingly passing a bill to restrict the employment of gays in state agencies. The governor vetoed the bill, but plans by several lawmakers to introduce a gay rights measure in the legislature were dropped.[56]

In 1977 another attempt was made in Philadelphia to amend the Fair Practices Ordinance to include sexual orientation. To muster greater council support, the proposal excluded the police and fire departments from the employment provision. These departments had vehemently opposed gay rights, contending that they could not entrust their lives to a gay person in a highly dangerous profession. Firefighters felt especially threatened because many of them would have to share sleeping quarters with gay firemen. Many gays, however, found the omission of these departments unacceptable and refused to support the bill. Lacking significant council support as well, the measure once again died in committee.[57]

With the second defeat of lesbian and gay civil rights, the political strategy of the gay movement changed. The new emphasis was on electoral politics, and the goal was to create a more supportive city lawmaking body. In 1978, gays were active at the polls in helping to reject a city charter change that would have allowed Mayor Rizzo to run for a third term. Rizzo had a reputation for being antagonistic to gays and to many other minorities as well. Thus the success of the "Stop Rizzo" campaign was considered a major victory. In the ensuing city elections in 1979, a politically moderate Democrat, William Green, was elected mayor, along with a more progressive city council. The visibility of gay and lesbian political efforts was very high during these election periods, and many liberal candidates for city office attended campaign forums in the gay community.[58]

The creation of the Philadelphia Lesbian and Gay Task Force in 1978 proved to be a major factor in the drive for a gay antidiscrimination amend-

ment. The task force quickly became the area's largest gay civil rights organization, and it played a key role in organizing, lobbying, fund raising, and
developing tactics necessary ultimately to gain passage of the legislation.
Somewhat later the task force also carried out periodic, systematic surveys of
Philadelphia's lesbian and gay citizens in order to document the degree of
antigay discrimination and violence. Rita Addessa, the executive director of
the task force, proved to be a shrewd and determined political organizer.[59]

By the early 1980s, not only had the local political landscape changed, but
nationally, more than forty communities had extended civil rights protections to gays and lesbians. In Philadelphia, the University of Pennsylvania, at
the urging of the Lesbian and Gay Task Force, adopted a nondiscrimination
policy in relation to sexual minorities in 1979. The university is the city's
largest private employer. A year later, Philadelphia's black managing director
(or chief administrator), W. Wilson Goode, a gay rights supporter, issued a
policy directive banning discrimination against lesbians and gays employed
by the city. These successes encouraged the drive for a comprehensive law
that would protect all gays in various areas of their lives.[60]

The task force, in collaboration with the Philadelphia Black Gays, a relatively new organization, began to galvanize grass-roots support for a gay
rights law. On June 30, 1982, a black city councilman, with a diverse group
of eight co-sponsors (there were seventeen members on the council), introduced a bill to attempt once again to amend the city's Fair Practices code.[61] In
public hearings before a council committee in late July, approximately fifty
witnesses gave testimony in support of the antidiscrimination measure. As
described by the *Philadelphia Daily News*, one of the city's major newspapers,
the endorsements at the hearings consisted of "a parade of witnesses from the
gay and religious communities, civil rights and women's groups, community associations, labor unions, Bell of Pennsylvania, and several prominent
public officials."[62] Goode, who later became mayor, praised the measure as
"reinforcement of basic human and civil rights."[63] In addition, Edward Rendell, the district attorney also later to become mayor, urged passage of the
bill in order to send a message to those who would discriminate and claimed,
"There is nothing in this bill not already guaranteed by the equal protection
clause of the U.S. Constitution."[64] Other witnesses testified that homosexuals had lost jobs, been evicted from their apartments, and suffered other forms
of discrimination because of their sexual orientation.[65]

Opposition to the bill formed late and was relatively unorganized. Gay
advocates had hoped that by moving the proposal along swiftly during the
quiet summer months they would catch opponents off guard and ill prepared. Indeed, during public hearings, no witness appeared to express opposition. The primary antagonist, as expected, was the Roman Catholic archdiocese. With an estimated 500,000 Catholics in the city, the church was a

potentially powerful political force. Cardinal John Krol, head of the arch-diocese, had claimed that the bill was not needed because antidiscrimination laws were already in place. The cardinal believed the city council was try-ing "to create an impression for the public that homosexuality is a normal way of living, that it is right, that it is not something immoral, as the scrip-tures tell us."[66] Cardinal Krol, however, was out of town during hearings, and diocesan officials urged the council to delay action on the measure to no avail.

The gay rights bill moved quickly out of committee with a favorable vote of 6–1. Although about fifty members of two fundamentalist religious groups appeared before the council in a last effort to thwart the bill, the city council voted, without delay, to approve the legislation by a decisive margin of 13–2 on August 5. Mayor Green, however, inexplicably refused to sign the legis-lation, nor did he veto it, and the measure quietly became law after the spec-ified waiting period.[67] The task force and gay activists had implemented a successful political strategy. In the words of one gay rights strategist, "Our tactic was to show this as 'the right thing to do,' as a 'nondiscrimination bill,' not as an endorsement of homosexuality."

Gay and lesbian political mobilization continued to affect Philadelphia's politics throughout the 1980s. Efforts by gays were instrumental in the ascen-sion of Wilson Goode to the mayor's post in 1983 and in his reelection four years later. In each campaign Goode defeated the former mayor, Rizzo, in hard-fought contests in the Democratic primary. Honoring campaign promis-es to gays, Goode appointed several lesbians and gays to city offices and cre-ated the Commission on Sexual Minorities as an advisory board to the mayor.[68] The establishment of the commission, characterized by the *Philadel-phia Inquirer* as a "bold step," provided the lesbian and gay community with a liaison to city hall and ensured that city services would be more adequate-ly distributed to gay people.[69]

Despite these political successes, the quest of gays for additional rights and policies met with considerable resistance. Only two years after granting homosexuals equal rights under law, the city council rejected a resolution recognizing Lesbian and Gay Pride Week. While some council members as well as gays saw this issue as more symbolic than substantive and therefore of no critical importance, others, including the Lesbian and Gay Task Force, perceived the resolution as a civil rights issue and a significant public recog-nition of the diversity and contributions of gay people. The task force also argued that Pride Week was an important occasion to educate society about gays and lesbians and thus to change antigay attitudes.[70] In spite of lobbying and even some protests by gays, the city council failed to approve the reso-lution until 1989, and even then by only a narrow 9–8 vote.[71] The most out-spoken critic of the Gay Pride resolution was Councilman Francis Rafferty, who asserted that homosexuality was "nothing to be proud of" and that "deviant" gay sex was to blame for the AIDS epidemic.[72] Gay activists mounted a major campaign against Rafferty, and in the early 1990s he was defeated in his next reelection bid.

Opposition to gay issues also proved to be intense in 1993, when gay and lesbian groups pushed for council consideration of domestic partners legislation. The proposed measure would have entitled gays to the same benefits as married heterosexual couples, including access to pension, health, and death benefits. On this occasion, unlike the political battle over the gay rights law in 1982, the Catholic archdiocese and other opponents were well organized. Cardinal Anthony Bevilacqua himself made a dramatic appearance during the committee hearings to denounce the legislation as "immoral" and a threat to the traditional family.[73] Many black ministers and other traditional church leaders were aligned with the Catholic Church. The black president of the city council also opposed the domestic partners bill as black leaders and council members divided over the legislation. A massive phone and letter lobbying campaign directed at the city council was indicative of the strength of the opposition, persuading even supportive Mayor Edward Rendell to request ultimately that the proposal be tabled.[74]

Despite this legislative setback, gay power has become a significant force in Philadelphia politics. In October 1993, the Pride of Philadelphia Election Committee, the local political action committee (PAC) for gays and lesbians, hosted a fund-raising dinner that included numerous state and local officials among its four hundred guests. The dinner raised almost $40,000, and Mayor Rendell, a speaker at the event, called the gay PAC one of the major political organizations in the city.[75]

Yet many lesbians and gays continue to face discrimination and even violence. The task force's 1995–1996 survey of almost 1,400 gay Philadelphians showed that 28 percent of the men and 33 percent of the women reported experiencing discrimination in employment, housing, or public accommodations in the previous year.[76] Fear and distrust of the police continues to be a sentiment of many gays, fueled perhaps by the well-publicized 1991 confrontation between gay protesters and the police when President George Bush visited the city. In that incident, homophobia and the fear of AIDS were the causes of the beating the protesters received at the hands of the police, according to an investigating panel.[77] In addition, the 1995–1996 survey indicated that large numbers of lesbians and gay men reported experiencing violence or harassment by classmates and teachers in junior and senior high school. Although Philadelphia's school board has passed two important policies that include sexual orientation and that potentially affect education and services relating to gay and lesbian youth, their implementation thus far has been negligible.[78] While the gay political movement has achieved some remarkable results during the last several decades, the "brotherly love" of Philadelphia remains an elusive goal for many lesbians and gay men.

Raleigh: "This Is the South"

Raleigh is in the heart of the South, where prejudice and discrimination have a long and enduring history. It is also the home of Jesse Helms, clearly the most virulently antigay member of the U.S. Senate. Yet North Carolina, especially the state's eastern, more urban Piedmont region, which includes Raleigh, has become a symbol of southern progressivism in the areas of industrial development, education, and race relations.[79] Raleigh in particular is seen as more liberal than most southern cities, partly because government and education are the major employers in the city. It is the state capital and home of North Carolina State University, which has more than 25,000 students. Raleigh is also part of the Research Triangle, which includes nearby Durham and Chapel Hill, and the host of high-tech companies located here have brought in moderately progressive people from all over the country.[80] As a result, Raleigh is one of the few areas in Dixie where gays and lesbians have felt relatively free to congregate, and in time, to organize politically.

The first stirrings of gay activity in the area took place in Chapel Hill in the 1950s. A college town dominated by the University of North Carolina, Chapel Hill had the reputation of "being liberal and a safe place for gays," according to a gay activist we interviewed. Homosexuals were attracted to the city, and gay bars appeared early on. Similar activity occurred in nearby Durham, the home of Duke University, by the 1970s. Students, many of whom were from the North, were at the center of the emerging movement in both communities. Although gays seemingly had no specific grievances in these fairly tolerant cities, the activist suggested that a "sense of identity" was the general issue of the period. During this phase, the gay movement was tied strongly to the black civil rights movement. Nourished by years of struggling for civil rights, southern liberals and gays in the area were keenly aware of oppression and how to respond to it.[81]

In 1975, Chapel Hill was the scene of the first notable political act by gays. Organized gays requested the city council to include lesbians and gays in the city's antidiscrimination personnel policy. The council approved the request with little debate.[82] A dozen years later an openly gay man was elected to the Chapel Hill city council. Durham, too, was affected by increased gay activism. In 1986 Durham's mayor proclaimed an Anti-Discrimination Week that specifically included gays and lesbians. In response, antigay Christian fundamentalists mobilized in an attempt to petition for a recall election to turn the mayor out of office. Gays organized in support of the mayor and, with the help of a progressive coalition of nongay whites and blacks, defeated the recall effort in an emotion-packed struggle.[83]

By the mid-1980s Raleigh began to feel the pulse of the gay movement, which had already affected neighboring communities. The incident that triggered the political mobilization of gays was a city official's cancellation of a park reservation for the annual Gay Freedom Day event in the spring of 1986. The park official discovered that the event would likely draw as many as five hundred gays and lesbians and reportedly said that he "didn't want a bunch of queers in his park." Gays complained to the city council, which then reversed the official's decision.

The park incident, however, convinced gay activists of the need for a city gay rights measure. Gays appealed to the city's Human Relations and Human Resources Advisory Committee, which in 1987 voted to ask the city council to approve a proposed state legislative resolution opposing discrimination against homosexuals. The council refused to act on the controversial state resolution but requested a report on crimes against gays in the city. In response to this request, the Advisory Committee held a public hearing on gay-related discrimination. Approximately twenty gays testified before the committee, telling of being fired from their jobs, harassed by police, and victimized by antigay violence. No one testified in opposition to gays, and the committee recommended to the city council that they pass an ordinance prohibiting discrimination against homosexuals.[84]

The gay community organized a group called Raleigh Citizens for Gay and Lesbian Equality to fight for the protective legislation. The group realized that it needed one city council member who was fully committed to gay rights and who would take the lead in passing legislation. Such a person emerged as a council candidate prior to the 1987 local elections. Mary Nooe, a married public relations director for Goodwill Industries, embraced the gay rights issue. With support from the relatively large number of gays and blacks in her district, she won a seat on the city council. In the process, gays and lesbians gained recognition as a political force in Raleigh.[85]

Soon after her election, Nooe began to lobby other members of the council for legislation protecting gays. "I don't call it gay rights," she said in an interview, "but constitutional rights." She also stated, "I was of the opinion that the people of Raleigh did not want to be perceived as discriminating against any group of people—gays included."[86] A liberal coalition, composed of various lesbian and gay organizations, the American Civil Liberties Union (ACLU), the North Carolina Council of Churches, the National Organization for Women (NOW), the National Association for the Advancement of Colored People (NAACP), and the Human Resources and Human Relations Advisory Committee, supported the proposed legislation and began a letter-writing campaign to the city council. Ministers representing twelve Raleigh churches, mostly liberal denominations but including some southern Baptists and Roman Catholics, organized as a group called the Religious Network for Gay and Lesbian Equality and also urged passage of an ordinance.[87]

At a city council meeting in early January 1988, Mary Nooe introduced a motion to amend the city's antidiscrimination law to include sexual orientation. With no organized opposition and little debate, the council voted 7–1 in favor of the amendment. Only the mayor voted against it, claiming that he did not believe that discrimination was a problem for gays in Raleigh. Some African Americans, especially those who were older or Baptist, also opposed gay rights, but the lone black council member supported the amendment, defining it as a human rights issue. The new ordinance was somewhat limited, prohibiting discrimination against gays only in city employment, city-funded housing, the use of city facilities, and businesses that had contracts with the city. Two weeks later, the council appointed an openly gay man to the Human Relations and Human Resources Advisory Committee, which was charged with monitoring adherence to the legislation. The appointee was nominated by Nooe and was the first openly gay person to serve on the committee.[88]

The passage of a gay rights measure provided an impetus to further gay political action. In June of 1988, the annual statewide Lesbian and Gay Pride March and Celebration was held in Raleigh for the first time. The march attracted some two thousand gays and their supporters, whose goals were not only to proclaim openly their homosexuality but also to push for more support for persons with AIDS and for a statewide law banning discrimination against gays. In addition, the marchers announced their strong opposition to Sen. Jesse Helms because of his stand against homosexuality and funding for AIDS education.[89]

Helms had long been the focus of gay political attacks, and in his next election bid in 1990, gays were particularly active in opposition. Although Helms won the election in a close race with the black candidate Harvey Gantt, the North Carolina Pride PAC, a statewide lesbian and gay political organization, and local gay activists proved to be effective political forces.[90] In Raleigh Council elections, gays were a significant factor in several reelections of Mary Nooe, including in 1993, when Nooe ran as an at-large, or citywide, candidate. By 1991, almost all local candidates for office were showing up at the public forums sponsored by gays, an indicator of the emerging political influence of the gay community.

One of the additional primary goals of gay activists was reform of the state's antisodomy, or crime-against-nature, law. Such laws are most commonly found in southern and more conservative states. Although the law in fact criminalized both heterosexual and homosexual oral and anal sex, the law had been applied in a discriminatory manner primarily against lesbians

and gay men. In addition, by defining homosexuals as lawbreakers and suggesting that they are "outside the human community," the crime-against-
nature law was often used as a legal rationale for antigay efforts and served
to justify hate crimes against gays.[91] Despite repeated efforts to modify the
measure in the state legislature, such actions failed because many lawmakers interpreted reform bills as "attempts to legitimize homosexuality and to
help gays and lesbians become more widely accepted."[92]

In Raleigh, gays also suffered a major setback in 1993, when the attempt
to extend the city's gay rights ordinance to the private sector failed in a city
council vote. Responding to some complaints that the application of the 1988
antidiscrimination measure primarily to city employees made it too limited,
Mary Nooe introduced a motion to expand the law to all private firms. The
process for doing so was more complicated than in 1988 because the council
had to ask the state legislature for enabling legislation. (It is a North Carolina state requirement that cities cannot exceed the boundaries of state law
without legislative approval.) The motion, however, immediately met with
stiff resistance locally from both business owners and fundamentalist churches. In a committee hearing on the proposal, local merchants argued that further regulation would harm their businesses, deter future business development, and even force them to hire gays. Other business persons maintained
that antigay discrimination was not a problem in Raleigh. Several ministers,
moreover, presented moral arguments against homosexuality and expressed
fears that they too would have to employ gays.[93] The Raleigh Christian
Academy, for example, upset about the prospect of having to hire gays, sent
fliers home with its seven hundred students urging parents to protest against
the city council proposal.[94]

The combination of significant, organized opposition and too little planning and mobilization by gay rights advocates doomed the attempt to extend
the city's antidiscrimination ordinance. But the expansion to the business
sector also failed because many policymakers and citizens saw the proposal
as an unacceptable intrusion into the private sector. There was, they felt, a big
difference between the city making a law to monitor its own employee practices and the city extending the law to employers in the larger community.
For many, the private sector is typically considered beyond the pale of government power, particularly when that public intrusion is considered unnecessary.

Despite these legislative defeats, gays and lesbians in Raleigh and the
Research Triangle area were able to forge ahead in the early 1990s. Gays and
their supporters continued to coordinate their campaigning and lobbying
efforts in local politics, and the North Carolina Pride PAC was increasingly
able to raise money to support local as well as statewide candidates. Partly as
a result of these political activities, an openly gay man was elected to the

Board of Aldermen in nearby Carrboro, and both the Chapel Hill and Durham city councils moved to expand their gay rights measures.[95] Lobbying from gays was also helpful in persuading Northern Telecom, one of the largest employers in the area, to offer domestic partner health benefits to its workers.[96] As the ultimate indicator of progress, a few area churches, including a Baptist church in Raleigh, blessed gay marriages without substantial local retribution.[97]

Although all these changes were important, political resistance was still alive, and gays continued to confront harassment and even violence. A 1991 study of antigay discrimination and hate crimes conducted by the North Carolina Coalition for Gay and Lesbian Equality found that North Carolina reported the highest number of such incidents in the nation. This statewide study was supported by local reports of gays and lesbians being verbally harassed, fired from their jobs, or physically attacked.[98] Even at North Carolina State University, gay students reported significant amounts of hateful graffiti and personal threats.[99] In 1995 the city council turned increasingly conservative, and Mary Nooe lost her bid for the mayorship to an antigay Republican. Shortly thereafter city officials closed Raleigh's most popular gay bar, suddenly deciding to enforce more selectively the city's ordinance dealing with adult establishments.[100] These incidents suggested that, as a Raleigh political leader put it, "Many people here still don't accept them [gays]. . . . [T]hey object to who they are and how they act." The extent of this nonacceptance is clearly reflected in Raleigh's school system, where no significant programmatic offerings beneficial to gay and lesbian youth have been proposed. As summarized by the head of a parent organization, "There is resistance to providing sex education of any kind. . . . Teachers are afraid to come out or to mention anything about homosexuality for fear of losing their jobs." Raleigh is considered progressive, but it is also very southern, and the pace of political change has clearly been influenced by the traditional culture of the South.

Santa Cruz: Little San Francisco

"It's hard to imagine a community that has changed more since the days of the charming little seaside community of the 1950s," stated the editor of the *Santa Cruz Sentinel*.[101] Santa Cruz is still the idyllic, upper-middle-income, distant suburb (approximately 100 miles south) of San Francisco. Nonetheless, its transformation to an "exciting, forward-thinking, and progressive community" of 49,000 residents is attributed to its proximity to San Francisco as well as to the establishment of a University of California branch campus in 1965.[102] These 10,000 students, however, nestled in the surrounding but remote redwood hills, reside somewhat apart from the city. Students attending the University of California at Santa Cruz do not tend to be involved in local politics. Thus the university lends a "tone to the town" but does not dominate local politics. Illustrative of this situation, the university-based initiative that resulted in the first county gay rights ordinance in the United States, one passed by the commissioners of Santa Cruz County in 1975, excluded the city.[103]

The relatively large number of gays and lesbians in Santa Cruz began to coalesce politically in the late 1970s in reaction to Miami's repeal of its ordinance and in order to fight passage of California's Briggs Initiative. State senator John Briggs's controversial proposal sought to mandate that California school boards fire teachers who engaged in, advocated, or promoted homosexuality.[104] This initiative was successfully defeated in the 1978 elections. Shortly thereafter university personnel and city residents established the Santa Cruz Action Network to elect liberal candidates to local office. The Action Network succeeded in electing a liberal city commission beginning in the early 1980s, and in 1983 it elected John Laird, a progressive, well-liked, coalition-building—and gay—Democrat as mayor. As an openly gay candidate, he was reelected in 1986 to serve a second consecutive term. A gay-friendly climate in the city emanated from Laird's election.

Known as a "lesbian mecca" since the early 1980s, Santa Cruz provided the safety and numbers for lesbians to become politically active. They had been a visible presence in the city's annual Gay Pride Parade since its inception in 1984.[105] More important, beginning in the mid-1980s many were actively involved in the Bay Area Municipal Elections Committee, a political action committee in behalf of gays and lesbians.[106] In contrast to the gay movement in other cities, it was lesbian activists in Santa Cruz who became primarily responsible for the passage of its antidiscrimination ordinance.

As mayor, Laird instituted several policies and procedures that addressed gay and lesbian needs. In his first term he issued an administrative order that prohibited discrimination in employment based on sexual orientation. In 1984 he instituted a directive that included sexual orientation in the city's sexual harassment policy. He also met regularly with the chief of police to relay concerns on behalf of gay and lesbian citizens and actively participated in the mandatory sensitivity training sessions for police.

One of Laird's most important accomplishments as mayor was to establish the city's Human Rights Commission in 1986 to document discrimination against gays and lesbians. Santa Cruz had a history of "gay bashing" incidents. Although mainly attributed to tourists and outsiders, these incidents included gay men beaten by area residents in 1991 and 1992.[107] In 1988 a front-page newspaper article, "Four Gay Killings in a Year," described the extreme dangers faced by gays as a result of homophobia within the community. Such documented violence against gays and lesbians substantiated the impetus for local legislation. Several arrests of gays resulting from entrapment authorized by the county sheriff further supported gays' claims of bias and injustice. The Human Rights Commission became the body to recommend the antidiscrimination ordinance to the city commission in 1992.[108]

The greatest motivation for instituting the city's ordinance, however, was attributed to the betrayal of gays by the California governor Pete Wilson, a Republican elected with significant support from the gay and lesbian community. As a candidate, Wilson promised to sign a statewide employment antidiscrimination law that included sexual orientation. His veto of that legislation in 1991 instigated riots and angry marches around the state and mobilized the gay community in Santa Cruz to rally strongly for passage of an antidiscrimination ordinance at the local level.[109]

Lesbian activists secured broadly based grass-roots support, formed the Santa Cruz Anti-Discrimination Coalition, and lobbied the city council for the protective legislation proposed in January 1992.[110] Despite documented cases of harassment and violence, and strong political support, the ordinance did not escape controversy. In fact, because of its extensive coverage, the proposed antidiscrimination legislation propelled Santa Cruz into the national spotlight—it would protect groups on the basis of age, race, color, creed, religion, national origin, ancestry, disability, marital status, sex, gender, sexual orientation, and physical appearance. The inclusion of "physical appearance" in particular proved to be most disturbing to the community, especially business leaders, and subjected Santa Cruz to national attention and ridicule.[111] Although proposed mainly to address the issue of weight, debates centered on "whether government should protect job rights for people who color their hair purple and wear nose rings."[112] On the whole, the business community did not express opposition to the inclusion of sexual orientation in the proposed ordinance, and even the Chamber of Commerce was moderately supportive.[113]

A task force under lesbian activist leadership was appointed by the council to rewrite the ordinance to allay the expressed fears. The revised ordinance was reconsidered in the fall, and some opposition to sexual orientation coverage then emerged. One member of the state Republican Party wrote an article for the *Sentinel* that claimed that the right to choose one's associations in work would be violated.[114] Some business representatives contended that the law was not necessary and would initiate bias in favor of homosexuals, and others expressed fears of the cost of additional government regulations.[115]

The revised legislation, however, maintained strong, broadly based support, which included Democratic clubs, civil rights organizations, women's groups, some churches, and the *Sentinel* newspaper, in addition to local and regional gay and lesbian organizations. The proposed ordinance was viewed as promoting fairness, and its coverage of sexual orientation had the support of all council members. "Arguing against the need for a level playing field in getting jobs and housing is not just 'politically incorrect,' it's a step backward to a time when people were judged . . . by the color of their skin and not the content of their characters," editorialized the *Sentinel*.[116] Problems that Santa Cruz lesbians and gays had faced, documented over years, and testimony in legislative hearings by gay men and lesbians about personal experiences of abuse and harassment provided examples of discrimination ranging from job loss to physical assaults. Although opponents packed the council meeting that considered the revised ordinance, they represented only the Christian right, expressing objections based primarily on the immorality of homosexuality. A long list of local churches that were *not* opposed to its passage was presented in rebuttal.[117] Council members passed the ordinance by a vote of 5–2 on April 28, 1992.[118]

Since passage of the law, no formal complaints have been filed on the basis of sexual orientation. The primary reason for this dearth of charges is the cost of litigation. The complainant and the offending organization are required to pay equally the mandated mediation process fees. Second, Governor Wilson reversed his decision and signed a bill protecting homosexuals from job discrimination in September 1992, stunning local activists and breaking with his Republican Party platform.[119] Thus, California acquired statewide statutes pertaining to hate crimes, domestic violence, and fair employment and housing that protect on the basis of sexual orientation, and these state laws have overriding jurisdiction at the local level. Since passage of the state hate crimes law in 1987, Santa Cruz police had begun collecting data documenting hate crimes, including those against gays and lesbians. The police also became more aggressive in their investigations and prosecutions of such incidents. Publicity about active law enforcement, particularly for arrests under the hate crimes law for violations against gays and lesbians, has served to increase gays' confidence that they can trust the police.[120]

Discrimination against lesbians and gays in Santa Cruz has not, however, been eliminated. Some verbal harassment on the streets, incidents of gay bashing, and ostracism persist. Gay and lesbian youths interviewed in 1994 claimed they faced lack of support as well as prejudice in school. Triangle Speakers, a gay, lesbian, and bisexual group formed in 1992 to provide education and support for youths, aroused significant local controversy, and its speakers were banned from certain area schools.[121]

Nonetheless, many gays and lesbians feel free to hold hands with their partner in public and to join the networking organization Gays and Lesbians in Business. City employees have had domestic partner benefits since 1987. The annual Gay Freedom Day Parade is supported by the city each June, and some local officials march in it. A few open lesbians serve on the police force.[122] In addition, in its schools the city offers the most extensive educational and support services beneficial to gays and lesbians of all the cities within this study, including nondiscrimination and antiharassment policies and teacher training and curriculum materials for education about sexual orientation. Efforts have recently been made to establish support groups and special counseling services within at least one high school. Several openly gay and lesbian individuals serve in school district administrative positions, and gays continue to play a significant role in local politics. Although only one other openly gay city council member has been elected, candidates in general routinely seek the endorsement of the Action Network and the Bay Area Municipal Elections Committee, and the council is uniformly categorized as liberal or progressive. Thus, as summed up by John Laird, Santa Cruz has "come a long way, and we still have a long way to go."[123] Clearly this San Francisco suburb by the sea is a significant step beyond most American cities in its acceptance and, more important, inclusion of gay and lesbian citizens into local life.

Cincinnati: City without Sin?

Sitting astride the Mason-Dixon line on the banks of the Ohio River, Cincinnati has a dual personality that is part northern and part southern. In the 1800s immigrants from western Europe, especially Germany and Ireland, settled in the area, drawn by the city's bustling trade and commerce. Following the Civil War, freed blacks from the South also flocked to Cincinnati, a migration that would continue well into the twentieth century. This cultural diversity is characteristic of most large northern cities. But Cincinnati's regional duality—being both a northern and a southern city—has provided a tension and a degree of unreconciled conflict that are unique among major American cities.[124] In this environment, the quest for gay rights was not only slow to develop, but once achieved, faced opposition that was unprecedented in major urban settings.

The traditional southern influence dictated that Cincinnati's politics would have a conservative and moralistic strain. The city's reputation in the mid-twentieth century was that of a reformed, good-government metropolis. Republican dominance of city government in the 1960s, however, asserted a conservative tone that exacerbated racial and ethnic cleavages. The eruption of a major race riot in 1967 played a key role in altering the political balance, as Democrats in a coalition with a liberal third party (the Charter Party) gained control in the early 1970s. This coalition maintained its dominance until the mid-1980s, when it fell apart and a more conservative majority came to rule once again.[125] Throughout this period Republicans controlled county government and, in conjunction with more traditional elements in the city, provided Cincinnati with its contemporary reputation as a "bastion of traditional family values" and as the "'smut-free' capital of the country." [126] "We ridded the city of pornography, massage parlors, and sex shops over the years," claimed a local conservative politician. "It's now a decent place to live—very pro-family." Not surprisingly, the city's schools offer no educational or support services designed to benefit gay and lesbian students.

One of the city's major political battles over morality was the 1990 controversy surrounding the local exhibit of the photographs of the late Robert Mapplethorpe. The photographs, some of which showed homoerotic acts, had been exhibited in other cities in the United States without much fanfare. Local officials in Cincinnati, however, indicted the director of the city's Contemporary Arts Center on charges of obscenity for showing Mapplethorpe's pictures. Although the director was ultimately acquitted, the controversy was an indication of the city's moral fervor and antigay mentality. [127]

This repressive atmosphere thwarted the development of an active gay movement. Many gay and lesbian organizers were lured to more liberal cities, and the gay political community remained relatively small. In the late 1960s, a small, local Mattachine Society and Homophile Organization were created, and among women, a chapter of the Daughters of Bilitis was formed. These groups focused primarily on education, political change, and some social functions. Their major political effort was lobbying to repeal the Ohio sodomy law that made homosexual acts a crime. With the help of gay organizations in Cleveland and Columbus, the law was overturned in 1973. [128]

These nascent gay groups were short-lived, however, as leaders left and other organizations emerged. By the late 1970s the Lesbian Activist Bureau and the Greater Cincinnati Gay Coalition were the major groups coordinating lesbian and gay activities. They organized annual gay pride days, sponsored newsletters, and worked on political issues, such as the picketing of movies they perceived as antihomosexual. Their most significant political activity, however, was the proposal in 1977 of an antidiscrimination ordinance that included gays and lesbians. Spurred on by Anita Bryant's well-publicized crusade against gay rights, gay leaders developed the Coalition for Cincinnati Human Rights Law, which included the ACLU, NOW, the city's Human Relations Commission, and other progressive groups. Cincinnati had no human rights legislation of any kind, and the proposed measure backed by the coalition would have protected a variety of groups, in addition to gays. [129]

The proposed ordinance, as it related to sexual orientation, generated opposition almost immediately. Landlords and realtors complained about the prospect of being unable to refuse to rent to homosexual couples, thus losing a right that they considered important. They also feared the loss of other tenants, who might object to having gays live nearby. [130] City council members voiced objections as well. "My personal moral persuasion is that it [homosexuality] is not acceptable," declared one black councilman.[131] Another stated he believed that there were relatively few cases of discrimination against gays and lesbians. Several council members, moreover, perceived the measure as "potentially explosive" politically, mentioning the recent controversy surrounding a similar proposal in Dade County, Florida.[132] The city's major newspaper, the *Enquirer*, expressed opposition as well, editorializing that "any such 'rights' law seems to put a stamp of legitimacy on an aberrant behavior for which those affected, to be sure, may not be totally responsible."[133]

The *Enquirer's* view of gays was reinforced in some people's minds by a massive police crackdown in the spring of 1978 on male homosexuals in city parks. In a series of police raids, more than sixty men were arrested and charged with public indecency or sexual imposition. Such antigay activity by the police was not uncommon, but this crackdown was unusually large. Gays protested the raids, contending that the police used illegal tactics and that the crackdown was politically inspired in an attempt to discredit homosexuals while the city council was considering a human rights law. The police denied that the crackdown was politically motivated and claimed they were simply enforcing the laws of the community in the process of protecting citizens in the public parks. The raids, however, sealed the fate of the proposed ordinance, which died in committee not long thereafter.[134]

This controversy with the police served to unify and mobilize the gay community. Gays began to carry out voter registration drives, and in 1981 an openly gay man ran for city council as a write-in candidate. He received only a few hundred votes, but his candidacy was an indication of the political awakening of the gay community.[135] In 1982, gays and lesbians united to found the city's most influential gay interest group, Stonewall Cincinnati. The organization's primary goal was to work for the passage of a local gay rights law, but its efforts soon broadened to include election and campaign activities, educational programs, and assistance to victims of discrimination and violence.[136]

Stonewall's first major political action was to confront attempts by members of the city council and other officials to fire gay city employees. With a letter-writing campaign and testimony given at a council hearing by Stonewall members, the organization was able to halt such antigay discrimination by the city.[137] In 1987 Stonewall carried out a month-long boycott of three local restaurants to protest the firing of gay employees. The boycott proved successful and the owner of the restaurants agreed to rehire the dismissed workers, thus showing the organizational capabilities and economic clout of the gay community.[138] The Stonewall organization also attempted to focus attention on alleged mistreatment of gays by the police and helped to create a county AIDS education program.[139]

By 1991 Stonewall Cincinnati was the state's second largest gay organization with four hundred active members, and the *Enquirer* called it "one of the most powerful special-interest groups in the city."[140] Its annual dinner that year drew more than 1,200 guests, including many local politicians. The substantial gay vote controlled an estimated five of Cincinnati's twenty-six Democratic ward clubs and was influential in the elections of several city council members. As an indication of Stonewall's growing political importance, for the first time since 1979 the mayor issued a proclamation in June honoring the city's lesbian and gay communities.[141]

In the spring of 1991 the city council took the first significant step toward the adoption of a comprehensive human rights law. After months of lobbying by the gay and lesbian community, the council added homosexuals and those infected with the AIDS virus to the city's Equal Employment Opportunity legislation. This law prohibited discrimination in city jobs, services, and contracts. The inclusion of sexual orientation faced virtually no opposition, but the legislation was narrowly confined to the public sector and therefore attracted little attention.[142] In the meantime the city's schools had adopted in the mid-1980s an antidiscrimination statement that specifically included sexual orientation, and gay and lesbian teachers had organized an active chapter of the national association called the Gay-Lesbian-Straight Teachers Network.

A little more than a year later the Human Rights Ordinance Task Force, a coalition of gay and lesbian organizations that included Stonewall Cincinnati, proposed a far-reaching human rights ordinance to the city council. The proposal prohibited discrimination in housing, public accommodations, and employment and covered a variety of disadvantaged groups in addition to gays and lesbians. This time the opposition was better mobilized. In a public hearing on the proposed ordinance in July 1992, more than seven hundred people filled the city council chambers and hallways in an emotional battle that lasted almost three hours. A network of religious, pro-family, black, and conservative groups, led by Charles Winburn, an influential black minister who later was elected to the city council, made up the opposition. Many argued that gays and lesbians should not receive special protection that would, for instance, prevent landlords from evicting gay couples.[143] Others, especially African Americans and including Winburn, maintained that homosexuality is a choice and not an immutable characteristic and therefore that gays cannot make the same claim for civil rights as can blacks or women.[144]

Somewhat later, the Chamber of Commerce and some business leaders joined the opposition, contending that most businesses already followed antidiscrimination policies and that the ordinance would impose special hardships on small businesses.[145] The *Enquirer* as well urged the council not to include sexual orientation in the ordinance, asking rhetorically, "What right does government have to trample fundamental rights, such as moral discretion and privacy, to make room for new rights?"[146]

Advocates of the human rights legislation, however, included a relatively broad coalition of forces. In addition to various gay organizations, supporters included the ACLU; NOW; the Council of Jewish Women; the National Women's Political Caucus; the American Federation of Labor-Congress of Industrial Organizations (AFL-CIO); the local Democratic Party; the clergy and some members of the Unitarian, Episcopal, and Presbyterian churches; and Appalachian-PAC (people from the nearby Appalachian region were included in the proposed ordinance). Most important, the election and campaign work of gay rights advocates had finally produced a city council majority that favored an ordinance. As a result, the opposition was able only to delay a council verdict. When the council finally voted in November 1992, it approved the ordinance by a 7–2 margin.[147]

Adoption of a human rights law that included sexual orientation enraged and further mobilized opponents. They vowed retribution at the polls, both against council members who approved the ordinance and for a local voter referendum to repeal the law. Organized as a group called Take Back Cincinnati, opponents mounted a successful petition drive that put a charter amendment on the November 1993 ballot. Known as Issue 3, the proposed amendment would revoke protection from discrimination for homosexuals and would also prohibit the city from creating any gay rights legislation in the future.[148]

To push for the passage of Issue 3, many pro-family, religious, and conservative groups came together in an umbrella organization known as Equal Rights, Not Special Rights (ERNSR). As the group's name suggests, proponents of Issue 3 asserted that it was necessary to prevent gays and lesbians from getting preferential treatment, or "special rights." While the charter amendment campaign was largely devoid of religious rhetoric, it did have ties to national Christian right forces. ERNSR also received advice and financial support from anti-gay rights activists in Colorado, where an initiative similar to Issue 3 had passed in 1992. The group Colorado for Family Values, for example, contributed approximately $390,000 of the $505,000 spent on the pro-Issue 3 campaign. A portion of this contribution, however, was allegedly "laundered" for Cincinnati businessmen opposed to gay rights.[149]

In addition to conservative whites, ERNSR targeted the black community for support. African Americans constituted 38 percent of Cincinnati's population, and "no special rights" were words of protest used throughout the campaign. An attempt was also made to arouse black wrath by characterizing the gay community as trying to "steal" the black civil rights legacy. Furthermore, ERNSR cast the issue of gay rights as one of blacks versus "privileged" whites by suggesting that gays were relatively well off economically.

A number of black ministers were enlisted in these efforts and were effective in communicating these messages to the African-American community.[150]

Anti-Issue 3 activists, in turn, characterized the matter as one of extreme prejudice against gays and lesbians and argued that the city ordinance was necessary to protect a class of citizens that suffered discrimination. Although being outspent by a 5:2 margin in the campaign, gay rights supporters focused their efforts on trying to identify the initiative as a "manifestation of hateful propaganda by the right wing."[151] Its primary advertising campaign featured images of Hitler, the Ku Klux Klan, and the 1950s anticommunist Sen. Joseph McCarthy appearing with the slogan, "Never Again." This ad created a good deal of controversy and criticism, especially in the black and Jewish communities, where some alleged that gays were inappropriately comparing themselves to other oppressed minorities.[152] On election day, Issue 3 passed with 62 percent of the votes; an estimated 55–60 percent of African-American voters supported the initiative.[153]

The battle over gay rights in Cincinnati did not end with this voter repeal, however. Gay rights advocates filed suit in U.S. District Court in an attempt to declare Issue 3 unconstitutional. They also called for a convention business boycott of Cincinnati in a protest tactic similar to that carried out earlier by gays in Colorado.[154] In August 1994, the federal district court ruled that Issue 3 was unconstitutional, but opponents of gay rights appealed the decision, bringing in the former federal appeals court judge Robert Bork and the former U.S. attorney general Edwin Meese to join the battle. In May 1995, the U.S. Court of Appeals overturned the district court's decision. By this time, however, the issue was moot because political turmoil over Issue 3 had led the city council to reconsider its position, and in March 1995 the council voted to delete "sexual orientation" from the Human Rights Ordinance.[155] Thus in Cincinnati the opponents of gay rights legislation have so far proven to be successful.

NOTES

Because of the controversial nature of this study, we promised the persons we interviewed that they would not be identified by name. Unless otherwise noted, all interviews pertaining to Iowa City took place in Iowa City in June 1994; all those pertaining to Philadelphia took place in Philadelphia in July 1994; all those pertaining to Raleigh took place either in Raleigh or Chapel Hill, N.C., in May 1994; all those pertaining to Santa Cruz took place in Santa Cruz in June 1994, and all those pertaining to Cincinnati took place in Cincinnati in November 1994. All quotations and information not otherwise documented are from these interviews.

1. John D'Emilio, *Sexual Politics, Sexual Communities: The Making of a Homosexual Minority in the United States, 1940–1970* (Chicago: University of Chicago Press, 1983), 13.
2. Randy Shilts, *The Mayor of Castro Street: The Life and Times of Harvey Milk* (New York: St. Martin's Press, 1982), 43.
3. D'Emilio, *Sexual Politics*, 10–11; Steven H. Haeberle, "Gay Men and Lesbians at City Hall," *Social Science Quarterly* 77 (March 1996): 190.

4. Barry D. Adam, *The Rise of a Gay and Lesbian Movement* (New York: Twayne, 1995), 42–43; Lillian Faderman, *Odd Girls and Twilight Lovers: A History of Lesbian Life in Twentieth Century America* (New York: Columbia University Press, 1991), 62–64.

5. Allan Berube, *Coming Out under Fire: The History of Gay Men and Women in World War Two* (New York: Free Press, 1990), 255–257; Faderman, *Odd Girls and Twilight Lovers*, 119–126.

6. D'Emilio, *Sexual Politics*, 24.

7. Berube, *Coming Out under Fire*, 271–272; D'Emilio, *Sexual Politics*, 31–33.

8. D'Emilio, *Sexual Politics*, 40–51; Faderman, *Odd Girls and Twilight Lovers*, 139–145.

9. Warren J. Blumenfeld and Diane Raymond, *Looking at Gay and Lesbian Life* (Boston: Beacon Press, 1988), 252–253; Toby Marotta, *The Politics of Homosexuality* (Boston: Houghton Mifflin, 1981), 15.

10. Marotta, *Politics of Homosexuality*, 8–12.

11. Faderman, *Odd Girls and Twilight Lovers*, 148–150.

12. Urvashi Vaid, *Virtual Equality: The Mainstreaming of Gay and Lesbian Liberation* (New York: Doubleday, Anchor, 1995), 50–51.

13. D'Emilio, *Sexual Politics*, 149–175.

14. Vaid, *Virtual Equality*, 52.

15. Faderman, *Odd Girls and Twilight Lovers*, 195.

16. D'Emilio, *Sexual Politics*, 236.

17. Adam, *Rise of the Gay and Lesbian Movement*, 81–89; D'Emilio, *Sexual Politics*, 237–238.

18. D'Emilio, *Sexual Politics*, 238.

19. Adam, *Rise of the Gay and Lesbian Movement*, 128–131; Vaid, *Virtual Equality*, 106–109, 137–138.

20. Adam, *Rise of the Gay and Lesbian Movement*, 109–115; Shilts, *Mayor of Castro Street*, 212–250.

21. Paul Gibson, "Gay and Lesbian Youth Suicide," in *Report of the Secretary's Task Force on Youth Suicide*, vol. 3, *Prevention and Intervention in Youth Suicide*, ed. M. R. Feinleib, no. (ADM)89-1623 (Washington, D.C.: U.S. Department of Health and Human Services, 1989), 3–110; Karen M. Harbeck, introduction to *Coming Out of the Classroom Closet: Gay and Lesbian Students, Teachers, and Curricula*, ed. Karen M. Harbeck (Binghamton, N.Y.: Harrington Park Press, 1992), 3, 16.

22. Adam, *Rise of the Gay and Lesbian Movement*, 139–141; Faderman, *Odd Girls and Twilight Lovers*, 295–300.

23. Joseph P. Shapiro, "Straight Talk about Gays," *U.S. News and World Report*, July 5, 1993, 46.

24. Martha Miller, "Iowa City 'Cool Place' for Gays, Lesbians," *Iowa City Press-Citizen*, June 25, 1988.

25. Ibid.

26. Barbara O'Reilly, "Supervisors Should Condemn Anti-Gay Graffiti, Oleson Says," *Iowa City Press-Citizen*, October 3, 1984; Jerry Heth, "UI's Freedman Openly Deplores Anti-Gay Graffiti," *Iowa City Press-Citizen*, October 9, 1984; Jerry Heth, "City Panel Approves Statement on Graffiti," *Iowa City Press-Citizen*, October 30, 1984.

27. Maudlyne Ihejirika, "Complaint Charges UI Fails to Protect Gay Rights," *Daily Iowan* (University of Iowa), October 30, 1984; Andrew Lersten, "Preference Clause Gets Support," *Daily Iowan*, February 5, 1985.

28. Kanchalee Svetvilas, "Letter to Rawlings Asks for Response on Rights for Gays," *Iowa City Press-Citizen*, October 23, 1990; Kanchalee Svetvilas, "2nd Steps Down from Rights Panel," *Iowa City Press-Citizen*, October 27, 1990; "Suits and Debate Follow Display of Cartoon Poster," *New York Times*, November 25, 1990.

29. James Arnold, "Iowa City Gays Claim to Be Victims of Discrimination," *Daily Iowan*, April 23, 1991.

30. Ibid.

31. Ibid.

32. Mark F. Rohner, "City Rights Ordinance Discussed," *Iowa City Press-Citizen*, February 15, 1977; Larry Eckholt, "Iowa City Council Urged to Ban Bias toward Gays," *Des Moines Register*, March 16, 1977; Mark F. Rohner, "Rights Ordinance Approval Urged," *Iowa City Press-Citizen*, March 16, 1977.

33. Rohner, "Rights Ordinance Approval Urged."

34. Ibid.

35. Ibid.
36. Two Iowa City officials, interviewed by the authors, Iowa City, June 7–8, 1994; Mark F. Rohner, "Protection for Homosexuals Changed," *Iowa City Press-Citizen*, March 22, 1977; Larry Eckholt, "Iowa City Passes Measure Protecting Gays, Singles," *Des Moines Register*, April 20, 1977.
37. Ford Clark, "Iowa City Gays Fear Repeat of Dade Battle," *Cedar Rapids (Iowa) Gazette*, June 19, 1977; "Bryant Visit Prompts Statements," *Iowa City Press-Citizen*, October 7, 1977.
38. John Campbell, "Council Clears Rights Compromise," *Iowa City Press-Citizen*, April 24, 1984.
39. Svetvilas, "Letter to Rawlings"; Valoree Armstrong, "University's Gay Staff, Faculty Group Fills Void," *Iowa City Press-Citizen*, no date available.
40. Lesbian activist, interviewed by the authors, Iowa City, June 6, 1994; Monica Mendoza, "Iowa Moving Closer to Gay Rights Bill, State Senator Says," *Iowa City Press-Citizen*, September 2, 1991; Valoree Armstrong, "Gay Groups Launch Campaign for State Civil Rights Bill," *Iowa City Press-Citizen*, April 8, 1992.
41. Mona Shaw and Robert J. Burns, "Should Health Insurance Be Provided for Same-Sex Couples?" *Iowa City Press-Citizen*, June 9, 1994.
42. Iowa City school official, telephone conversation with authors, May 21, 1996; Iowa City official, telephone conversation with authors, September 10, 1996.
43. Lisa Swegle, "Council Candidates Find Being Gay a Political Risk," *Iowa City Press-Citizen*, October 12, 1993.
44. Scott Tucker, "Philadelphia: Home of Great Spirits," *Advocate*, September 2, 1982, 26.
45. Joseph S. Clark Jr. and Dennis J. Clark, "Rally and Relapse, 1946–1968," in *Philadelphia, A 300-Year History*, ed. Russell F. Weigley (New York: Norton, 1982), 649–703.
46. D'Emilio, *Sexual Politics*, 123, 161. See also Marotta, *Politics of Homosexuality*, 48.
47. D'Emilio, *Sexual Politics*, 174.
48. Marotta, *Politics of Homosexuality*, 165; "Pickets Aid Homosexuals," *New York Times*, July 5, 1967.
49. D'Emilio, *Sexual Politics*, 200–201; Clark and Clark, "Rally and Relapse," 664.
50. "Homosexuals Hold March," *New York Times*, June 12, 1972.
51. "Philly Bill May Tiptoe to Passage," *Advocate*, April 10, 1974, 13; "Fitzpatrick Backs Proposed Gay Rights Bill," *Philadelphia Daily News*, April 11, 1974.
52. John Zeh, "Bible-Beaters Replace the Firemen in Philly," *Advocate*, July 3, 1974, A3; Philadelphia Commission on Human Relations, news release, August 6, 1974.
53. Ibid.
54. "Elections: Philadelphia," *Advocate*, December 3, 1975, 9.
55. "75 Gay Activists Disrupt Council, Protest Delays on Rights Bill," *Philadelphia Inquirer*, December 5, 1975.
56. Keith Clark, "Governor Shapp Vetoes Anti-Gay Bill Passed in Unanimous Senate Vote," *Advocate*, November 14, 1975, 9.
57. Philadelphia Lesbian and Gay Task Force, strategy report, circa 1982.
58. Stephanie G. Wolf, "The Bicentennial City, 1968–1982," in Weigley, *Philadelphia*, 722–725; Tucker, "Philadelphia: Home of Great Spirits," 27.
59. Philadelphia Lesbian and Gay Task Force, "10 Pride: The Celebration of a Decade, 1982–1992," report, 1992. Philadelphia Lesbian and Gay Task Force, "Major Gay Rights Bill Drive—1980," press release, December 27, 1979.
60. Philadelphia Lesbian and Gay Task Force, "Penn Acts to Prohibit Discrimination against Gays," press release, January 17, 1979; Philadelphia Lesbian and Gay Task Force, "New City Policy Bans Discrimination on Basis of Sexual Preference," press release, October 9, 1980.
61. Jane Eisner, "Bill to Outlaw Bias toward Gays Is Introduced," *Philadelphia Inquirer*, July 1, 1982.
62. Bob Warner, "Committee OKs Gay Rights Bill," *Philadelphia Daily News*, July 28, 1982.
63. Ibid.
64. Ibid.
65. Bob Warner and Tom Cooney, "A City of Real Brotherly Love," *Philadelphia Daily News*, August 5, 1982.
66. Ibid.

67. Ibid.; Tommy Avicolli, "1358 Passes in Council, 13–2; Archdiocese Plea Given Last Rites," *Gay News,* August 20–September 2, 1982, 6–7; Jane Eisner, "Gay-Rights Bill Becomes Law in Philadelphia," *Philadelphia Inquirer,* September 10, 1982.

68. "Nov. 8 Mayoral Election in Philadelphia—Goode for Gays?" *Advocate,* November 10, 1983, 10; "Is Mayor Goode Indeed the Gay Community's 'Mutual Friend'?" *Advocate,* March 6, 1984, 14; "Philadelphia's Goode Creates Long-Awaited Sexual Minorities Panel," *Advocate,* April 3, 1984.

69. "Sexual Minorities Commission" (editorial), *Philadelphia Inquirer,* March 5, 1984.

70. Joe Logan and William W. Sutton Jr., "City Council Rejects 'Gay Pride Week,'" *Philadelphia Inquirer,* May 25, 1984; Philadelphia Lesbian and Gay Task Force, "A Call to Action . . . Action," press release, June 1, 1984.

71. Dan Meyers, "A Bitterly Split Council OKs Gay Pride Month," *Philadelphia Inquirer,* June 16, 1989.

72. Dick Pothier, "Gay-Rights Activists Rally to Protest Council's Rejection of Pride Month," *Philadelphia Inquirer,* June 29, 1988.

73. Doreen Carvajal, "Cardinal Confronts Council, the Domestic Partners Bill Is Immoral, He Said at a Hearing," *Philadelphia Inquirer,* May 26, 1993.

74. Vernon Loeb, "Street Opposes Gay Rights Measure," *Philadelphia Inquirer,* May 28, 1993.

75. Katharine Seelye, "Gay Philadelphia Displays Its Clout at a Political Dinner," *Philadelphia Inquirer,* October 15, 1993.

76. Larry Gross and Steven K. Aurand, *Discrimination and Violence against Lesbian Women and Gay Men in Philadelphia and the Commonwealth of Pennsylvania: A Study by the Philadelphia Lesbian and Gay Task Force* (Philadelphia: Philadelphia Lesbian and Gay Task Force, 1996), 6.

77. "Philadelphia Police Attack," *New York Times,* March 20, 1992.

78. Gross and Aurand, *Discrimination and Violence,* 20.

79. William H. Chafe, *Civilities and Civil Rights: Greensboro, North Carolina, and the Black Struggle for Freedom* (New York: Oxford University Press, 1980), 4–6.

80. Rick Harding, "Gays Win Protection in Raleigh, N.C.," *Advocate,* March 1, 1988, 11.

81. Jaleh Hagigh, "Triangle Gays Tear Down Some Southern Stereotypes," *Raleigh News and Observer,* November 14, 1993.

82. Guy Munger, "Gays Say Life's Good, But Not Perfect," *Raleigh News and Observer,* September 15, 1988.

83. Dave Walter, "Durham: The Dust Settles," *Advocate,* September 16, 1986, 10–11, 24.

84. Harding, "Gays Win Protection in Raleigh," 10–11; Kema Soderberg, "Committee Hears of Violence, Harassment of Homosexuals," *Raleigh News and Observer,* August 13, 1987.

85. Harding, "Gays Win Protection in Raleigh," 11.

86. Ibid.

87. Ibid.

88. Paul Gaffney, "City Passes Law Protecting Gays," *Raleigh News and Observer,* January 6, 1988; Harding, "Gays Win Protection in Raleigh," 11; "Solid Coalition Brings Resolution," *Raleigh Front Page,* February 2–15, 1988, 1, 10.

89. Debbi Sykes, "Homosexuals, Supporters March in Pride Celebration," *Raleigh News and Observer,* June 26, 1988.

90. Sarah Friday, "Gays, Lesbians Plan to Hold Special March," *Raleigh News and Observer,* June 21, 1990.

91. Ann Burlein, *Homophobia and Human Rights in North Carolina: Rending the Fabric of Human Community* (Raleigh: North Carolina Coalition for Gay and Lesbian Equity, 1994), 6.

92. Joe Dew, "House Panel Kills Sodomy-Law Change," *Raleigh News and Observer,* April 23, 1993.

93. Jane Stancill, "Gay Rights Proposal Sparks Hot Debate," *Raleigh News and Observer,* January 27, 1993.

94. Donna Seese, "Gay Rights Proposal Decried, Christian Schools Dislike Plan to End Hiring Prejudice," *Raleigh News and Observer,* February 1993.

95. Susan Kauffman, "New Alderman No Political Novice," *Raleigh News and Observer,* November 4, 1993; Jane Stancill, "Chapel Hill Debate on Gays May Be Quiet," *Raleigh News and Observer,* February 20, 1993; Tim Vercellotti, "Council Backs Effort to Ban Bias against Gays," *Raleigh News and Observer,* April 19, 1994.

96. Dennis Rogers, "When Gay People Express Love, Why Do Others Vent Hate?" *Raleigh News and Observer,* April 26, 1994.

97. Ibid. The local Baptist church was, however, expelled by the Southern Baptist Convention for performing a gay marriage ceremony.
98. Lisa Bellamy, "Coalition Again Ranks N.C. First in Violence against Homosexuals," *Raleigh News and Observer*, May 21, 1992. See also Burlein, *Homophobia and Human Rights in North Carolina*.
99. Trish Wilson, "NCSU Grapples with Hate Speech Issues," *Raleigh News and Observer*, April 20, 1993; Debbi Sykes, "Tunnel Ignites Debate, NCSU Free Speech Used against Gays," *Raleigh News and Observer*, February 25, 1994.
100. Matthew Eisely, "Gay Club Files Suit against Raleigh," *Raleigh News and Observer*, May 11, 1996.
101. Tom Honig, "Challenges to Traditional Values Constantly Test a Community," *Santa Cruz Sentinel*, August 4, 1991.
102. Ibid.
103. Tom Sater, "First in U.S.—County Bans Bias," *Advocate*, August 13, 1975, 13.
104. Paul Beatty, "Gays Here Urge a Fight against Move by Briggs," *Santa Cruz Sentinel*, March 13, 1978.
105. Tracie White, "Lesbian Community Has Become an Established Part of Santa Cruz," *Santa Cruz Sentinel*, September 12, 1993; Robin Musitelli, "Lesbians Claimed Place in Headlines," *Santa Cruz Sentinel*, December 26, 1993.
106. Glen Schaller, "The Ballot According to BAYMEC," *Lavender Reader* (gay magazine), summer 1994, 9.
107. Steve Perez, "Suspects in Gay Beating Face Hate-Crime Charges," *Santa Cruz Sentinel*, September 19, 1991; John Laird, "City's Debate on Ordinance Lacks Quality," *Santa Cruz Sentinel*, January 24, 1992.
108. "Nine Arrested on Sex Charges," *Santa Cruz Sentinel*, October 30, 1980; Mark Bergstrom, "Four Gay Killings in a Year," *Santa Cruz Sentinel*, February 18, 1988.
109. Amy Zuckerman, "Gays, Lesbians Gather for Legislative Update," *Santa Cruz Sentinel*, December 12, 1991.
110. Brenda Starr and Scotty Brookie, "Queers Victorious: Anti-Bias Bill Passes, 5–2," *Lavender Reader*, summer 1992, 19.
111. John Robinson, "Looks-Law Group Takes Media to Task," *Santa Cruz Sentinel*, January 24, 1992; John Robinson, "Council Split on Appearance," *Santa Cruz Sentinel*, February 8, 1992; "City Council Stumbles toward a Right Decision" (editorial), *Santa Cruz Sentinel*, February 13, 1992; Martha Snyder, "Anti-Bias Protection Scaled Back," *Santa Cruz Sentinel*, March 17, 1992.
112. "It's Time to Heal Wounds from Bias-Law Debate" (editorial), *Santa Cruz Sentinel*, April 30, 1992.
113. "City Council Stumbles"; Robinson, "Council Split on Appearance."
114. Timothy Morgan, "Coonerty's Law Flouts Individual Rights," *Santa Cruz Sentinel*, January 14, 1992.
115. "Council Should Approve Anti-Discrimination Law" (editorial), *Santa Cruz Sentinel*, January 14, 1992; Kathy Krieger, "Activists Stunned by News," *Santa Cruz Sentinel*, September 26, 1992.
116. "Council Should Approve," A11.
117. Starr and Brookie, "Queers Victorious," 19.
118. Martha Snyder, "Council Passes Anti-Bias Law," *Santa Cruz Sentinel*, April 29, 1992.
119. Krieger, "Activists Stunned by News."
120. Donna Kimura, "Hate-Crime Reports Increasing," *Santa Cruz Sentinel*, February 19, 1992.
121. Musitelli, "Lesbians Claimed Place"; John Laird, "Taking Stock," *Lavender Reader*, winter 1994, 11–12; Merrie Schaller, "Has the Movement Made It Easier? On Being Young and Queer," *Lavender Reader*, winter 1994, 18–21, 26, 29; Katherine Edwards, "Triangle Speakers Visit Classrooms for Frank Talks on Homosexuality," *Santa Cruz Sentinel*, December 2, 1992.
122. Musitelli, "Lesbians Claimed Place"; Laird, "Taking Stock," 11.
123. Laird, "Taking Stock," 11.
124. Henry Louis Taylor Jr., ed., preface to *Race and the City: Work, Community, and Protest in Cincinnati, 1820–1970* (Urbana: University of Illinois Press, 1993).
125. Zane L. Miller and Bruce Tucker, "The New Urban Politics: Planning and Development in Cincinnati, 1954–1988," in *Snowbelt Cities*, ed. Richard M. Bernard (Bloomington: Indiana University Press, 1990), 91–108.

126. Leigh W. Rutledge, *The Gay Decades* (New York: Plume, 1992), 340.
127. "Gay-Rights Activists Plan Protest for Trial," *Cincinnati Enquirer,* August 17, 1990; Ben L. Kaufman, "City Steps in Rights Ring Again," *Cincinnati Enquirer,* October 3, 1994.
128. Barbara Zigli, "Political Clout Lacking, Negative," *Cincinnati Enquirer,* April 4, 1982; Mark Thompson, ed., *Long Road to Freedom: The* Advocate *History of the Gay and Lesbian Movement* (New York: St. Martin's Press, 1994), 52, 83; D'Emilio, *Sexual Politics,* 199–200.
129. Zigli, "Political Clout Lacking"; Michelle Horak, "Gay Rights in Cincinnati," *Cincinnati Enquirer,* July 26, 1977.
130. Robert Webb, "Must Cincinnati Guard Homosexual 'Rights'?" *Cincinnati Enquirer,* April 9, 1978.
131. Dave Krieger, "Chances for Proposed Rights Ordinance Doubtful," *Cincinnati Enquirer,* April 15, 1978.
132. Ibid.
133. Webb, "Must Cincinnati Guard Homosexual 'Rights'?"
134. "Police Arrest 62 Gays in Eight-Day Crackdown," *Cincinnati Enquirer,* April 13, 1978; "Human Rights Unit to Investigate Police Crackdown on Homosexuals," *Cincinnati Enquirer,* April 14, 1978; "Police Used 'Enticement' in Crackdown, Gays Say," *Cincinnati Enquirer,* April 15, 1978.
135. Zigli, "Political Clout Lacking"; Dave Krieger, "Homosexuals Unite in Face of Controversy," *Cincinnati Enquirer,* April 23, 1978.
136. *Stonewall Cincinnati: Ten Years of Challenge, Change, and Championing Our Rights* (Cincinnati: Stonewall Cincinnati, 1992); Camilla Warrick, "Politicians Recognizing Power of Gays," *Cincinnati Enquirer,* April 23, 1987.
137. *Stonewall Cincinnati: Ten Years of Challenge;* J. Frazier Smith, "Lesbian Fire Recruit Wins Right to Be Considered for Position," *Cincinnati Enquirer,* May 26, 1984; Sharon Moloney, "City Peeks Behind Applicants' Closed Doors," *Cincinnati Post,* June 14, 1985.
138. Elizabeth Neus and Valerie Bailey, "Gay Group Settles Dispute with Restaurants," *Cincinnati Enquirer,* June 7, 1987; *Stonewall Cincinnati: Ten Years of Challenge.*
139. Chris Graves, "Gay Activists Lash Out at Prosecutor," *Cincinnati Enquirer,* December 17, 1991; *Stonewall Cincinnati: Ten Years of Challenge.*
140. Richard Green, "Gay-Rights Groups Gaining Clout," *Cincinnati Enquirer,* April 28, 1991.
141. Ibid.; "Mayor Proclaims Today Gay Tolerance Day," *Cincinnati Post,* June 15, 1991.
142. Sharah Sturmon, "City Council to Consider Gay Bias Ordinance," *Cincinnati Post,* February 28, 1991; "New Bill Protects Gays, Appalachians," *Cincinnati Enquirer,* March 14, 1991.
143. Smita Madan Paul and Geoff Hobson, "700 Take Sides on Gay Rights," *Cincinnati Enquirer,* July 30, 1992.
144. Charles E. Winburn, "Gays Don't Need City Protection," *Cincinnati Enquirer,* May 25, 1992.
145. Sarah Sturmon, "Chamber Opposes Gay-Rights Ordinance," *Cincinnati Enquirer,* September 10, 1992.
146. "The Human Rights Ordinance: Good Name for Bad Government" (editorial), *Cincinnati Enquirer,* August 4, 1992.
147. Jeff Harrington, "Council Approves Gay-Rights Ordinance," *Cincinnati Enquirer,* November 26, 1992.
148. Howard Wilkinson, "City's Gay Rights Battle Is Taking Shape," *Cincinnati Enquirer,* August 20, 1993.
149. Charlene J. Allen, "Strange Bedfellows: Cincinnati's Anti-Gay Rights Initiative 'Issue 3' as a Test for a Christian Right and African-American Political Alliance?" (paper delivered at the Annual Meeting of the American Political Science Association, Chicago, August 31–September 3, 1995), 8–10; and Howard Wilkinson, "Money Talked in Gay-Rights Vote," *Cincinnati Enquirer,* December 11, 1993.
150. Allen, "Strange Bedfellows," 10–12.
151. Ibid., 12.
152. Howard Wilkinson, "Issue 3's Intent Lost Somewhere between Hitler, 'Gay Takeover,'" *Cincinnati Enquirer,* October 10, 1993; Allen, "Strange Bedfellows," 12–13.
153. Lew Morres and Steve Bennish, "Voters Reject Rights Law," *Cincinnati Enquirer,* November 3, 1993; Allen, "Strange Bedfellows," 18.

154. Jane Preudergast and Jeff Harrington, "Gays Call for City Boycott," *Cincinnati Enquirer,* November 7, 1993; Ben L. Kaufman and Adam Weintraub, "Gay-Rights Advocates Sue Cincinnati," *Cincinnati Enquirer,* November 9, 1993.

155. Allen, "Strange Bedfellows," 13–16; Mark Curnutte and Christine Wolfe, "Gay Rights Foes Enlist Big Names," *Cincinnati Enquirer,* September 14, 1994; Laura Goldberg, "Gay Rights Law Thrown Out," *Cincinnati Enquirer,* March 9, 1995.

CHAPTER 3

The Politics of Gay Rights Laws

It was one of the proudest moments of my public life.
—Philadelphia City Council member, commenting on addition of
sexual orientation to the city's human rights ordinance

T he struggle for equality for lesbians and gay men has been a major
issue in many American communities for more than two decades. The
primary emphasis of the modern gay movement has been to create or
change various laws and policies in order to secure basic civil rights for gays
and lesbians. These fundamental rights include the abolition of discrimination
in employment and housing, the repeal of sodomy laws, the reduction in
hate crimes directed toward gays, the attainment of domestic partner employment benefits, and the legalization of same-sex marriages. Throughout U.S.
history the sexual relations of gays have been a concern of the legal system.
Until recently, government human rights codes purposely excluded gays and
lesbians, and therefore jobs, housing, and access to public places could be
and often were denied to persons because of their sexual orientation. Thus
the law has been the primary arena in which the struggle for gay rights has
been waged.[1]

Within the legal arena, gay rights advocates have pushed for the introduction of sexual orientation into human rights laws. Barry Adam, a noted
sociologist of the gay movement, has asserted that by the 1980s this emphasis was clearly "the cutting edge of legislative change" in a movement that
was increasingly preoccupied with state power.[2] By comparing their status
to that of African Americans before the civil rights movement, gays hoped to
claim political legitimacy as a minority entitled to demand basic rights.[3] By the
1970s, moreover, nearly every state and many local governments had some
type of human rights ordinance that prohibited discrimination in employment and typically other institutions on the basis of race, ethnic background,
religion, sex, and certain other characteristics. One of the principal goals of
the gay rights movement was to include sexual orientation in the list of protected groups in these laws. The purpose of this chapter is to provide a close
look at why and how gays were able to secure legal protection in the form of
local gay rights legislation.

The Rationale for the Legal Protection for Gays

Historically the United States has depended on social norms, rather than law, to ensure that people are treated fairly. The fundamental assumptions here have been not only that most people are committed to fairness but that in a competitive capitalistic system those people who are consistently unfair will fail. For example, business people who base employment decisions on issues other than merit will suffer economically because they will be less efficient than competitors. This theory underlies our laissez-faire economic system, and it may indeed be a relatively accurate description of how society works much of the time. Still, there have been eras in which some groups of people have suffered economically and socially for reasons that have nothing to do with merit or ability. African Americans and women are two obvious examples. When such injustices do occur and society is unable or unwilling to correct them, it is appropriate and even necessary that the state intervene to rectify the situation. Thus, civil rights laws are the most common, and some might argue the most effective, means by which government attempts to protect groups of people who are subject to irrational discrimination.[4] The Civil Rights Act of 1964, an important federal law designed to protect African Americans and women against discrimination in employment, is a good illustration of this method.

The first, and perhaps most important, hallmark of a group in need of civil rights protection is a history of systematic discrimination. The legislative campaign for black civil rights, for example, was fueled by evidence of discrimination against African Americans in employment, housing, education, public accommodations, and other institutions. To what extent have gays and lesbians suffered from similar kinds of discrimination because of their sexual orientation? This has been a crucial issue in the quest for gay civil rights. Not only is such proof of discrimination necessary legally for protected-class status, but opponents of gay rights have long contended that there is no substantial evidence of a pattern of oppression against gays and lesbians.[5]

Systematic surveys and official documentation of various forms of anti-gay discrimination have not been available until relatively recently. Historically, however, violence against gays and lesbians has been both widespread and continuous according to numerous accounts. Beatings, burnings, various kinds of torture, and execution of gays were not uncommon in eighteenth-century America, where laws against homosexuality often included the death penalty.[6] Although the nineteenth century marked the turning point for ending legally prescribed violence against gays, the increased visibility of lesbians and gay men after World War II made them easy targets of extralegal violence by the police and private citizens.

Since the beginnings of the gay liberation movement of the late 1960s, a great deal of data has been compiled on antigay violence and victimization. The first national study of violence against gays, reported in 1984, surveyed 2,074 gay men and lesbians in eight major cities. Among those surveyed, 94 percent reported that they had experienced at least once in their lives some type of victimization because of their sexual orientation, including verbal abuse; physical assault; abuse by police; assault with a weapon; vandalized property; and being spat upon, chased, stalked, or hit with an object. Forty-four percent reported that they had been threatened with physical violence, and 62 percent said that they feared for their safety. Many respondents had been victimized more than once; for example, nearly half (47 percent) of those who stated they had been physically assaulted reported multiple episodes.[7]

Other surveys of gays and lesbians in various other cities and states have depicted similar patterns of victimization.[8] Data on antigay murders are less prevalent (mainly because the victims are not available to be surveyed), but they indicate that such homicides are extremely brutal and less likely to be solved by the police than other murders.[9] One recent study of 151 antigay slayings, for example, reported that 60 percent of the murders were marked by "extraordinary and horrific violence" of a sort "fueled by rage and hate."[10]

Although law enforcement officials are, at least in theory, responsible for protecting gays and lesbians from violence and assault, in reality they have frequently contributed to these illegal actions. As enforcers of social and sexual norms, the municipal police have often harassed and even physically assaulted those they consider to be lawbreakers and sexual deviants.[11] Having little protection under the law until relatively recently, gays were often the target of police entrapment and victimization through periodic raids on their bars and other social meeting places. In addition, the police commonly responded slowly, or not at all, to requests for aid from gay persons.[12] In a summary of numerous surveys of antigay violence and victimization undertaken from 1984 to 1991, Kevin Berrill concluded that a median of 20 percent of lesbians and gay men claimed some form of victimization by police because of their sexual orientation. Berrill reported "numerous documented cases of police verbal and physical abuse, entrapment, blackmail, unequal enforcement of the law, and deliberate mishandling of anti-gay violence cases."[13] It is no surprise, therefore, that gays and lesbians do not readily seek out or rely on the police for protection.

Although physical assault is obviously the most terrifying form of victimization, many lesbians and gay men endure various other forms of discrimination in their daily lives. Discrimination in employment and housing has been particularly widespread. Between 1980 and 1991 at least twenty-one local surveys explored these and other forms of gay victimization.[14] They revealed that between 16 and 44 percent of respondents reported some kind of discrimination in employment due to their sexual orientation. Such discrimination included not being hired or promoted, being fired, getting harassed at work, and fearing reprisals if their sexual orientation were known. In housing, 8 to 32 percent of respondents had met with antigay bias in the process of renting, and between 40 and 72 percent concealed their sexual orientation to avoid the possibility of such discrimination. Finally, with regard to public accommodations, 4 to 30 percent reported that they had faced antigay discrimination in restaurants, 5 to 27 percent in motels or hotels, 6 to 16 percent in bars or nightclubs, and 8 to 24 percent in other public establishments. Again, between 46 and 80 percent claimed that they feared discrimination or purposely hid their orientation to avoid discrimination in public accommodations. Concealing one's sexual identity often creates a painful discrepancy between one's public and private life, typically resulting in negative psychological consequences that may endure for years.[15]

Without civil rights legislation that expressly includes protection based on sexual orientation, gay men and lesbians face overt acts of discrimination with no legal recourse. In the quest for gay rights, public attitudes toward gays and lesbians in general, as well as public perceptions of antigay discrimination and civil rights protections, are considered to be important factors. It is virtually impossible politically to extend civil rights laws to gays without a reservoir of citizen support. In regard to citizen attitudes, it is important to understand, as we pointed out in Chapter 1, that a majority of the U.S. public believes that homosexuality is unacceptable or immoral. Yet despite this high level of disapproval, there is, at the same time, an equally strong public perception that gays and lesbians face discrimination and that most such discrimination is wrong. Although there is a certain ambiguity about where most Americans stand on these issues, there has been a growing trend toward greater acceptance of at least some basic rights for gays. According to a 1993 national survey, 65 percent of respondents said they wanted to ensure equal rights for gays. Many opponents, however, believe that such laws would tend to endorse the gay subculture. Moreover, most Americans mistakenly think that gays and lesbians are already granted protection by existing federal law. Thus, fully half (50 percent) *opposed* extending current civil rights laws to cover gays.[16]

One of the most important factors influencing attitudes about civil rights protections is beliefs about the origin of sexual orientation. People who believe that homosexuality is genetically determined are more likely to support gay rights than are those who believe that such an orientation is learned or chosen. Another significant factor in alleviating negative attitudes is actually knowing someone who is gay or lesbian. According to the same survey, 53 percent of adult Americans who said they personally knew someone who was gay favored gay rights, compared with a 46 percent approval rating among those who said they did not know any gay men or lesbians. This suggests that the increased visibility of gays is likely to have a positive effect on their battle for civil rights protection. Indeed, by 1993 a majority of respondents (53 percent) claimed to know someone personally—a relative, friend, or co-worker—who was identified as gay. As recently as 1985, pollsters indicated that only 25 to 30 percent of Americans knew an open lesbian or gay man.[17]

For gay rights advocates, the most significant finding of public opinion surveys has been the dramatic increase in the proportion of citizens who are supportive of equal job opportunities for gays. In 1977, only 56 percent of those surveyed said homosexuals should have equal rights in job opportunities, whereas 33 percent opposed this position. By 1992, however, those agreeing with gay rights in employment had increased to 74 percent (and by 1996 to 84 percent), and only 18 percent were opposed. Not surprisingly, this high level of support drops for some job categories, particularly those involving close physical contact and work with children.[18] Yet even after the 1994 elections and the creation of a Republican majority in Congress, a voter poll indicated continuing broad support for equal rights for lesbians and gays, especially in the area of job opportunities. The survey also showed that a specific federal bill to extend current civil rights laws in the workplace to cover gays (termed the Employment Non-Discrimination Act) was endorsed by 57 percent of the voters.[19] Although the U.S. Senate narrowly defeated (50–49) this bill in 1996 (it was not voted on in the House), the indication of popular support may well serve to refuel efforts at both the federal and local levels to further antidiscrimination legislation.

The final, and perhaps most important, rationale for protective legislation for gays revolves around the value and influence of law in American society. If one views gays and lesbians as similar to other disadvantaged minorities, the conventional liberal solution is to extend to homosexuals the same legal protections granted to blacks, women, and other minorities. The analogy often deemed most appropriate is to the civil rights movement and the resulting achievement of significant legislation prohibiting discrimination against African Americans.[20] Accordingly, the legislative solution is to add sexual orientation to the list of protected minority groups in local human rights ordinances. Some critics challenge the assumption that sexual orientation is equivalent to race in regard to status and degree of discrimination, but this assumption does provide a powerful and persuasive logic for extending civil rights protections to lesbians and gay men.[21]

Invoking the analogy of blacks and civil rights also suggests the use of law for protecting the basic rights of minorities. Current federal civil rights law bars discrimination in housing, employment, and public accommodations on the basis of race, national origin, ethnicity, religion, age, and disability. Such law, and additional legal restrictions in most states and communities, have proved to be helpful in reducing discrimination in basic institutions. To the extent that one's general prosperity and happiness are greatly influenced by one's work, housing, and entertainment, these legal barriers to unjustified discrimination are extremely important for many groups.[22]

The value of protective law for gays as well as other groups extends well beyond this utilitarian dimension, however. The psychological and educational influence of civil rights legislation is perhaps its most significant function. The passage of such protective legislation for a group tends to extend greater legitimacy to that group in the eyes of society as a whole. In this sense, it creates a kind of "public affirmation."[23] Thus the mere presence of such a statute, along with the public awareness that gays can invoke the power of the state for protection, often has a major influence on cultural perceptions of lesbians and gay men. By changing public consciousness and awareness, the law itself provides an educational function. Moreover, improvement in the legal status of gays tends, in return, to promote their collective self-esteem and self-respect.[24]

For gay rights advocates, the ultimate rationale for including sexual orientation in civil rights legislation is the moral argument for doing so. They contend that equality for gays is something society ought to recognize and extend because it is morally right to do so. The emphasis here is on the notion of rights and of law that appeals to some higher moral principles—to a sense of justice. This claim to moral rightness rests on the assumption that all Americans are guaranteed basic rights. Without legal protection against various forms of discrimination, however, lesbians and gays face serious restrictions in their access to the fundamental rights enjoyed by all other citizens.[25]

Awakenings: The First Legal Protections

The Stonewall rebellion of 1969 signaled the beginning of the mass political movement for gay rights. Earlier organizations of homosexuals rarely challenged directly the legal and social norms that relegated gays and lesbians to second-class status. As late as 1968, homosexual acts (even between consenting adults in private) were illegal in every state but Illinois. Many occupations, most notably teaching, law, medicine, and the military, were closed in virtually the entire country to those known to be gay or lesbian. Even in New York, San Francisco, Washington, and other large cities with sizable concentrations of gay citizens, job discrimination and police harassment continued to be major issues for many gays.[26] Furthermore, not a single law or known policy prohibited discrimination on the basis of sexual orientation in any public or private entity in the nation.

By the late 1960s and early 1970s, however, numerous lesbian and gay liberation organizations came into being. More radical in tone and tactics than previous homosexual groups, these new organizations began to challenge antigay policies as well as focus on the sexual oppression of all people to some degree. The emphasis on "coming out" gave the movement additional political clout.[27]

Within a few years of the Stonewall riots the gay liberation movement began to achieve some political successes, as mentioned in Chapter 2. The American Psychiatric Association, for example, removed homosexuality from its classification as a mental disorder. In addition, several states repealed their sodomy laws. Between 1969 and 1973, for example, six states decriminalized same-sex sexual acts.[28] Although such antisodomy laws were not well enforced, their greatest significance lay in the fact that they declared all gays and lesbians as criminals by virtue of their sexual conduct and thereby created greater opportunities for police harassment.

One of the foremost goals of the gay rights movement was the introduction of sexual orientation into human rights laws. Discrimination in employment, housing, public accommodations, and other institutions was a significant concern of many gays, as we have indicated. Beginning in 1974, Congress attempted to amend the 1964 Civil Rights Act to include gays and lesbians in the federal ban on discrimination, but it failed to do so. Indeed, the enactment of national or even statewide gay rights legislation appeared extremely unlikely. The gay political movement was a nascent one, still relatively small and with few powerful allies. Moreover, most organized gays and lesbians were concentrated in large cities and various university communities. For these reasons, the focus of initial attempts to enact or amend antidiscrimination legislation to include sexual orientation was at the local, particularly city, level.

The first gay rights ordinances were adopted in the early 1970s in primarily university communities, such as Berkeley and Palo Alto, California; Boulder, Colorado; Ann Arbor and East Lansing, Michigan; and Austin, Texas. In fact, of the twenty-eight cities or counties that passed such laws or policies before 1977, more than half (eighteen) could be reasonably classified as college communities.[29] Clearly, students and faculty were in the vanguard of this social movement, as they have been for many other challenges to cultural traditions. Several large cities with sizable and organized gay and lesbian populations, including Detroit, Minneapolis, San Francisco, Seattle, and Washington, also adopted legislation early on. Other large cities with similar characteristics, such as Atlanta, Chicago, Los Angeles, New York, and Philadelphia, had at least initiated political discussions of such laws prior to 1975. Thus, localities that pioneered gay rights laws had significant supportive constituencies (large numbers of students or significant gay populations), which were necessary for the extension of civil rights to unpopular minorities.

East Lansing as the First City

In March 1972, East Lansing became the first community in the country formally to adopt a policy or law that legally banned discrimination on account of sexual orientation.[30] It was significant that the first gay rights code was passed in this midwestern college community of approximately 50,000 citizens. Most analysts and gay activists had expected such a legal breakthrough in a larger metropolitan area, like San Francisco or New York, where gays and lesbians were not only more concentrated but had long sought gay rights protection. In fact, as expected, San Francisco became the second city to adopt such a legal code less than two months later. East Lansing, however, proved to be more typical of the kind of community that passed gay rights legislation early on and of the process by which such policies or laws achieved passage. For that reason, the story of the adoption of antidiscrimination protection for gays in East Lansing is worth telling.

An officially recognized student group at Michigan State University, the Gay Liberation Movement, first started the campaign for gay civil rights protections in East Lansing in late 1971. At that time the group actively supported two city council candidates, both later elected, who pledged support for gay rights. Shortly thereafter, the Gay Liberation Movement and an allied human rights organization presented proposals to the city's Human Relations Commission, a data-gathering arm of the city council. The proposals were to add both gender and sexual orientation as protected classifications to the city's civil rights law. The commission approved and recommended to the council the proposal to add gender to the code, and this was eventually adopted by the city council. But the more controversial sexual orientation provision stalled for several months as the commission debated it. In the meantime, as a result of lobbying by the Gay Liberation Movement, the city council voted 3 to 2 to amend the city's personnel rules to ban discrimination in city hiring on the basis of sexual orientation. The adoption of a policy and not an ordinance, the extension of coverage to city employees only, and the split council vote (even the mayor was opposed) all suggested the limited and incremental nature of the city's first legal step. Indeed, council opposition was sufficient at the time of this initial adoption to pass a provision (soon after repealed) specifying that homosexual solicitation by a city employee would be grounds for dismissal even though homosexuality itself would not.[31]

After a long series of meetings and debates, East Lansing's Human Relations Commission recommended that the sexual orientation provision be

included in the city's antidiscrimination ordinance. The commission also recommended that legal coverage be extended beyond municipal employment
to include private sector jobs, housing, and public accommodations. Such
coverage was similar to that already granted to other protected groups such
as blacks and women. The commission's recommendation to the city council was unanimous. The council, however, delayed action on the recommendation, referring it to the city attorney for an opinion. The gay student
organization and its allies put continuous and intense political pressure on
the council, and the council finally approved the addition to the city's civil
rights ordinance in May 1973—but only after removing the housing provision, which was considered to be the most controversial area of bias protection. There was only one dissenting council vote on the final measure.[32] The
mayor supported the addition to the antibias law on the basis of "humani-
tarian considerations," but he did so reluctantly and declared, "Some say
homosexual behavior is acceptable in our society. I am not ready to accept
that."[33]

The tale of East Lansing's pursuit and ultimate passage of gay rights legislation was fairly typical of what took place in many communities that initiated similar laws or policies in the early to middle 1970s. Gay and lesbian
campus organizations were often the first to initiate political discussion of
such proposals, at least in college-dominated communities. Their political
efforts were commonly directed at both electing city officials who were supportive of gay rights as well as lobbying for the adoption of legal protections.
Approval of the proposal by a city's human rights commission or board, composed of a representative group of appointed citizens, was usually the initial
required step. These commissions grew out of the black civil rights era of
the 1950s and 1960s and were established to ensure the protection and fair
representation of minority interests. The human rights boards often held
public hearings on such new proposals, and the testimony of gay and lesbian
citizens was essential to demonstrate the necessity for antidiscrimination
laws.

The incremental approach to achieving legal protection on the basis of
sexual orientation was common to other communities as well. As in East
Lansing, the adoption of a city policy that extended only to municipal
employees, not an all-encompassing law, was the typical first step. A policy
did not have the legal standing, nor the legitimacy and public recognition,
that attached to an ordinance. It was, however, easier to get passed, especially when the protected group was as controversial as gays and lesbians.
Adoption of a policy initially was also a means by which the city council could
test the political waters to see how acceptable gay rights might be in the larger community. The next step, again as in East Lansing, was to urge the adoption of a law or ordinance, limited if necessary in its coverage of institutions.

A law itself, as we have suggested, has intangible as well as substantive importance. Municipal employment was the first and most likely institution for such an ordinance and was most acceptable politically because relatively few employees were involved. Later the ordinance might be amended to include some additional institutions like public accommodations, private employment, and housing. As was true for earlier civil rights legislation, the private sector demonstrated greater political resistance to government interference than the public sector. In general, people were most opposed to antidiscrimination codes that included workplaces, public accommodations, and housing, where they were most likely to encounter gays. An incremental approach of adding one institution at a time enabled city officials to ascertain gradually how the new change in the law was working and how politically feasible it was.

Clearly the attempt by gay activists to link gay rights with the civil rights of African Americans and other protected groups was an astute strategy. By the 1970s a widespread sense of legitimacy attached to the civil rights movement and to the granting of basic rights to blacks. Many municipalities, including East Lansing, had adopted earlier some kind of human rights law, often fashioned after the federal 1964 Civil Rights Act, that typically banned discrimination on the basis of race, sex, ethnicity, religion, and sometimes other characteristics. To argue that discriminating against gays and lesbians was as unjustified as discriminating against African Americans was an effective way to gain sympathy and political support. In addition, the presence of such municipal civil rights laws meant that similar antidiscrimination protections on the basis of sexual orientation were possible by merely *amending* the present code. Not having to pass a new ordinance simplified the political process, and linking basic rights for gays and lesbians to guaranteed civil rights for other minorities gained an essential legitimacy for the movement. This process proved successful in East Lansing and in many other communities thereafter.

Finally, East Lansing fit the norm of communities that pioneered the adoption of gay rights in that proponents faced little organized opposition. Gays, students, and their allies were relatively well mobilized in these so-called bastions of liberalism and often dominated the local political process. As an indication of such political dominance, in the fourteen communities that formally passed by council vote an antidiscrimination policy or ordinance covering sexual orientation between 1972 and 1974, all but four did so with a unanimous or near-unanimous (only one dissenting council member) vote. No organized opposition was reported in most of these communities, and only the Catholic Church was known to offer organized resistance in San Francisco and a few other cities.[34] Often, potential opponents were caught by surprise, since gay rights provisions were new and had never been proposed anywhere before. As a result, they were unable to mobilize quickly enough to provide more than token opposition. Without much organized resistance and debate, and even without much fanfare and controversy, the first anti-gay bias policies and laws were adopted rather easily.[35] Because of the high level of support and ease of passage, moreover, the early gay and lesbian protection codes tended to be broad in scope, covering a range of institutions in both the public and private spheres.

The Backlash to Gay Rights

The early legal successes of gay activists, achieved relatively easily in most communities, proved to be the calm before the virulent political backlash that occurred in the later 1970s. As early as 1974, traditional religious groups and other opponents of gay rights began to react to the first adoptions of local policies and laws prohibiting discrimination on the basis of sexual orientation. In that year, even some university communities were affected as gay rights proposals failed in Columbus, Ohio, and Eugene, Oregon, liberal cities that typically would have endorsed such bills.[36] Although legislation was adopted later in each community, those defeats were the first clear indication that opposition to gay rights was emerging. Later in 1974, Boulder, the home of the University of Colorado, passed an antidiscrimination amendment that included gays and lesbians, only to have it repealed shortly thereafter by a nearly 2 to 1 margin as conservatives mobilized against the new measure.[37] In addition, mayors who had supported controversial gay rights laws narrowly survived recall elections in Columbus and Boulder, and in Seattle the popular mayor was almost unseated in his reelection bid when the city's legal code protecting gays became an issue.[38]

Organized reaction to the quest for gay rights reached its zenith in June 1977, when voters in Dade County, Florida, repealed a recently enacted ordinance by a margin of more than 2 to 1. As mentioned in Chapter 2, this referendum on, and the repeal of, a law that protected gays and lesbians from discrimination was the first of its kind that affected a major U.S. city (Miami). The Save Our Children organization, which led the repeal, provides a profile of the antigay forces of this period. The organization was formed by the popular singer Anita Bryant, a devout Baptist and former Miss America candidate. She used her national reputation, media access, and church ties to raise almost $200,000 in campaign funds, most of it coming from outside Florida. Bryant maintained that the Dade County ordinance was a religious abomination and a license for gays to molest children, asserting that "Homosexuals cannot reproduce so they must recruit." [39] Bryant garnered support from the National Association of Evangelicals, which represented more than three million people from some sixty denominations. The Christian Cause, a right-wing direct-mail political organization, also mobilized a large national contingent, and there was additional local support forthcoming from other religious groups. Antiabortion and anti–Equal Rights Amendment (ERA) activists, police representatives, leaders of the Young Men's Christian Association (YMCA) and Kiwanis, and politicians, including Florida's governor and several state legislators, joined the campaign to defeat the gay rights law.[40] Aligned against this coalition of right-wing forces was Miami's gay and lesbian community, which was not particularly large or vocal, and their liberal allies. The larger gay communities in San Francisco and New York raised sizable sums of money in support, and political organizers came from several cities to help, but the opposition proved to be implacable.[41]

The repeal of the Dade County antidiscrimination law attracted national attention and propelled Anita Bryant on an anti–gay rights crusade across the country. Within a year, voters in Eugene, Oregon; St. Paul, Minnesota; and Wichita, Kansas, had similarly rescinded local ordinances that protected the basic rights of gay citizens. In each city fundamentalist churches constituted the organizational backbone of the antigay movement, often supplemented by financing from business interests. According to Barry Adam, the successful "ideological formula equated the no-discrimination law with 'child molesting,' 'gay recruiting,' 'boy prostitution,' 'threat to the family,' and a 'national gay conspiracy,' adding the argument that 'the majority has the right to do business with and rent to people of their choice.'"[42] The opposition drew on a well of public concern that extended beyond the religious community.

Thus by 1978 conservative opposition to gay rights legislation had asserted itself. Sparked initially by Bryant and the momentous victory in Dade County, opponents began to organize and work vigorously to repeal what many saw not as a civil rights issue but as the imposition of an immoral "lifestyle."[43] The opposition, however, was not invincible. Unlike the 1950s and the McCarthy era, the times were more tolerant of diversity. Rather than withdrawing, gay activists used the attacks on them to politicize their cause and publicize their grievances further. In this vein, Bryant's campaign infuriated and mobilized gays and lesbians across the country, and in November 1978 two significant challenges to gay rights went down to defeat. In California, the hotly contested Proposition 6, which would have permitted school boards to expel gay teachers, was soundly rejected by the voters. At the same time, citizens in Seattle voted to retain their legal protection for gays by a margin of 63 to 37 percent.[44] Moreover, despite the political backlash of the late 1970s, a number of cities, including Hartford, Connecticut; Los Angeles; San Jose, California; and Tucson, Arizona, passed antidiscrimination legislation that included sexual orientation. By 1980 some forty U.S. communities could claim legal protection for gays and lesbians.

The 1980s: Political Accommodation and Progress

Reflecting on the decade of the 1980s, the scholar Lillian Faderman has stated, "While the 1970s rode on the steam of the social revolution that had been set in motion by the flower children of the '60s, the momentum appeared to have been lost in the '80s as mainstream America returned to more conservative times."[45] The tone of American politics shifted distinctly to the right in the 1980s. The trend was both symbolized and prodded by the New Christian Right movement that emerged as a coherent and organized constituency. Many attributed the defeat of Democratic presidential candidates in 1980 and 1984 at least in part to the emerging political power of this movement. The Democrats had included gay rights as part of their national platform beginning in 1980. No figure better epitomized the new political mood than President Ronald Reagan, who openly courted the New Right with promises to resist government support for homosexuals.[46]

By the mid-1980s public recognition of the AIDS epidemic added a new dimension to the debate over civil rights. Gay men were now marked by the stigma of a potentially fatal disease. According to public opinion polls, the fear of contracting AIDS made Americans less tolerant of homosexuals, and support for gay rights lessened.[47] The opponents of gay rights were able to capitalize on the fear surrounding the virus to refuel their efforts. Gay men were charged with causing the problem by "overindulging in 'immoral' sexual activity," and some New Right leaders called AIDS "just retribution" and "God's punishment" for a sinful lifestyle.[48] Partly as a result of the increased anxieties and resentment surrounding the new disease, reported incidents of harassment and crimes against gays increased in the middle to late 1980s.[49]

The climate of concern surrounding AIDS affected local politics as well. Some public officials cited constituents' fears about the spread of the virus as a rationale for opposing legal protection for gays. This phenomenon was most clearly evident in the mayoral campaign in Houston in 1985. Gays and lesbians were a large and politically powerful force in this city, having helped Mayor Kathy Whitmire, an ardent supporter of gay rights, win landslide victories in 1981 and 1983. As concern over the outbreak of AIDS began to grow, however, city voters turned out in large numbers in early 1985 to repeal by referendum a recently passed gay rights ordinance. Encouraged by the overwhelming defeat of the ordinance, a former mayor, stressing "morality" and his opposition to gay rights, challenged the incumbent in the mayor's race. During the campaign, the challenger responded to a question about what to do about the AIDS problem by stating that he would "shoot the queers." The gaffe seemed to delegitimize antigay feelings and Mayor Whitmire won reelection.[50] Nonetheless, *Newsweek* magazine opined that support for legal protection for homosexuals was "politically hazardous in the AIDS-altered climate" of this period.[51]

Although the AIDS epidemic hardened political attitudes against gays, it also served as a political awakening for many lesbians and gay men. Clearly the disease pushed many homosexuals out of the closet, served to mobilize others, and ultimately thrust many into the political arena.[52] Openly gay and lesbian politicians began to compete for and win election to office, particularly at the local level. Such politicians, although confronting significant barriers to approval, proved successful at the ballot box by developing populist platforms with support from a variety of other outgroups, including racial minorities, feminists, neighborhood activists, labor union members, environmentalists, and liberal church groups. By the mid-1980s, several cities, including Bunceton, Missouri; Key West, Florida; and Laguna Beach and Santa Cruz, California, had even elected openly gay mayors.[53]

Despite the shift to the right in the country generally, gays were confident that most Americans were still sensitive to issues of civil rights. Although national legislation to protect gays and lesbians from discrimination continued to languish in Congress, two states (Wisconsin and Massachusetts) successfully adopted such legislation in the 1980s. In several other states executive orders were issued or civil service rules were amended to bar discrimination in public employment.[54] In addition, the decade found some forty cities and counties passing gay rights legislation, a total that equaled the number of communities that had adopted such laws or policies in the 1970s (Figure 3-1).

Unlike the decade of the 1970s, when many of the pioneering efforts to achieve gay rights took place in university communities or big cities, the communities that adopted legal protection in the 1980s comprised a mix of large cities, suburban communities adjacent to major cities that already had ordinances, and some ten counties. Atlanta, Chicago, Philadelphia, and New York had been debating gay rights legislation for more than a decade. Well-organized opposition groups, however, as well as lack of cohesion among gays and their allies, had delayed passage in each of these cities. In New York, for example, the city council adopted a gay rights law in 1986 with a divided 21–14 vote some fifteen years after the bill was originally introduced. Right-wing Catholics, Orthodox Jews, and fundamentalist Protestants had waged an effective campaign against the bill, keeping it tied up in committee since 1974. With the election of new leadership to the city council (partly resulting from the mobilization of lesbian and gay voters), and with gay activists' agreement to create a more moderate bill, the political conditions propitious for passage were finally achieved.[55] In Philadelphia too, as we have seen, gays and lesbians toiled in local elections for several years before contributing to the formation of a city council that was receptive to protective legislation.

FIGURE 3-1 Adoption of Gay Rights Ordinances or Policies, 1972–1993

Number adopted

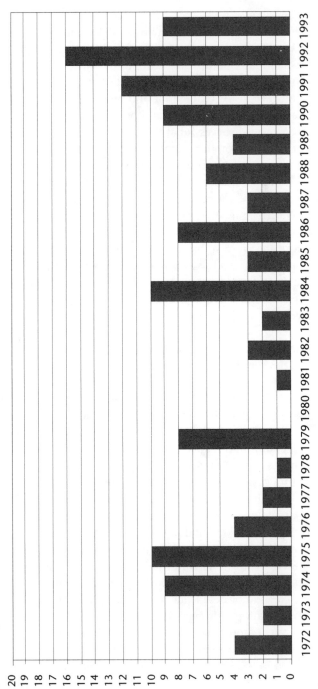

Year

Source: National survey by authors.

Note: The data for 1993 are for the first six months of that year.

The adoption of ordinances in the 1980s was also marked by an apparent "diffusion of innovation" process whereby suburban communities began to accept the new legislation from larger and more dominant nearby cities.[56] Thus, suburban locales near Los Angeles (Long Beach, Pasadena, Riverside, Santa Monica, West Hollywood), San Francisco (Brisbane, Alameda County, San Mateo County), Seattle (King County), and Washington, D.C. (Alexandria, Arlington County), passed gay rights legislation following earlier adoptions by central cities. According to this theory of policy innovation, local decision makers look to officials in other nearby communities for guides to action in many policy areas. Uncertainty and the fear of unanticipated consequences tend to limit policy change and reform. Once a policy has been adopted by a large number of communities or by a dominant nearby city, however, it is increasingly recognized as a legitimate public responsibility. When this occurs, public officials find it difficult to resist demands to implement the new policy. As the political scientist Jack Walker states it, "once a program has gained the stamp of legitimacy, it has a momentum of its own."[57] Clearly this theory helps to explain the process and pattern of many adoptions of gay rights legislation in the 1980s and, as we shall see, in the early 1990s as well.

An Upsurge in the 1990s

The 1990s has seen a significant increase in homosexuals coming out of the closet and more urgently demanding an end to gay bias. A new militance began to replace the politics of moderation that characterized much of the 1980s. ACT-UP was formed in New York in 1987 by a group of gay men and some lesbians who were angered with slow governmental response to the AIDS crisis. Their political tactics were more confrontational than those used by other gay organizations. So were the direct action strategies of Queer Nation, established in 1990 in New York and quickly disseminated to other major cities.[58] These groups were relatively small, but they attested to the less moderate tone of the movement. Many of these activists went back to the Stonewall era, but many others were born after Stonewall and grew up in a world in which homosexuality was not a dirty secret. Not only was the gay movement larger and more politicized in the 1990s, but it had also spread from the major cities of the East and West Coasts into the heartland. An indication of this proliferation was the celebration of gay pride events each year in places like Columbus, Memphis, Omaha, and Phoenix.[59]

Perhaps the best illustration of the new political primacy granted to gays and lesbians was the 1992 presidential election. During the primaries, all five leading Democratic contenders actively courted the gay vote. All five also endorsed a repeal of the ban on homosexuals in the military, as did the inde-

pendent candidate Ross Perot. After extensive gay-sponsored voter registration drives, the number of lesbian and gay voters was estimated at nine million, a figure exceeding the Jewish vote. Moreover, gays demonstrated their
financial willingness to support helpful politicians. The Human Rights Campaign Fund, one of the fastest-growing political action groups in Washington,
raised an estimated $4.5 million in 1992.[60] In the presidential race, the gay
and lesbian community united behind Bill Clinton, who campaigned as a
strong advocate of homosexual rights. Gays poured more than $2.5 million
into the Clinton campaign, and on election day, an estimated 72 percent of
the openly gay vote went to this candidate. Clinton's election was unques-
tionably a historic event in gay politics, in which, as recently as a decade earlier, support of gay rights was considered political suicide for most candidates,
and certainly for one seeking the presidency.[61]

As lesbians and gay men felt more comfortable in being open about their
sexual orientation, more Americans reported that they knew someone who
was gay and thus seemed to feel more comfortable around homosexuals.
And those who knew gay people were most likely to support civil rights protections. Given this atmosphere of acceptance, it was not surprising that by
1993 some 120 openly gay elected officials held local public office. Although
this figure was less than one-tenth of 1 percent of all elected officials in the
United States, the number of gay officeholders had more than doubled in the
previous two years. In addition, six more states had passed gay rights laws
since 1990.[62]

One of the most remarkable, as well as contentious, aspects of gay political progress has been the significant upsurge in community antidiscrimination ordinances. In the first three and a half years of the decade, at least forty-
six cities and counties added sexual orientation to their civil rights codes (Figure 3-1). This period represented the highest adoption rate by far of the twenty-one years of local gay rights legislation. The 1990s also showed great variation in communities according to size, type, and region. As in the 1980s
many were relatively small and suburban in nature, like Brighton, New York;
Oak Park, Illinois; Pacifica, California; Rockville, Maryland; and Stamford,
Connecticut. The Midwest and South claimed increased numbers of communities as the gay movement spread beyond its original coastal confines.
Several large cities, where lesbians and gay men were just beginning to organize and flex their political muscle, also adopted antidiscrimination legislation
that covered sexual orientation. These major cities included Cincinnati, Denver, Kansas City, New Orleans, Phoenix, Pittsburgh, and San Diego. In addition, trendy resort communities like Crested Butte, Colorado; East Hampton,
New York; Key West, Florida; and Telluride, Colorado, as well as several university cities, including Corvallis, Oregon; New Haven, Connecticut; and State
College, Pennsylvania, were among those communities that adopted gay

rights legislation in the 1990s. Finally, nine counties, many of which encompassed cities that already had such policies or laws, also numbered among this broad array of localities that passed legislation in this decade.

Not surprisingly, communities that pioneered antidiscrimination ordinances on sexual orientation in the 1970s differ in several striking respects from those that came late to this particular reform. The differences tell us much about the changing environment that is supportive of gay rights. The communities that adopted legislation in the 1990s were much less likely to be university oriented. College and university students accounted for less than half the share of population in the late adopters of gay rights protection as they had in the early adopters (14 percent versus 30 percent). The disparity is even more striking when we consider that the pioneering communities were home to such major universities as the University of California-Berkeley, the University of Minnesota, Ohio State University, Stanford University, the University of Texas, and the University of Washington. If we define "college towns" by either enrollment as a sizable proportion of the population or the presence of a large institution of higher learning, the label fits eighteen of the twenty-eight early adopters but only nine of the last twenty-five places to enact legal protection based on sexual orientation.

In addition to college students, the communities that adopted legal protection later in time also appear to have fewer gay residents and government employees. On the admittedly imperfect census measure of households headed by unmarried partners of the same sex, the first twenty-eight ordinance communities averaged one and one-half times the figure for the last twenty-five adopters and were twice as likely as the latecomers to exceed the average for all ordinance communities on this datum. Similarly, one-fourth of the cities and counties in the early-adopting category were government centers, whereas none of the places that adopted in the last three and one-half years were such centers. Overall, then, the three qualities of large higher-education enrollment, substantial numbers of government employees, and significant gay populations characterize three-fourths of the early adopters but only one-third of the localities that have adopted gay rights protection more recently.

In large measure, these traits identify supportive constituencies for the extension of civil rights to unpopular minorities. This would suggest that the two types of communities also differ in the scope of their commitment to gay rights, an assumption confirmed by empirical analysis. Four communities in the late-adoption category (as opposed to two of the pioneers) implemented equal rights through administrative policies, which are typically much less far-reaching than statutory reforms. Comparing the ordinances in the two categories affirms the greater breadth of the antidiscrimination effort in the pre-1977 communities. The ordinances in the pioneer communities covered, on average, two more institutions or sectors than the ordinances in the late-adopting communities.

Although many more communities adopted gay rights legislation in the 1990s, these localities often contained a less supportive environment than did cities and counties that had passed legal codes much earlier. The political atmosphere surrounding lesbian and gay issues was clearly much different in the 1990s compared with the early to middle 1970s. The antigay backlash that was apparent from the late 1970s and continued through the decade of the 1980s seemed to gain momentum in response to the gay successes of the 1990s. As increased numbers of homosexuals came out of the closet to become part of mainstream America, gay subcultures and gay rights became a chief target of the political right. Many of the battles waged over these issues took the form of voter referendums on proposals to deny homosexuals protection against discrimination. In Colorado, Idaho, and Oregon, and in cities like Cincinnati; Portland, Maine; and Tampa, Florida, voters were asked to repudiate gay rights. In perhaps the most widely publicized referendum of the early 1990s, for instance, voters in Colorado passed decisively a ban on all local antidiscrimination laws that protected homosexuals.[63] This measure, which was overruled by the U.S. Supreme Court in 1996, was an attempt to override gay rights ordinances in Aspen, Boulder, Denver, and other Colorado communities.

The Nature and Diversity of Communities with Discrimination Laws

By mid-1993 approximately one in five Americans lived in a community that forbade discrimination on the basis of sexual orientation. What kinds of communities have adopted ordinances or policies since the 1970s? Figure 3-2 shows the location of the cities and county seats that had enacted legislation protecting sexual orientation by mid-1993. The 126 governmental units in our sample seem to exhibit, at first glance, a bewildering diversity. They range in size from villages and towns of fewer than 10,000 inhabitants to megalopolises incorporating millions of residents. With apologies to Woody Guthrie, they are scattered across the country from California ($n = 28$) to the New York islands (East Hampton, Long Island), from the redwood forests (near Santa Cruz) to the Gulf Stream waters (New Orleans). The list of cities with ordinances or policies includes citadels of the cybernetic revolution (Cupertino, California, and Cambridge, Massachusetts), resort towns (Aspen), affluent bedroom suburbs (Stamford, Connecticut, and Oak Park, Illinois), and gritty industrial centers like Flint and Saginaw, Michigan. There are ordinances in historic bastions of liberalism—Berkeley; Yellow Springs, Ohio; Chapel Hill—and in such conservative southern cities as Raleigh and

FIGURE 3-2 The Location of Cities and Counties with Gay Rights Ordinances and Policies, as of Mid-1993

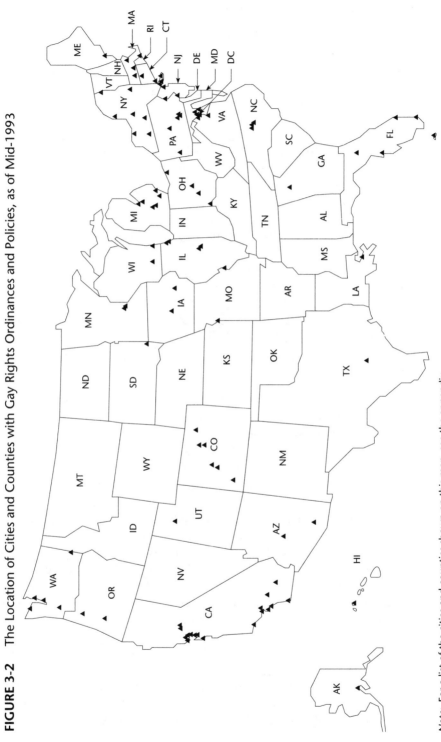

Note: For a list of the cities and counties shown on this map, see the appendix.

TABLE 3-1   ALL CITIES AND CITIES WITH GAY RIGHTS
ORDINANCES OR POLICIES, BY SIZE OF
POPULATION

| | All cities [a] | | Cities with gay rights ordinances or policies | |
Population	%	No.	%	No.
Less than 25,000	83.2	5,965	0.2	12
25,000–49,999	9.4	678	2.8	19
50,000–99,999	4.7	337	5.9	20
100,000–249,999	1.8	131	13.7	18
250,000–499,999	0.6	40	42.5	17
500,000–1 million	0.2	16	56.3	9
Over 1 million	0.1	8	75.0	6
Total	100.0	7,175	1.4	101 [b]

Source: Data for all cities are from International City/County Management Association, Municipal Yearbook 1993 (Washington, D.C.: ICMA, 1993), xii.

[a] Includes all U.S. municipalities of 2,500 and over and smaller municipalities with professional management.

[b] Excludes the twenty-five counties with antidiscrimination ordinances based on sexual orientation.

Tampa. Apart from the common denominator of a gay rights law or policy, these communities seem to share only diversity.

The four models or theories of public policy innovation that we introduced in Chapter 1 can help us to understand why some communities were more likely than others to adopt legislation. These theories refer to social and political forces that are considered important in the policy process. The names of the models, which reflect their primary emphasis, are urbanism/social diversity, political opportunity structure, resource mobilization, and communal protest. The first quality that clearly distinguishes these communities is population size. As noted previously, the principal stimulus for gay political action was the social dislocation that occurred during and after World War II. The war and its aftermath induced massive geographical migrations, uprooting people from familiar surroundings, cutting off traditional patterns of social interaction, and permitting individuals to construct their social identities anew. In this tolerant setting, gays—like other minorities—found an environment in which they could develop communities that were somewhat insulated from the larger culture. Because the anonymity of large cities afforded gays a measure of freedom from the scrutiny of family and traditional social institutions, gays tended to concentrate in certain neighborhoods of large cities, facilitating the emergence of a critical mass for political mobilization.[64]

Large communities fit with our urbanism/social diversity model and seem to be the most promising environments for assertive gay power and the adoption of gay rights legislation. The data in Table 3-1 clearly demonstrate that city size is indeed highly correlated with the adoption of ordinances. Gay rights ordinances are unknown in 99.8 percent of the communities with populations under 25,000 (which comprise more than 80 percent of all American communities). In contrast, such laws are the rule in six of the eight American cities with populations of at least 1 million. There is a steady, monotonic increase in the relative frequency of such legislation between these extremes. We find ordinances in exactly half of all cities of 250,000 or more.

Larger cities also tend to be culturally diverse in regard to the socioeconomic makeup of their populations. Thus, communities with gay rights legislation are not only larger but much more diverse than our randomly selected sample of communities without such laws or policies. As portrayed in Table 3-2, ordinance cities and counties have on average a higher growth rate; a greater proportion of African Americans and nonfamily households; and a younger, better-educated, and more affluent citizenry. Such social con-

TABLE 3-2   DIFFERENCES BETWEEN COMMUNITIES WITH AND WITHOUT GAY RIGHTS ORDINANCES OR POLICIES

Variable	Communities with gay rights ordinances or policies (N=126)	Communities without gay rights ordinances or policies (N=125)
Population	434,214	18,388
Population growth, 1970–1990 (%)	16.2	6.6
African Americans in community (%)	15.4	8.3
Per capita income ($)	16,514	12,576
Individuals with 12 or more years of education (%)	81.2	72.6
Individuals with 16 or more years of education (%)	33.3	16.5
Median age	31.6	34.5
Nonfamily households (%)[a]	42	29

Source: Data are from U.S. Department of Commerce, Bureau of the Census, 1990 Census of Population: Social and Economic Characteristics (Washington, D.C.: GPO, 1993).

Note: All figures are averages.

[a]Defined as households composed of unrelated persons.

TABLE 3-3   REGIONAL DISTRIBUTION OF COMMUNITIES WITH
AND WITHOUT GAY RIGHTS ORDINANCES OR
POLICIES

Region	Communities with gay rights ordinances or policies (%) [a]	Communities without gay rights ordinances or policies (%) [b]
Northeast	24	22
Midwest	22	32
South	18	32
West	37	14

Source: Data are from authors' national survey.

Note: Regions are defined by the U.S. Census Bureau.

[a]$N = 126$.

[b]$N = 125$.

ditions are typically associated with urbanism, and these findings reinforce our urbanism/social diversity hypothesis. Further analysis of our survey findings, moreover, indicated that city size and the concentration of nonfamily households are the strongest predictors among these factors in differentiating ordinance communities.[65]

If size and diversity are correlates of such legislation, what about regional patterns? We would anticipate finding proportionately the fewest ordinances in the more traditional and conservative South and industrial Midwest, and we would expect the Northeast and West to be more hospitable. The patterns that emerge in a regional comparison generally fit these predictions (Table 3-3). Both the South and Midwest report fewer cities with laws or policies than they should have on the basis of population alone. Although the Northeast offers more legislation than the South or Midwest, surprisingly it offers only a little more than would be expected, despite its reputation for liberalism.

Most striking is the enormous regional skew evident in the American West. There are almost as many communities with gay rights laws in the West as in the midwestern and southern regions combined—despite the fact that western cities constitute only 14 percent of all American cities. Western cities are overrepresented among communities with sexual orientation ordinances by a ratio of better than two to one. The prevalence of western cities among communities with legislation lends weight to both the social dislocation hypothesis and the moral traditionalist argument. The West has long been known for its attractiveness to people from elsewhere, its communities serving as magnets for internal migration. The West, moreover, often welcomed people

TABLE 3-4   RELIGIOUS COMPOSITION OF COMMUNITIES WITH
AND WITHOUT GAY RIGHTS ORDINANCES OR
POLICIES

Religious composition	Communities with gay rights ordinances or policies [a]	Communities without gay rights ordinances or policies [b]
Level of church adherence as percentage of population	47.7	56.6
Evangelical Protestants as percentage of all church adherents	26.8	38.5
Liberal Protestants as percentage of all church adherents	22.8	18.7
Black Protestants as percentage of all church adherents	15.5	8.7

Source: Data are from Martin B. Bradley, Norman M. Green Jr., Dale E. Jones, Mac Lynn, and Lou McNeill, comps., Churches and Church Membership in the United States, 1990 (Atlanta: Glenmary Research Center, 1990).

[a] $N = 126$.
[b] $N = 125$.

fleeing intolerance of all sorts, and these people in turn were more likely to be tolerant. This lack of rootedness has also produced the lowest level of religious attachment in the country (Utah excepted, of course), and the West has proportionately fewer evangelicals among its church members.

The final quality we examined was the religious composition of the communities. We gauged the religious climate of our sample communities from their church membership statistics.[66] We used two measurements, one identifying membership in churches professing fundamentalist Christianity and issuing policy statements disapproving of gays and gay rights, the other indicating the strength of churches with strong reputations for openness to gays and lesbians.[67] The religious differences between ordinance communities and the communities without such legislation are summarized in Table 3-4. We have reported figures on church adherence, a concept that includes both formal membership and affiliation. Because some churches restrict membership to adults who have made a particular profession of faith, the broader concept of adherence is more comparable across different religious traditions.

We start by determining whether religiosity per se—equated here with the share of the population recognized as church members or communicants—is associated with a disposition toward or against gay rights legislation. Conventional wisdom suggests that places with strong religious communities would be inhospitable to antidiscrimination policies based on sexual orientation and that, by contrast, legislation would be more common in areas that are unchurched. This assumption is based on widespread evidence that most branches of organized religion in the United States reject homosexuality. Table 3-4 seems to confirm conventional wisdom. Rates of church adherence are 9 percent lower in communities with gay rights protection than in the localities that do not provide legal protection based on sexual orientation.

Apart from differences in the level of religious attachment, the data in Table 3-4 reveal striking variations in the balance of religious forces between the two types of communities. The cities and counties that have adopted gay rights ordinances have significantly lower concentrations of people attached to the predominantly white denominations of evangelical Protestantism.[68] Furthermore, the local governments that have extended antidiscrimination legislation to cover sexual orientation are found in communities with proportionately more members of liberal Protestant and historically black denominations. As we will elaborate later, both religious groups contribute to the political opportunity structure supportive of civil rights for gays. If we treat the evangelical churchgoers as the primary locus of potential opposition to gay rights and combine the liberal and predominantly black Protestants as the core of potential supporters, the differences between the two types of communities are even clearer. In places that do not provide a legal basis for gay rights, churchgoers associated with evangelical Protestantism far outstrip the number of liberal and African-American Protestants. But in communities with gay rights laws or policies, the pattern is reversed. In those communities, churchgoers drawn from liberal and African-American denominations are much more numerous than evangelical Protestants. As we shall see, both in the section on gay allies in this chapter and in Chapter 6, these statistics help us pinpoint the sources of support and opposition to gay rights legislation.

Taken together, the evidence tends to paint a pattern that is consistent with our principal theoretical expectations. The existence of gay rights legislation is most common in larger, diverse cities; in the West and Northeast; and in places where liberal Protestants are overrepresented. The urbanism/social diversity perspective in particular provides a firm foundation for understanding the adoption of laws or policies protecting sexual orientation. It is important to recall that these are sociological affinities rather than deterministic laws. Many large cities have ordinances—but not all do—and some small communities defy the patterns among their peers to pass comprehensive ordinances providing legal protection of gays.

The Political Mobilization of Gays

Another crucial factor promoting the adoption of civil rights protections for lesbians and gay men was the political mobilization of the gay community. Although the actual size of the gay population did not contribute independently to the passage of such legislation, it did matter greatly if the gay community was organized and politically active.[69] This finding fits with what many scholars have been suggesting about mass movements. According to resource mobilization theory, society generates a good deal of discontent, but only some groups possess the necessary means to translate discontent into public policy. At a minimum, successful social movements require a large and energized constituency with a common sense of identity and a strong feeling of grievance. Success is also enhanced by having sophisticated leadership, resources, sound strategy, and helpful allies.[70] Given the effort required to achieve passage of a local civil rights law or policy, it is not surprising that one of the essential ingredients was a committed and politically organized gay community, a factor that fits with our resource mobilization model.

Little data exist on the political activities of gay and lesbian citizens, especially at the community level. Our surveys of communities both with and without gay rights legislation, however, provided some evidence on the degree of gay political mobilization. The surveys asked questions about the local electoral activities, candidacies for public office, and actual officeholding of lesbians and gays. Although the responses were provided by a "knowledgeable" public official in each community, officials' perceptions within the same community may differ, especially when estimating the political activities of a largely closeted population. Nonetheless, the results, shown in Table 3-5, are useful for comparing communities that had gay civil rights protections with communities that did not. The responses to each question indicate a much greater degree of gay political mobilization in the communities with antidiscrimination legislation.

We also employed another indicator of the political organization of gays and lesbians. Using a standard reference, we calculated the number of gay bars and gay-oriented services in each community.[71] The lack of recognized institutions puts lesbians and gays at a disadvantage in the development of a collective identity. Still, "to the degree that gay people . . . or at least gay men . . . have a functional equivalent of the ghetto, the factory, or the church, it is the gay bar."[72] Although not intended to serve primarily as a political base, gay bars and other services constitute at least potential institutions for the promotion of political and social action. These measures are biased to some degree in favor of gay males and higher socioeconomic groups. Nonetheless, gay bars and other services provide another indicator of the organizational capability of the homosexual community. We found an average of more than eight bars and three services in ordinance communities, none of either in the control group. These results portray a much better mobilized gay population in cities and counties that have gay rights legislation.

Our final evidence comes from answers to an open-ended question in our national survey. When respondents in communities with such laws were

TABLE 3-5   RESPONSES TO SURVEY QUESTIONS INDICATING GAY POLITICAL MOBILIZATION: A COMPARISON OF COMMUNITIES WITH AND WITHOUT GAY RIGHTS ORDINANCES OR POLICIES (PERCENT)

Questions asked in survey	Communities with gay rights ordinances or policies [a]			Communities without gay rights ordinances or policies [b]		
	Yes	No	Don't know	Yes	No	Don't know
Is there any evidence that gays and lesbians made a difference in any local election (including school board elections) in the past 10 years?	31	41	28	0	93	7
Aside from officeholders, within the past five years, have there been any other openly gay men or lesbians who have been *candidates* for public office in your city or county?	42	55	2	3	90	6
Is there currently an openly gay member of the city or county legislature?	21	76	2	1	95	4

Source: Data are from authors' national survey.

[a] $N = 126.$
[b] $N = 125.$

asked which local groups most actively supported gay rights legislation, gay and lesbian organizations were listed most frequently by far. Although other supportive groups were also mentioned by many officials, gay organizations were listed, in the aggregate, more than four times more frequently than the next most popularly nominated group.

In Philadelphia, the political battle to amend the Fair Practices Act to outlaw discrimination against lesbians and gays was a fine illustration of the crucial importance of a mobilized gay population. The gay rights bill was conceived in the late 1960s by the city's two primary gay organizations. In 1970 these groups sponsored a series of forums to educate the public on the need for such a measure. They also began to lobby local politicians to support the bill. The Philadelphia chapter of the Gay Activists Alliance was formed in 1971 and soon became the city's largest gay political organization. The alliance urged the city's Commission on Human Relations to recommend the bill to the city council. The commission did so in 1974, but despite a petition campaign and organized protests, both sponsored by the alliance and other gay groups, the bill failed even to clear committee for council consideration. A similar measure died in committee in 1977 as well.[73]

The early defeats of gay rights proposals in Philadelphia served to stimulate the formation of even more gay organizations. In 1978 the city's Lesbian and Gay Task Force was established, and it provided the organizational base and coordination of groups that were necessary for an effective political campaign. The primary strategy was to elect city officials who were supportive of civil rights legislation for gays. Thus, in 1978, gays were an instrumental part of the voter rejection of a charter change that would have allowed Mayor Frank Rizzo, an opponent of gay rights, to run for a third term. A year later, gays and lesbians played an active political role in helping to elect four new council members and to reelect three others, all of whom were perceived as bill supporters. With a more sympathetic city council and mayor in place, the task force began a major campaign to enact a gay rights bill. Through public education, lobbying, fund-raising, and a massive letter-writing and phone call effort directed at city officials, the gay campaign proved effective. Essential to this strategy was the strong coalition of forces in both the gay and nongay communities, a coalition forged largely by the task force. An indication of the breadth of political support was the fact that the successful bill was cosponsored by several city council members, including a Jewish representative and an African-American councilman.[74]

As in Philadelphia, Cincinnati's gay population suffered a setback when it first attempted to persuade city officials to adopt a human rights ordinance in the late 1970s. Spurred on by this defeat and by anger over reports of significant police harassment, gay leaders founded Stonewall Cincinnati in 1982.[75] The organization's primary goal was to work for passage of lesbian and gay civil rights in order to protect gays from discrimination and the overall oppressive atmosphere. Using conventional political action and education methods, Stonewall developed its own political action committee to screen and endorse local candidates. By the early 1990s Stonewall had become one of the most powerful interest groups in the city and was estimated to control five of Cincinnati's twenty-six Democratic ward clubs. Following the 1991 city elections, candidates endorsed by Stonewall controlled a majority of council seats and the mayor's post. To gain approval of the ordinance, the movement built a coalition with other supportive groups such as NOW, the AFL-CIO, liberal churches, and some African-American organizations. Significant efforts were also made to ensure the neutrality of the city's Catholic archbishop. In 1992, despite significant political opposition from some religious and business leaders, the council passed Cincinnati's first human rights law that included protections based on sexual orientation.[76]

The political mobilization of gays was perhaps more extensive and certainly better documented in Philadelphia and Cincinnati than elsewhere, but it was a key factor in the adoption of gay rights legislation almost everywhere. Often this mobilization was sparked by a political event or a notable act of discrimination, such as the denial of public park use for the celebration of Gay Freedom Day in Raleigh. Because gay rights organizations were most successful when they flexed their political muscles during election campaigns and at the ballot box, building a supportive majority on the city council was crucial. Yet such a strategy typically meant years of political involvement and effort, as was seen in Philadelphia and Cincinnati. Moreover, these electoral gains could not be accomplished alone. They called for generating, or sometimes simply joining, broadly based liberal coalitions.

The successful organization of gays was often the product of dynamic, shrewd, and inspired gay and lesbian leaders. Rita Addessa, the longtime director of the influential Philadelphia Lesbian and Gay Task Force, played a pivotal role in that city's ultimate adoption of gay rights as well as in many other issues affecting gays and lesbians. Addessa spent countless hours directing surveys of gays to document the prevalence of antigay discrimination, producing perhaps the most comprehensive data of any city in the country. She was also able to use the media effectively to publicize the plight of lesbians and gays and to educate the public about gay political concerns. Finally, Addessa was a master political strategist and lobbyist who put together a massive coalition of supporters for gay rights and then successfully managed the bill through the maze of interests that dominated the city's politics.

Another gay political figure with consummate leadership skills, John Laird, was a council member and eventually the mayor of Santa Cruz. With a reputation as a bright, knowledgeable, Democratic Party loyalist, Laird was the first openly gay mayor in this city (and one of the first in the country when

elected in 1983). His election meant that gays had gained a measure of acceptance in Santa Cruz, and his being open about his homosexuality "helped
destigmatize the issue of being gay."[77] Many local lesbians and gay men first
became involved in politics during his initial campaign, and many would stay
politically active. Being a skilled political "insider" with an awareness and
commitment to gay issues, he was instrumental in the city's adoption of two
of the first domestic partner benefits programs in the nation. Laird also promoted the passage of an AIDS nondiscrimination law and helped found the
Santa Cruz AIDS Project, which he directed for several years.[78]

Lesbian and gay political activists in the mold of Addessa and Laird are
somewhat exceptional, but every community we studied had gay leaders
who played pivotal roles in effectively mobilizing the gay community and
their allies. Such leaders were not necessarily the most skilled, especially in
their initial organizational efforts, and were almost always political neo-
phytes. The stigma of homosexuality has been, as a rule, too great for career
politicians to step forward and provide leadership in these campaigns. Yet
gay leaders often compensated for these disadvantages with their abundant
energy, enthusiasm, and strong sense of commitment. Leaders who were not
gay—typically liberal sympathizers and other minority group activists—were
often instrumental in mobilization efforts as well. All such political activists
proved to be important components of the resource mobilization model of
policy innovation.

Gay Allies and the Peculiar Case of Blacks

The mobilization of gays alone would not usually have been sufficient in
any community to ensure the adoption of an antidiscrimination law. With
few exceptions, self-identified lesbians and gay men number something less
than 10 percent of the population everywhere.[79] Although an absolute
majority of citizen support is not necessarily required for the passage of such
a community ordinance, the political opportunity structure theory suggests
that having allies and coalitions with additional groups greatly enhances the
chances for success. This is especially the case when the antibias legislation
involves an unpopular minority.

In the late 1960s, gay liberation groups developed coalitions with other
progressive forces, including feminists, blacks, Hispanics, radical students,
and hippies. At this time, the gay movement conceived of itself as a "revolutionary struggle to free the homosexuality in everyone."[80] As the movement
shifted to emphasize more politically moderate goals, it began to focus on
civil rights measures and legislative reform. In this vein, gays and lesbians
were classified as a disadvantaged minority, much like African Americans,
and they inherited many of the liberal coalitions that blacks and other dis-

possessed groups enjoyed. Thus, when we surveyed officials in communities with gay rights legislation about groups that had actively supported an ordinance, many different liberal organizations were specified. These included, in addition to gays and lesbians, the following political interests (with frequency of listing): human rights groups, including the American Civil Liberties Union (18); local human relations commissions or boards (15); liberal religious and church groups (13); black civil rights organizations (13); women's groups (12); Democratic Party organizations (6); university or student groups (5); business establishments (5); and environmental organizations (4).

Early on, gay strategists discovered that the recipe for success involved coalition politics. At the beginning of the 1970s in Washington, D.C., for example, the Gay Activists Alliance spent two years in demonstrations, confrontations, and private discussions with public officials trying to persuade the city to legislate against gay discrimination. It was all to no avail until the alliance formed a coalition with the local NOW chapter, student groups, Democratic Party organizations, and several other local groups. The alliance also obtained endorsements of the proposed gay rights bill from key black leaders in the city and in Congress. This broad coalition was able to win swift approval of a human rights bill that covered gays and two other classes of individuals and was one of the most comprehensive ordinances in the country.[81]

In Philadelphia, too, gay leaders understood that broad support, or at least the perception of such, was necessary for success in a city known for its pluralistic politics. By the mid-1970s some sixty-six local groups had endorsed civil rights for gays, and in public hearings that took place in 1982 just prior to council approval of the bill, more than fifty witnesses testified in support.[82] The *Philadelphia Inquirer,* the city's major newspaper, also endorsed the gay rights bill. An editorial stated:

[T]he bill seeks only to right an offensively discriminating wrong. It has been endorsed by an immense number of organizations and individuals, ranging from District Attorney Emmett Fitzpatrick to the Philadelphia Bar Association, from the Lutheran Church of America to the Episcopal Diocese of Pennsylvania, from the American Federation of Teachers to the Anti-Defamation League of B'nai B'rith.[83]

Clearly such legislation gains a greater sense of political legitimacy when support is widespread.

Liberal women's organizations were among the most consistent supporters of gay rights. The National Organization for Women in particular was a strong advocate in almost every community we investigated. Interestingly, Betty Friedan, the founder of NOW in 1966, originally feared a lesbian "takeover" of the women's movement, rejecting lesbians as a "lavender menace" that would tarnish the image of the organization. By 1971, however, NOW had affirmed that the "oppression of lesbians" was an important concern and had defined lesbianism as both a civil rights and women's issue. Feminists' attack on traditional sex roles tended to align them politically with lesbians, and in turn, many lesbians found the freedom and support in the feminist movement that was necessary to proclaim more openly their sexual identity. In 1973 NOW endorsed civil rights legislation to ban discrimination based on sexual orientation. Other liberal women's groups, including the National Women's Political Caucus and the National Women's Agenda, soon followed the lead of NOW.[84]

Although the gay movement for equal rights was in many ways modeled after the earlier civil rights movement, and many gays and their allies were transplants from this movement, African-American leaders and various civil rights groups were often seriously divided on the issue of gay rights. In the late 1960s many radical blacks joined in the revolutionary movement that demanded, among other things, greater freedom for gays and lesbians. The Black Panthers, the vanguard of black militance, supported the gay movement, and the Panther leader, Huey Newton, declared that homosexuals "might be the most oppressed people in the society."[85] In the late 1970s moderate African Americans were an important element in the political coalitions that swept Harvey Milk into office as San Francisco's first openly gay supervisor and that helped to defeat the antigay Briggs Initiative in a California statewide referendum.[86] In 1984 the black presidential candidate Jesse Jackson embraced lesbians and gay men as part of his Rainbow Coalition and issued a call for their civil rights at the Democratic National Convention.[87] Various black civil rights leaders and groups, including the NAACP and the Southern Christian Leadership Conference, have also endorsed basic rights for gays as a matter of compelling justice.

Many African Americans, however, have strongly opposed civil rights for gays and lesbians and have deeply resented the suggestion that antigay sentiment was as pernicious as racism. Some conservative blacks, especially Baptists, opposed homosexuality on religious grounds, as did their white coreligionists. They saw gays as practicing a sinful lifestyle by choice and believed that gays had therefore forfeited any claim for legal redress. Other African Americans claimed that the discrimination that gays experienced was not equivalent to the racism most blacks faced. By comparing the conditions of the two groups, according to these blacks, gays were "misappropriating the spirit and legacy of the black civil rights movement."[88] Vernon Jarrett, a black columnist for the *Chicago Sun-Times*, declared, "I consider it offensively disrespectful of the recorded and unchronicled sufferings of millions of my people who were kidnapped, chained, shipped and sold like livestock. Gays were never declared three-fifths human by the Constitution."[89]

Even some African Americans who were more sympathetic to the plight of homosexuals resented gays, especially white men, whom they perceived as hiding their sexual orientation as long as it was beneficial to do so. Other blacks feared that gays and lesbians were the latest minority to emerge and compete for their jobs. There was also the recognition, certainly among black homosexuals, that racism existed in the gay community itself. Gays reflected the larger society from which they came, and so black and ethnic homosexuals were often found in separate all-black gay clubs or Latino gay clubs. This was particularly the case because of the combination of residential segregation and the presence of gay bars in residential neighborhoods. Gay African Americans, moreover, who might have been expected to educate and help gain the political support of the nongay black population, were typically more outcast in black communities than in many white communities. This occurred because many black communities tended to be working class and fairly rigid about machismo and sexuality.[90] In the words of a black leader we interviewed in Raleigh, "There's more of a stigma—a real viciousness— in the black community about sexual orientation than in the majority community. As a result, black gays are not very open."

Despite their differences with homosexuals on civil rights and other issues, most African Americans support guaranteed equal rights for gays and have often been an important component of the political opportunity structure. A 1993 national opinion poll, for example, indicated that 53 percent of blacks thought gay rights legislation was necessary (as against only 40 percent of whites).[91] Another poll in the same year showed African Americans to be the largest group in the country to say that the AIDS crisis had made them *more sympathetic* to gays.[92] Numerous black city officials, especially big city mayors, were strongly supportive of legal protections for gays and lesbians. The black former mayors Tom Bradley (Los Angeles), Harold Washington (Chicago), and W. Wilson Goode (Philadelphia) all played important roles in mobilizing political support for gay rights issues. Even in the South, where black opposition to gays is probably greatest, Raleigh's only African-American council member voted in favor of the city's antidiscrimination law. Although he was criticized by some black constituents and by many black ministers for this vote, he felt it was important to protect the basic rights of all, including gays, and was fearful that any failure to guarantee human rights might ultimately jeopardize the rights of blacks. Thus, it seems that on some basic level, most African Americans, certainly those outside the South, do understand the gay struggle and sympathize with their cause.

The opponents of gay rights, however, attempted to exploit the conflicts between some African Americans and gays, both to diminish black support and to persuade whites that a commitment to civil rights did not have to entail support for gay rights. In Cincinnati, well-organized and financed white conservatives were able to persuade many black church leaders and their communities to join them in their campaign to repeal the sexual orientation provision in the city's antidiscrimination ordinance. Many old-guard black leaders and civil rights proponents continued to support basic rights for gays, but their advocacy was insufficient as an estimated 55 to 60 percent of voters in Cincinnati's black precincts cast ballots in favor of the repeal.[93] This important and unique political phenomenon will be discussed in more detail in Chapter 6, which focuses on the opposition.

Liberal Churches

We noted earlier that gay rights ordinances were more common in communities with higher concentrations of liberal Protestants, a term we used for Protestant denominations that had developed gay-friendly policy statements. Such supportive environments, including religious settings, are important, according to the political opportunity structure theory. Thus we were not surprised to find that liberal churches were often identified as part of the coalition favoring gay rights in our national survey. The churches that provided much of the support for these local efforts tended to be affiliated with denominations that have taken public positions welcoming gays and lesbians—such churches as the Episcopalians, Unitarians, Friends, Evangelical Lutherans, and the United Church of Christ.[94] The most gay-friendly of such denominations, the Unitarians, not only treat homosexuality as a fully legitimate form of human bonding but recognize gays and lesbians as an oppressed minority that warrants such strong measures as affirmative action within the church structure. Hence the four Unitarian churches in the Cincinnati metropolitan area declared themselves "hate-free" zones and strongly endorsed the original gay rights ordinance. The other churches within this broad heading have not taken such steps but nonetheless welcome homosexuals and affirm their worthiness without insisting that they repent of their sexual orientation as a condition for admission. That stance is also commonly found within much of the non-Orthodox wing of American Judaism, especially the Reform and Reconstructionist movements.

This stance of openness to gays and lesbians is often anchored in a theological position that affirms homosexuality as part of the divine plan. To establish this position requires that many churches confront biblical passages that appear to condemn homosexuality as a severe sin (see Chapter 6). The first of three such strategies, prevalent among Unitarians but also evident in other liberal religions, is simply to reject Scripture as the sole or primary source of moral norms. But for those who do regard the Bible as the font of their faith, the task is to provide a different understanding of the relevant passages. Many such interpreters argue that the passages commonly cited as antihomosexual are primarily intended as condemnations of the pagan faiths that were displaced by Judaism and Christianity. Thus, they argue, the Bible does not condemn homosexuality per se but rather certain forms of homosexual behavior that were widely practiced by groups in competition with monotheism. In a similar vein, these interpreters contend, the terrible fate that befell the inhabitants of Sodom was not retribution for the practice of anal sex but for the sexual assaults on strangers permitted by the citizens. When it was pronounced "an abomination" for a man to "lie with a male as one lies with a female" (Lev. 18:22), revisionists argue, the founders of the Judeo-Christian tradition envisioned homosexual acts performed by heterosexuals in flagrant disregard of their marital vows.

The third and final response to traditional biblical understanding is to contend that the writers of Scripture sometimes confused cultural norms with divine intention. The types of homosexuality described in the Bible were not acts of affection within the context of stable, loving relationships. Indeed, such long-term same-sex relationships were essentially unknown to the authors of the Bible. Had they been aware that it is possible for gay couples to form bonds of affection as strong and stable as the links between heterosexuals, revisionists believe the authors of the Bible would regard such ties as part of God's gift to humankind. Thus, the grace promised to married couples is equally available to same-sex couples that form permanent unions marked by love and fidelity. In all these ways, it is argued, the Judeo-Christian traditions are fully compatible with a condition of civic equality for gays and lesbians.

Despite the availability of these strategies to combat the apparent antihomosexual orientation of the Bible, such views do not find uncritical acceptance by all members of liberal Protestant churches. Many of the mainline Protestant churches with generally liberal dispositions still bar homosexual individuals from positions of responsibility. In fact, churches that do not maintain such formal provisions also harbor leaders with more traditionalist mentalities. For example, despite the generally affirming stance of the Episcopal Church toward homosexuality, several bishops recently brought heresy charges against another church leader who had ordained a noncelibate gay man as a deacon.[95] Even if the religious elite subscribes to the revisionist views outlined above, there is no guarantee these attitudes will be adopted by the laity. As a rule, the people in church pews are not particularly well versed in contemporary theology and may understand the Bible and their religious tradition much as traditionalist Christians do.

Scholars of American religion have long noted the substantial gap between clergy and laity on social issues, a gap especially apparent in many liberal Protestant churches. During the height of social conflict over civil rights, the Vietnam War, and other battles in the 1960s, many Protestant congregations were rocked by their own little wars between liberal clergy and appreciably more conservative congregants.[96] Liberal clergy often discovered that the

price for advocating social change was internal conflict within the congregation and a real possibility that parishioners would revolt against clerical leadership. Many clergy who sympathized with the social trends of the 1960s
found they were more comfortable in campus ministries or in denominational bodies where they did not have to placate congregations. The same
pattern has been found in many congregations as they struggle with the issue
of homosexuality in the 1990s. We found instances in our case study communities in which ministers who challenged denominational sympathies to
ordain gays or perform symbolic gay marriages were forced out of their pul-
pits because of the resistance of their congregations.[97] Perhaps this recognition of internal disunity accounts for the rather limited role of liberal churches in the political opportunity structure supportive of gay rights. Although we
often found that the churches identified themselves as supporters of gay
rights ordinances, they were seldom tapped as strong moving forces. The
word *sympathy* better describes the role of liberal churches than does a
stronger term like *activist.* Compared with the massive mobilizing efforts
against gay rights policies that were located in many of the evangelical
churches (see Chapter 6), the liberal churches were hardly centers of activity on this issue. We learned from a Cincinnati gay activist that apart from the
Unitarians and some Jewish organizations, the only support for the ordinance
from the religious community came from the testimony of individual ministers. The same pattern repeated itself in Iowa City, Santa Cruz, and Philadelphia. The one conspicuous exception to this pattern was in Raleigh, where a
group of church leaders formed the Raleigh Religious Network for Gay and
Lesbian Equality following hearings in 1987 on antigay discrimination. This
association of religious professionals and lay activists meets monthly and
holds an annual conference. The goal of these activities is, as stated in an
undated pamphlet describing the organization and its activities, to create "a
climate of support for basic human and civil rights for gay men and lesbians"
and to focus particularly on the need to provide pastoral care and ministry to
homosexuals. Although the group was not mentioned as a strong force in
lobbying the city council to pass the gay rights ordinance, it apparently
worked quietly behind the scenes.[98]

Students, Universities, and the Political Opportunity Structure

The successes of the gay rights movement were due as well to the influential allies and favorable political environment provided by university communities. As we have seen, many of the first cities to adopt antidiscrimination legislation that included sexual orientation were communities largely
influenced by institutions of higher learning. Students were often in the vanguard of this social movement, especially in its initial strivings but also to a

lesser degree later on, and so the role of gay and liberal students is worth exploring as another key ingredient of the political opportunity structure.

With the freedom guaranteed by a university setting and the liberal atmosphere of the times, gay students in the late 1960s began to proclaim their homosexuality and to organize openly. Even before the Stonewall riots, the gay movement's presence in New York spawned the Student Homophile League at Columbia University in 1967. It was the first campus gay organization in the country. The media attention it received aided in the formation soon after of similar groups at Cornell University, New York University, Stanford University, and the University of Minnesota. For the most part the gay student groups emerged without major controversy to become generally accepted on campus, and by 1974 there were an estimated 200–250 such organizations across the country. The early emphasis of homosexual campus groups was both political and personal. By organizing, lesbian and gay students hoped to build a sense of community and to educate their nongay classmates and others about the damaging myths concerning homosexuals. In this vein, their first activities consisted of social events like dances and parties, the establishment of gay lounges and offices on campus, the operation of telephone "hot lines" for emergencies and counseling services, and the publishing of newsletters.[99]

As gay and lesbian students began to come out, they discovered that their mere presence often qualified them for arrest because of the prevalence of state antisodomy laws. Many also faced harassment and outright hostility from other students and townspeople. These infringements of basic rights induced many gay and lesbian students to become politically active. Two of their primary goals were to repeal laws against sodomy and to extend local and university antidiscrimination legislation to cover sexual orientation.[100] Other liberal and radical heterosexual students sometimes joined this political cause as the gay movement became a successor for some to the civil rights and antiwar movements of the 1960s. In many cases students who were the initial activists in the gay cause had been activists in these other social movements. They had been mobilized and energized by these prior movements and had learned political tactics that they adapted to the struggle for gay rights.

In the early and middle 1970s, lesbian and gay students and their supporters played a key role in the gay rights movement, often taking the lead in demanding protective legislation from local governments. As we noted earlier, many of the first communities to adopt gay rights measures were university communities, including Alfred, New York; Ann Arbor; Berkeley; Boulder; Columbus; East Lansing; Ithaca, New York; and Minneapolis. Iowa City passed its gay rights ordinance just a few years later and is a good example of student involvement in this political process. In the late 1960s gay activists at the University of Iowa created the Gay Liberation Front (now the Gay People's Union). The organization was a response to the Stonewall riots as well as a byproduct of the antiwar and student activism of this period. One of the goals of the campus group was to encourage the community to amend its antidiscrimination ordinance to include gays and lesbians. To accomplish this, gay students appealed to the city's Human Rights Commission in the mid-1970s to recommend the amendment to the city council. There were no students on the commission, but gay students knew several commission members personally and persuaded them to make the recommendation. The gay rights initiative, although controversial, was not considered a major political issue in this liberal, university atmosphere, and it was passed by the council in 1977.[101]

Although influential allies and advocates such as students were important, political opportunity structure theory suggests that the "openness of government to new interests" is also a crucial factor for success of the gay rights movement.[102] Thus, the local political climate is essential in providing the "political opportunity" conducive to gay concerns. Universities generally promote tolerance and understanding, including greater acceptance of homosexuality.[103] Iowa City, for example, was considered an "island of liberalism" in the otherwise conservative and traditional Midwest. Indeed, the lead sentence in a local newspaper article about gays was "Being gay in Iowa City is OK," and the article further stated, "Its reputation as a tolerant city has spread throughout the state and the Midwest."[104] Moreover, almost everyone we interviewed claimed that the University of Iowa had influenced the city greatly. As one city official put it, "The university makes the city more diverse and creates an atmosphere of acceptance and understanding that would not normally be here." This receptive political climate enabled Iowa City to adopt a gay rights measure without the considerable mobilization of gays and lesbians that was typically required. Santa Cruz, too, was more open to unconventional social movements because of the presence of its University of California campus. In the words of one local political leader, "The university gives a tone to the town." A Santa Cruz minister went even further, suggesting that "since the arrival of the University of California campus, this resort community has been transformed. Students here are to the 'left' of Berkeley."

Additional elements, beyond a university atmosphere, enhanced the political opportunity structure and thus the likelihood of legal protection for gays. According to our analysis, communities that adopted such legislation were significantly more likely to be represented by a member of Congress who had cosponsored a national civil rights bill for gays and lesbians. Although the relation between constituency and representative opinion is not invariably close, it seems likely that elected officials will hold views similar to constituents on such an emotionally charged issue as sexual orientation. These legislative votes, therefore, can be viewed as proxies for community sentiment. In addition, communities with gay rights ordinances or policies were more likely to have voted Democratic in the 1992 presidential election, be covered by a state gay rights law, and have a state hate crimes statute that includes sexual orientation. These are all indicators of a favorable political environment, and they reinforce the importance of the political opportunity structure.

The Role of the Media

The media is no doubt one of the most important institutions in our society in influencing public sentiment on significant social issues. It clearly plays a major role in socially defining lesbians and gays and therefore contributes to the political opportunity structure. Until relatively recently, however, the media provided little coverage of gay issues, and what focus there was tended to portray gays in a stereotypic, biased fashion. Often the mainstream press, as well as the mass media in general, emphasized scandal and tragedy in regard to gays. Partly because most gays remained closeted, only rarely did lesbians and gay men have the opportunity to express their own views in the media. Opponents of gays, moreover, consistently attacked the media for anything they perceived as favorable attention to gay people.[105]

Beginning in the 1970s, and certainly by the 1990s, the degree and tone of most media coverage of gay life and politics changed. Gay issues were more commonly a media topic, and the depiction of lesbians and gay men became less negative. By 1993 the journalist Andrew Kopkind could claim that gay life "fills the media, charges politics, saturates popular and elite culture."[106] According to Kopkind, ten years earlier every month or so might have seen one gay issue in the news, but by the 1990s dozens of such issues were in the news at the same time. This was due in part to the increase in openly gay persons holding high and mid-level positions in journalism and publishing.[107] Despite these changes, however, a 1993 U.S. News and World Report poll found that 56 percent of voters thought that media portrayals of gays had a negative influence on society. Only 33 percent believed that such media images had a positive effect.[108]

In regard to the politics of gay rights, it does appear that media coverage increased significantly during the period when a community was actively debating the issue. This media focus, especially press coverage, seemed to arouse public concern, as well as educate the public, about civil rights for gays.[109] Whether media attention gained support for gay rights measures or not is less clear. In communities that had adopted such legislation, however, our survey results indicated that the primary local newspaper had either favored the legislation (37 percent) or remained neutral (38 percent) about the issue. In only 2 percent of these communities did respondents indicate that the local press had opposed this legislation. Furthermore, our case studies depicted local media as primarily supportive of equal rights for gays and lesbians. In every city except Cincinnati, the primary local newspaper endorsed gay rights legislation. In addition, the media generally had become more active in reporting gay issues and more sympathetic to gay and lesbian concerns. Raleigh's major newspaper, the *News and Observer,* is rather typical in this regard, and its transformation on gay issues was captured well in the comments of a gay activist there:

The *News and Observer* was reluctant at first to report gay issues or events in a favorable light. It perceived gays as primarily criminals prior to the early 1980s. But as public perceptions changed, the press changed and began to oppose sodomy laws. After all, it's a business and wants to make money. They now seek out gay leaders and others for interviews.

Conclusion

In the summer of 1995, some twenty-three years after East Lansing became the first community in the country to adopt a gay rights ordinance, another small Michigan city 200 miles west of Detroit debated the issue of legal protection based on sexual orientation. Saugatuck, primarily a resort community made up of conservative Dutch-American residents, families with children, and homosexuals, became seriously divided over gay rights. As in so many other communities across the land, this contentious issue pitted ethnic residents and more traditional groups against gay men, lesbian women, and their supporters. Saugatuck citizens opposed to the ordinance voiced fears that a gay-friendly statute would scare away conventional families and that enforcement of the law would sorely strain the city's already slim budget. Lesbians and gay men, involved in the city's business community, social life, and even city elections for years, contended that they still faced discrimination (especially in housing) and felt generally unaccepted. Discussion of the proposed law became so conflictual that at one point the city manager angrily told a gay resident that if he did not like the council's decision to delay action on the bill, he should move out of town.[110] In the meantime, debate over gay rights legislation continues.

Events in Saugatuck are illustrative of the political debates over gay rights that have been waged in countless U.S. cities and counties for more than two decades. By 1996, approximately 160 communities had adopted some kind of legal protection for lesbians and gay men. The first places to pioneer legislative reforms were fairly liberal university towns or big cities with relatively large numbers of gay citizens. Political opponents had not yet coalesced, so passage was relatively easy with little conflict. By the late 1970s, the political atmosphere had changed, those who opposed gay rights were better organized, and the rate of adoption slowed as a result. In the 1980s, however, lesbians and gays were more open about their sexual orientation and more politicized, partly as a result of the AIDS crisis. A greater diversity of communities, including suburbs and counties, began to pass protective legislation. By the next decade, this diffusion of the innovation process led to a virtual explosion of adoptions in an even wider range of communities.

Our findings over these years of civil rights advancements for gays indicate the importance of the urban/social diversity model. Gay men and lesbians have settled in relatively large, socially mixed communities and in regions outside the more conservative South and Midwest, where they feel more secure and less threatened. These diverse and generally tolerant communities are much more likely to have adopted gay rights legislation than other locales across the country.

Resource mobilization theory, however, suggests that a large lesbian and gay population alone is not sufficient for political change. The gay community requires a strong sense of identity and significant political mobilization in order to be successful. This has proved to be a crucial factor. Where gays were active in local electoral politics as voters, organizers, candidates, or officeholders, they were also most likely to be able to persuade local politicians to adopt antidiscrimination laws. Effective leadership and shrewd strategy were also important factors in such legislative achievements. Gay rights reforms were also made possible because of helpful political allies in the form of liberal coalitions that typically included human rights groups, African Americans, women, labor organizations, students, and some liberal religious groups. Finally, the media, especially the press, was generally supportive (or at least neutral) on the issue of gay rights. These findings conform to the political opportunity structure model, which indicates the importance of helpful allies and an environment conducive to policy innovation.

NOTES

Because of the controversial nature of this study, we promised the persons we interviewed that they would not be identified by name. Unless otherwise noted, all interviews pertaining to Iowa City took place in Iowa City in June 1994; all those pertaining to Philadelphia took place in Philadelphia in July 1994; all those pertaining to Raleigh took place either in Raleigh or Chapel Hill, N.C., in May 1994; all those pertaining to Santa Cruz took place in Santa Cruz in June 1994, and all those pertaining to Cincinnati took place in Cincinnati in November 1994. All quotations and information not otherwise documented are from these interviews.

1. William B. Rubenstein, ed., *Lesbians, Gay Men, and the Law* (New York: New Press, 1993), xv–xviii. See also David E. Newton, *Gay and Lesbian Rights: A Reference Handbook* (Santa Barbara, Calif.: ABC-CLIO, 1994), 6–7.

2. Barry D. Adam, *The Rise of a Gay and Lesbian Movement* (New York: Twayne, 1995), 129.

3. Dennis Altman, *The Homosexualization of America, the Americanization of the Homosexual* (New York: St. Martin's Press, 1982), 9.

4. Matthew A. Coles, "Homosexuals Need Civil Rights Protection," in *Homosexuality: Opposing Viewpoints,* ed. William Dudley (San Diego, Calif.: Greenhaven Press, 1993), 78–86.

5. Roger J. Magnuson, *Are Gay Rights Right?* (Portland, Ore.: Multnomah Press, 1990), 77–89.

6. Gary David Comstock, *Violence against Lesbians and Gay Men* (New York: Columbia University Press, 1991), 14–22.

7. National Gay and Lesbian Task Force, *Anti-Gay/Lesbian Victimization: A Study by the National Gay Task Force in Cooperation with Gay and Lesbian Organizations in Eight U.S. Cities* (Washington, D.C.: National Gay and Lesbian Task Force, 1984).

8. See summaries of surveys reported in Comstock, *Violence against Lesbians and Gay Men,* 31–46; and in Kevin T. Berrill, "Anti-Gay Violence and Victimization in the United States: An Overview," in *Hate Crimes: Confronting Violence against Lesbians and Gay Men,* ed. Gregory M. Herek and Kevin T. Berrill (Newbury Park, Calif.: Sage, 1992), 19–24.

9. "Survey Details Gay Slayings Around U.S.," *New York Times,* December 21, 1994; Brian Miller and Laud Humphreys, "Lifestyles and Violence: Homosexual Victims of Assault and Murder," *Qualitative Sociology* 3 (fall 1980): 169–185.

10. "Study: Gay Killings Are More Brutal," *Gainesville Sun,* December 21, 1994.

11. Comstock, *Violence against Lesbians and Gay Men,* 152–160.

12. Warren J. Blumenfeld and Diane Raymond, *Looking at Gay and Lesbian Life* (Boston: Beacon Press, 1988), 253–254. See also John D'Emilio, *Sexual Politics, Sexual Communities: The Making of a Homosexual Minority in the United States, 1940–1970* (Chicago: University of Chicago Press, 1983), 49–51.

13. Berrill, "Anti-Gay Violence and Victimization," 32.

14. National Gay and Lesbian Task Force Policy Institute, "Survey Results on Discrimination against Lesbians and Gay Men," draft, Washington, D.C., 1992.

15. See Gregory M. Herek, "Stigma, Prejudice, and Violence against Lesbians and Gay Men," in *Homosexuality: Research Implications for Public Policy,* ed. John C. Gonsiorek and James D. Wienrich (Newbury Park, Calif.: Sage, 1991), 73–75.

16. *U.S. News* poll conducted by Celinda Lake, cited in Joseph P. Shapiro, "Straight Talk about Gays," *U.S. News and World Report,* July 5, 1993, 42–48. See also Jeffrey Schmalz, "Poll Finds an Even Split on Homosexuality's Cause," *New York Times* (special supplement), March 5, 1993.

17. Shapiro, "Straight Talk about Gays," 44, 46.

18. Newton, *Gay and Lesbian Rights,* 26–27. See also Schmalz, "Poll Finds an Even Split," 1; David A. Kaplan and Daniel Klaidman, "A Battle, Not the War," *Newsweek,* June 3, 1996, 29.

19. Human Rights Campaign Fund, "Post-Election Poll Finds Consensus on Gay Issues: GOP, DEM, and Independent Voters Support Equal Rights," press release, November 17, 1994.

20. Andrew Sullivan, "The Politics of Homosexuality," *New Republic,* May 10, 1993, 33–35.

21. See Magnuson, *Are Gay Rights Right?* 72–101; Sullivan, "Politics of Homosexuality," 34–35.

22. Richard D. Mohr, *A More Perfect Union: Why Straight America Must Stand Up for Gay Rights* (Boston: Beacon Press, 1994), 77–96.

23. Peter M. Cicchino, Bruce R. Deming, and Katherine M. Nicholson, "Sex, Lies, and Civil Rights: A Critical History of the Massachusetts Gay Civil Rights Bill," *Harvard Civil Rights-Civil Liberties Law Review* 26 (summer, 1991): 627.

24. Ibid., 626–628. See also Mohr, *A More Perfect Union,* 77–80.

25. Cicchino, Deming, and Nicholson, "Sex, Lies, and Civil Rights," 630–631; Mohr, *A More Perfect Union,* 84–85. As was the case with the African-American movement, absent legislation, there was an emphasis on litigating constitutional issues.

26. Charles Alverson, "U.S. Homosexuals Gain in Trying to Persuade Society to Accept Them," *Los Angeles Advocate,* September 1968, 8.

27. D'Emilio, *Sexual Politics,* 231–239.

28. "Ohio Law Reform," *Advocate,* January 31, 1973, 1.

29. We analyzed the 28 communities that passed laws or policies before 1977 and the 25 localities that did so after 1991. These dates are not arbitrary; they indicate dates that are one standard deviation beyond the mean adoption date for all 126 communities surveyed.

30. "Oops, E. Lansing First with Hiring Law," *Advocate*, May 10, 1972, 1, 14; "Gay Rights Law May Be Upcoming in Michigan City," *Advocate*, November 22, 1972, 1, 9.
31. "East Lansing Okays Ban on Gay Bias," *Advocate*, December 20, 1972, 1; "E. Lansing Finally Gets Bias Ban," *Advocate*, July 4, 1973, 17.
32. "E. Lansing Finally Gets Bias Ban," *Advocate*, July 4, 1973, 17.
33. Ibid.
34. "Rights Law in San Francisco," *Advocate*, April 26, 1972, 1, 17.
35. See Donald P. Haider-Markel and Kenneth J. Meier, "The Politics of Gay and Lesbian Rights: Expanding the Scope of the Conflict," *Journal of Politics* 58 (May 1996): 332–349.
36. "Gay Rights Bills Run Aground," *Advocate*, January 2, 1974, 1.
37. "Gay Issue Fires Up Conservatives; A Friend Loses," *Advocate*, October 9, 1974, 13–14.
38. "Employment Rights Roundup—Where We Are, Where We're Going," *Advocate*, January 29, 1975, 8, 14.
39. Randy Shilts, *The Mayor of Castro Street: The Life and Times of Harvey Milk* (New York: St. Martin's Press, 1982), 156.
40. Adam, *Rise of a Gay and Lesbian Movement*, 109–111; B. Drummond Ayres Jr., "Miami Votes 2 to 1 to Repeal Law Barring Bias against Homosexuals," *New York Times*, June 8, 1977.
41. Ayres, "Miami Votes 2 to 1 to Repeal Law."
42. Adam, *Rise of a Gay and Lesbian Movement*, 111.
43. "Why Tide Is Turning against Homosexuals," *U.S. News and World Report*, June 5, 1978, 29.
44. Adam, *Rise of a Gay and Lesbian Movement*, 113. See also, "How Gay Is Gay? *Time*, April 23, 1979, 72–75; Lillian Faderman, *Odd Girls and Twilight Lovers: A History of Lesbian Life in Twentieth Century America* (New York: Columbia University Press, 1991), 198–200.
45. Faderman, *Odd Girls and Twilight Lovers*, 271.
46. Ibid., 270–271; "Democratic Platform Panel Adopts Carter's Stands," *New York Times*, June 25, 1980.
47. Newton, *Gay and Lesbian Rights*, 26; Shapiro, "Straight Talk about Gays," 46.
48. Blumenfeld and Raymond, *Looking at Gay and Lesbian Life*, 327.
49. "Are Homosexuals Facing an Ever More Hostile World?" *New York Times*, July 3, 1988.
50. James L. Gibson and Kent L. Tedin, "The Etiology of Intolerance of Homosexual Politics," *Social Science Quarterly* 69 (September 1988): 588; "Morality and Mayoralty," *Newsweek*, September 30, 1985, 34.
51. "Morality and Mayoralty," 34.
52. Jeffrey Schmalz, "Gay Politics Goes Mainstream," *New York Times Magazine*, October 11, 1992, 29.
53. Adam, *Rise of a Gay and Lesbian Movement*, 140–141.
54. "A Gay Rights Law Is Voted in Massachusetts," *New York Times*, November 1, 1989.
55. Peter Freiberg, "New York City: Victory!" *Advocate*, April 29, 1986, 10–11; Joyce Purnick, "Homosexual Rights Bill Is Passed by City Council in 21-to-14 Vote," *New York Times*, March 21, 1986.
56. Jack L. Walker, "The Diffusion of Innovations among the American States," *American Political Science Review* 63 (September 1969): 880–899.
57. Ibid., 890.
58. Faderman, *Odd Girls and Twilight Lovers*, 299–301.
59. Schmalz, "Gay Politics Goes Mainstream," 42.
60. Ibid., 20.
61. Jeffrey Schmalz, "Gay Areas Are Jubilant over Clinton," *New York Times*, November 5, 1992; Murray S. Edelman, "The Gay and Lesbian Vote and Estimates of Population Size" (paper presented at the annual meeting of the American Statistical Association, Toronto, 1994).
62. Shapiro, "Straight Talk about Gays," 46.
63. Schmalz, "Gay Areas Are Jubilant over Clinton," 8.
64. See D'Emilio, *Sexual Politics*, 9–40; Steven H. Haeberle, "Gay Men and Lesbians at City Hall," *Social Science Quarterly* 77 (March 1996): 190–197.
65. Kenneth D. Wald, James Button, and Barbara A. Rienzo, "The Politics of Gay Rights in American Communities: Explaining Antidiscrimination Ordinances and Policies," *American Journal of Political Science* 40 (November 1996): 1152–1178.
66. Martin B. Bradley, Norman H. Green Jr., Dale E. Jones, Mac Lynn, and Lou McNeill, comps., *Churches and Church Membership in the United States, 1990* (Atlanta: Glenmary Research Cen-

ter, 1990). These data are calculated for counties rather than cities and, thus, do not coincide exactly with the boundaries of our predominantly city-based units.

67. In identifying denominations as *evangelical,* we relied initially upon Kenneth J. Meier and Cathy M. Johnson, "The Politics of Demon Rum: Regulating Alcohol and Its Deleterious Consequences," *American Politics Quarterly* 18 (October 1990): 404–429. We added the churches classified as either fundamentalist or evangelical by Tom W. Smith, "Classifying Protestant Denominations," *Review of Religious Research* 31 (March 1990): 225–245, and Lyman A. Kellstedt, "Evangelical Religion and Political Behavior: A Validation Effort" (paper presented at the annual meeting of the Society for the Scientific Study of Religion, Salt Lake City, Utah, 1989). We also included the Presbyterian Church in America. The category of *liberal* churches includes only those Protestant denominations that have issued official statements generally sympathetic to gays. See J. Gordon Melton, comp., *The Churches Speak on Homosexuality* (Detroit, Mich.: Gale Research, 1991). This category does not include many churches that are part of the mainline Protestant tradition but that have put severe limits on the role that gays may play in church life. Nor does it include the Roman Catholic Church, which has staked out a position that differs from both the evangelical opponents of gay rights and the liberal Protestant denominations that support equal protection (see Chapter 6). While the Catholic Church offers special ministries to gays and maintains recognizably gay parishes in some large cities, its formal position on homosexuality does not meet the gay-friendly standard. The figures on African-American religion represent an estimate of the number of black Baptists, the single largest denominational tradition in the black community.

68. We are not surprised to learn that the West Bay area of San Francisco, including the city and some of its suburban communities, has both the lowest proportion of self-identified Christians and the highest concentration of gay rights ordinances in the United States. See Barry A. Kosmin and Seymour P. Lachman, *One Nation under God: Religion in Contemporary American Society* (New York: Crown, 1993), 79.

69. Wald, Button, and Rienzo, "Politics of Gay Rights."

70. John D. McCarthy and Mayer Zald, "Resource Mobilization and Social Movements: A Partial Theory," *American Journal of Sociology* 82 (May 1977): 1212–1241; Margit Mayer, "Social Movement Research and Social Movement Practice: The U.S. Pattern," in *Research on Social Movements,* ed. Dieter Rucht (Frankfurt am Main: Campus Verlag, 1991), 47–120.

71. *Damron Address Book '94* (San Francisco: Damron, 1994).

72. Kenneth Sherrill, "On Gay People as a Politically Powerless Group," in *Gays and the Military,* ed. Marc Wolinsky and Kenneth Sherrill (Princeton, N.J.: Princeton University Press, 1993), 112.

73. Tommy Avicolli, "A History of Gay Rights in Philadelphia," *Gay News,* March 19–April, 1982.

74. Jane Eisner, "Bill to Outlaw Bias toward Gays Is Introduced," *Philadelphia Inquirer,* July 1, 1982; "Council Victories Brighten Rights Bill Prospects," *Bulletin of the Philadelphia Lesbian and Gay Task Force* 2 (1979): 1–2.

75. Barbara Zigli, "Political Clout Lacking, Negative," *Cincinnati Enquirer,* April 4, 1982; *Stonewall Cincinnati: Ten Years of Challenge, Change, and Championing Our Rights,* Stonewall Cincinnati, 1992.

76. *Stonewall Cincinnati;* Richard Green, "Gay-Rights Groups Gaining Clout," *Cincinnati Enquirer,* April 28, 1991.

77. Robin Musitelli, "Laird Hopes to Make History," *Santa Cruz Sentinel,* August 25, 1993.

78. Ibid.; John Laird, "Journal of an Openly Gay Candidate," *Lavender Reader,* fall 1993, 11–12, 15.

79. Kenneth Sherrill, "The Political Power of Lesbians, Gays, and Bisexuals," *PS: Political Science and Politics* 29 (September 1996): 469.

80. Adam, *Rise of a Gay and Lesbian Movement,* 84.

81. David L. Aiken, "D.C. Rights Law Gets Preliminary Nod," *Advocate,* August 29, 1973, 5; "D.C. Rights Bill Signed into Law," *Advocate,* December 19, 1973, 1, 17.

82. "Endorsements for Gay Civil Rights," Philadelphia Lesbian and Gay Task Force, listing, 1975; Bob Warner, "Committee OKs Gay Rights Bill," *Philadelphia Daily News,* July 28, 1982.

83. "Pass the 'Gay Rights' Bill," *Philadelphia Inquirer,* November 26, 1975.

84. D'Emilio, *Sexual Politics,* 236–237; Faderman, *Odd Girls and Twilight Lovers,* 211–213.

85. As quoted in Adam, *Rise of a Gay and Lesbian Movement,* 86.

86. Ibid., 112–113.
87. Ibid., 163.
88. Lana Williams, "Blacks Reject Gay Rights Fight as Equal to Theirs," *New York Times,* June 28, 1993.
89. As quoted in ibid.
90. Ibid.; David W. Dunlap, "60 Gay Public Officials Gather to Share Ideas," *New York Times,* November 23, 1994; Faderman, *Odd Girls and Twilight Lovers,* 240–241.
91. Williams, "Blacks Reject Gay Rights."
92. Shapiro, "Straight Talk about Gays," 46.
93. Jeff Harrington, "Anti-Gay Coalition Wants Political Clout," *Cincinnati Enquirer,* July 31, 1992; Donald Suggs and Mandy Carter, "Cincinnati's Odd Couple," *New York Times,* December 13, 1993.
94. The most gay-friendly of all religious denominations, the Metropolitan Community Church, was founded in Los Angeles in the late 1960s. This denomination was formed to provide a safe and affirming religious environment for gays and lesbians. As a sign of the controversy homosexuality poses for Christianity, the National Council of Churches, generally considered the organizational representative of mainline Protestantism, has refused to grant membership status to this church.
95. See David W. Dunlap, "Role of Openly Gay Episcopalians Causes a Rift in the Church," *New York Times,* March 21, 1996. The charges were dismissed by a court of Episcopal bishops, who found no "core doctrine" barring from the priesthood people involved in same-sex relationships.
96. Jeffrey Hadden, *Gathering Storm in the Churches* (Garden City, N.Y.: Doubleday, Anchor, 1969).
97. Erin Kelly, "Pastor Who Advocated Gay Rights Seeks Transfer," *Raleigh News and Observer,* April 19, 1990.
98. According to Rick Harding, "Gays Win Protection in Raleigh, N.C.," *Advocate,* March 1, 1988, 11, a group of clergy from the Network visited the pastor of the largest fundamentalist congregation in the area and successfully lobbied him to refrain from opposing the ordinance.
99. D'Emilio, *Sexual Politics,* 209–210; Robert Reinhold, "Campus Homosexuals Organize to Win Community Acceptance," *New York Times,* December 15, 1971; Iver Peterson, "Homosexuals Gain Support on Campus," *New York Times,* June 5, 1974.
100. Peterson, "Homosexuals Gain Support," 32; Tony Vellela, *New Voices: Student Activism in the '80s and '90s* (Boston: South End Press, 1988), 162–165.
101. James Arnold, "Iowa City Gays Claim to Be Victims of Discrimination," *Daily Iowan,* April 23, 1991.
102. Anne N. Costain, *Inviting Women's Rebellion: A Political Process Interpretation of the Women's Movement* (Baltimore: Johns Hopkins University Press, 1992), 14–15.
103. Ilsa L. Lottes and Peter J. Kuriloff, "The Impact of College Experience on Political and Social Attitudes," *Sex Roles* 31 (July 1994): 31–54.
104. Martha Miller, "Iowa City 'Cool Place' for Gays, Lesbians," *Iowa City Press-Citizen,* June 25, 1988.
105. D'Emilio, *Sexual Politics,* 109; Larry Gross, "Lesbians and Gays and the Broadcast Media," *SIECUS Report,* April/May 1996, 10–12; Richard D. Mohr, *Gays/Justice: A Study of Ethics, Society, and Law* (New York: Columbia University Press, 1988), 174–177.
106. Andrew Kopkind, "The Gay Movement," *Nation,* May 3, 1993, front cover.
107. Ibid., 590, 592.
108. Shapiro, "Straight Talk about Gays," 44.
109. Cicchino, Deming, and Nicholson, "Sex, Lies, and Civil Rights," 603.
110. Oscar Suris, "Saugatuck Attracts Many Gay Tourists, but There Is Friction," *Wall Street Journal,* August 22, 1995.

CHAPTER 4

The Impact of Antidiscrimination Legislation: What Difference Does It Make?

Legislation cannot dictate feelings to discriminate, but when government outlaws discrimination, it indicates it is important to treat people fairly.

—Gay activist, Philadelphia

L aw is a powerful force in American society. While a good deal of debate has occurred about the linkage of law and social change, there is general agreement that under the proper conditions state legislation can influence even the most deep-seated societal patterns and beliefs. The 1960s civil rights laws are often viewed not only as the supreme test of law as a catalyst to change, but also as the ultimate indicator of the transformative nature of stateways.[1] Even in the Deep South, entrenched patterns of race relations gave way to federal legislation. As Harrell Rodgers and Charles Bullock summarized the civil rights process, "New patterns of behavior required by law have helped produce significantly more tolerant attitudes toward black Americans."[2]

Although the evidence indicates that some laws, especially civil rights legislation, clearly have promoted social change, ample data also exist that suggest the substantial limitations of the law. Public policy operates in a social context that may seriously circumscribe compliance and therefore impact. The sociologist William Graham Sumner's famous aphorism that "stateways cannot change folkways" captures the essence of this societal constraint. Moreover, law is also limited by its intrinsic nature and the process by which it is put into effect. That statutes, including civil rights laws, have not always lived up to their expectations has focused attention on their implementation and impact.[3]

In the last chapter we discussed why and how gay rights legislation was adopted, emphasizing the politics of this process. In this chapter we examine the kinds of laws or policies that were passed and how they have been implemented and enforced. In addition, we explore the effects of such legislation on lesbians and gays themselves and on basic institutions in the community, such as the police and businesses (schools are discussed in a separate chapter), that were often targeted by enforcement bodies. Finally, the social, psychological, and educational effects of antidiscrimination measures will be discussed in an attempt to investigate more fundamental and intricate influences of the law.

Clearly, one of the most contentious issues for both proponents and opponents of gay rights laws and policies was the probable effect of such legislation. Gays and their advocates argued that protective codes were necessary and would help to prevent unjustified discrimination in employment, housing, and other areas of life. More basically, government actions were thought to be essential for gaining greater acceptance, even a sense of legitimacy, for gays in a largely homophobic society. In contrast, those opposed to gay rights contended that most gays and lesbians, because of their supposed middle-class status and ability to hide their identity, did not face serious discrimination and therefore had no need of civil rights legislation. Such unnecessary legislation, it was argued, would unduly hamper local governments, schools, businesses, landlords, and others directly affected by such measures. Furthermore, opponents agreed that laws lend greater legitimacy to groups afforded protective status but asserted that such acceptance was unwarranted for those who chose a clearly deviant "lifestyle." Obviously, the probable effect of gay rights legislation was as hotly debated as the politics of its adoption.

The Nature and Scope of Antidiscrimination Legislation

As we have seen, gay rights measures varied a great deal in how and when they were enacted. Reflecting the politics of its passage, the legislation showed important differences as well in its nature, scope, and coverage. Our national survey of 126 communities indicated that 89 percent, or 112, of them had enacted or amended laws or ordinances, whereas the remaining 14 cities or counties had adopted executive resolutions, plans, or policies. Nonordinances were limited in scope, covering only employment (typically just public employment) in all but 2 of these 14 communities. Antidiscrimination resolutions and policies were typically adopted later in time (mid-1980s to 1990s) in smaller cities and counties, such as Brighton, New York; Hayward, California; and Minnehaha, South Dakota. In addition, policies lacked the investigative and punitive aspects of law and were therefore considered less effective in preventing or dealing with antigay discrimination. Such policies, nonetheless, sometimes preceded the passage of an ordinance, as was the case in East Lansing, and thus served as an important first step in this incremental process. In other communities, where sufficient support for gay rights laws was lacking, policies or resolutions simply reflected the tenor of local politics.

The vast majority of antidiscrimination ordinances and policies (115 of the 126) were enacted by a vote of the city or county legislature. This is the normal method of local ordinance adoption or amendment. Another 7 codes were enacted by executive order, 5 of which were policies or resolutions and not laws. It is extremely rare for an ordinance to be adopted by executive authority alone. Finally, 4 gay rights laws resulted from a popular vote. Referendums on civil rights measures are highly unusual, except as attempts to repeal already-adopted laws. As an example of such a referendum, voters in Detroit adopted a new city charter in 1974 that included a gay rights provision. The protection of homosexuals drew little attention, however, because many voters were not aware it was a part of the comprehensive new charter.[4]

Gay rights ordinances are perhaps most diverse in their scope, or basic institutions covered. Table 4-1 lists the public and private institutions and activities covered and exempted in the 126 localities. Clearly the most frequently covered institution is public employment (91 percent), especially in executive divisions (meaning all basic city or county departments or agencies). This is significant not only because government is one of the largest employers in most communities but also because these policies establish standards for the rest of society. Special districts (separate government units outside of city hall) and public schools are much less commonly included in these protections, most likely reflecting the belief held by many Americans that homosexually oriented individuals should not hold positions that involve contact with youth. Private sector employment, which affects more citizens than any other work-related institution, is legally protected in only a little more than half (58 percent) of these communities.

The other primary institution of importance in everyday life is housing. Private rental housing is included in the human rights codes of two-thirds (66 percent) of these cities and counties. Yet all housing, including the sale of residential homes, is covered in a mere ten (8 percent) of these communities. The actual figure is probably somewhat higher; because this institution was not specifically listed in our survey and therefore had to be added following "other," this category was likely to be overlooked by some respondents. Realtors and some business leaders, however, are often strongly resistant to what they perceive as unnecessary government regulation, particularly civil rights laws. Public accommodations such as restaurants, hotels, and retail centers are granted coverage in most communities (64 percent), as are private businesses that have contracts with the city or county (57 percent). In contrast, only 38 percent of credit agencies, including banks, are covered, and hardly any private schools or unions are designated.

Clearly, gay rights laws extend much less protection in the private than in the public sector. This is generally true for civil rights legislation due to the prevailing free enterprise ideology that resists government interference in the private sector. This is particularly the case in regard to housing, where the general feeling that "a man's home is his castle" suggests a spirit of individualism beyond government control. Moreover, it is easier, and more acceptable

TABLE 4-1   SCOPE OF LOCAL GAY RIGHTS ORDINANCES OR
             POLICIES (*N*=126)

Institutions and organizations	Percentage covered by local ordinances or policies	Number covered by local ordinances or policies
Public institutions covered		
Public employment (executive divisions)	91	114
Public employment (special districts, authorities)	51	64
Public employment (schools)	36	45
Public services	11	14
Private institutions covered		
Private rental housing	66	83
Public accommodations	64	80
Private employment	58	73
Private contractors or suppliers performing publicly funded activities	57	72
Credit agencies	38	48
All housing	8	10
Educational institutions	3	4
Unions	2	2
Other	2	2
Public or private organizations specifically exempted		
Religious organizations	37	46
Private rental housing with relatively few units	21	27
Private schools	8	10
Small businesses	6	7
Federal agencies	6	7
Public schools	2	2
Youth services	2	2
Other	12	15

Source: Data are from authors' national survey.

politically, for government to make changes in the public sector, which is already under its direct influence, than to extend the scope of government to the private sector that is generally unregulated.[5]

The attempt in Raleigh in 1993 to extend employment protection for gays and lesbians to the private sector illustrates well the perilous politics of this issue. The city's initial gay rights measure, prohibiting discrimination in municipal employment, was enacted relatively easily five years earlier. Several council members, however, felt the legislation should be broadened to deal with allegations of antigay discrimination in the private sector. Their proposal met heavy opposition, particularly from the business community, which saw it as a "needless bureaucratic intrusion" by local government. Business owners maintained that it would add another layer of regulation and might discourage future business development. "Let's leave employers alone so they can best determine who can fulfill their duties," stated one businessman. "They have enough red tape to deal with already."[6] Not surprisingly, this extension proposal failed.

Iowa City faced similar circumstances when its city council was forced to drop housing from coverage in the struggle to enact its original gay rights ordinance in 1977. In public hearings on the proposed ordinance, housing proved to be the most controversial issue. Several landlords opposed the housing provision on moral grounds and on grounds that they should have the ability to choose their tenants. Some objected, for example, that the provision "would force landlords to condone sexual activity they consider immoral."[7] With local elections about to take place, a majority of the city council of Iowa City conceded the issue and adopted the antigay bias code without coverage of housing.[8] Seven years passed before the city council was able to reach an agreement to include housing. The agreement was reached only after two years of sometimes bitter debate and despite the protests of an apartment owners' group contending that gay tenants did not face enough discrimination to justify the changes.[9]

Gay rights legislation also varied a great deal in the number and kinds of exemptions granted. Almost half (46 percent) explicitly exempted one or more institutions. Discovering which organizations were specifically excluded from these ordinances can reveal which local interests were most significant in their opposition to such laws. Topping the list, as expected, were religious organizations whose leaders often expressed fears that they would be forced to employ gays and lesbians (see Table 4-1). Historically it was common for civil rights statutes to protect the freedom of religion by excluding religious institutions or by permitting these institutions to use religion as a factor in employment.[10] Small-scale rental housing (typically defined as fewer than four to six units) was also excepted in approximately one-fifth of communities. But very few other institutions, including private schools and small businesses, were specifically granted exemptions.[11] Some institutions, although not excluded in ordinances, were clearly not typically included in legal coverage either, which presumably had the effect of allowing communities to discriminate in some areas on the basis of sexual orientation despite enacting gay rights legislation.

The Issue of Enforcement

Until recently, scholars tended to neglect the implementation of legislative actions in favor of the process of policy adoption. Concern about the perceived failure of major legislation in the 1960s and early 1970s, however, has served to change this scholarly emphasis. This concern has spawned studies of the implementation of policies in many areas, including education, poverty, urban affairs, employment, health services, and civil rights.[12] Clearly the implementation and enforcement of civil rights codes, including gay rights, are important, for they are the keys to the successful prohibition of discrimination.

Social scientists have documented numerous factors and conditions related to the success of policies. In general, for policy or law to modify the status quo, attention must be given to the nature of the policy, how it is administered, and the environment in which implementation occurs.[13] Although our study does not provide a detailed look at the enforcement of gay rights legislation, it does offer more than a general glimpse of this process. Moreover, a basic understanding of implementation is essential to knowing how effective these laws and policies have been.

We have already discussed the nature and scope of gay rights legislation, so we now turn to its administration. In the 126 cities and counties we studied, the primary local organization charged with implementing these ordinances or policies varied tremendously. In fact, more than a dozen different enforcement organizations were listed in these communities. Most common by far was the human relations or human rights board or commission, which was the primary administering agency in 42 percent of the communities. These organizations were typically established during the black civil rights era of the 1950s and 1960s to help improve race relations and to enforce civil rights laws. Thus, human rights agencies were found in larger communities with sizable black populations (see Table 4-2). This suggests the importance of the urbanism/social diversity model in the enforcement process.

The second most frequently listed enforcement agency was the personnel or equal employment opportunity office (19 percent), reflecting the widespread legislative coverage usually given employment. Smaller communities were less likely to have separate enforcement agencies and were therefore more likely to place enforcement responsibility in the chief executive's office (6 percent) or in the city or county attorney's office (6 percent). Eleven percent of the communities provided no formal enforcement powers in local government but relied instead on state agencies (seven states had statewide gay rights laws in 1993) or private litigation through the courts.

Implementation was less effective in communities that lacked an independent enforcement organization or a public administering agency.[14] Larg-

TABLE 4-2   TYPE AND CHARACTERISTICS OF ENFORCEMENT
AGENCIES (N=126)

Type of enforcement agency	Average population size	Average percentage of blacks	Discrimination complaint rate [a]
Human rights board or commission	631,192	20	0.03
Regular city or county department or office [b]	324,465	14	0.01
Other than city or county government, or no specific enforcement agency	134,704	7	0.00

Source: Data are from U.S. Department of Commerce, Bureau of the Census, 1990 Census of Population: Social and Economic Characteristics (Washington, D.C.: GPO, 1993), and authors' national survey.

[a] The complaint rate is the number of formal complaints of discrimination based on sexual orientation divided by population size (per thousand).

[b] Includes departments such as personnel and equal employment opportunity, and offices such as city or county manager, attorney, or clerk.

er communities with more complex bureaucracies and fairly comprehensive antidiscrimination statutes were most likely to have independent administrative structures. These specialized agencies also encouraged a relatively high rate of complaints of discrimination based on sexual orientation (Table 4-2). The Philadelphia Commission on Human Relations (PCHR) is fairly typical of such agencies in both its makeup and the process it has employed. Created in 1951 to protect against discrimination and to enforce the city's civil rights law, the PCHR established regulations that described how the law was to be enforced. Its nine commissioners, appointed by the mayor, make judgments in cases of alleged discrimination brought before it. Formal complaints are investigated by staff and then reported to the commission. When a respondent and complainant are unable to reach a voluntary settlement of a complaint, and after a finding of probable cause has been determined, the PCHR is empowered to hold a public hearing and can legally order a settlement. The emphasis, however, is on the mediation of disputes, and most cases are settled prior to a public hearing.[15]

In addition to the disposition of individual complaints of discrimination, the PCHR is allowed to investigate any conditions that adversely affect intergroup relations and is able to study more generally the problems of prejudice and discrimination. Focusing on broad patterns of discrimination, as well as handling individual cases, is considered an optimum approach for fully enforcing civil rights legislation. Not surprisingly, Philadelphia's enforcement agency, at least in its early years, was considered one of the most active and effective oversight organizations in the country.[16]

Smaller communities, with less elaborate and specialized bureaucracies, tended to enforce gay rights provisions through a regular department, the chief executive or city attorney, or civil court. These enforcement mechanisms were less formalized and emphasized individual complaints to the exclusion of discrimination patterns. Resort to the courts for resolution was most costly, especially for lesbian and gay plaintiffs, and the burden of proof was often more demanding than administrative enforcement.[17] Strategies of implementation outside of city or county government generated little publicity and education about the legislation, and predictably, the numbers and rates of formal complaints by lesbians and gay men were low (Table 4-2).

Litigation of alleged sexual orientation discrimination also depends on access to lawyers with experience in cases of discrimination in employment. Smaller cities and counties were less likely to have such lawyers. These communities tended to have "general practitioner" lawyers who were unskilled at arguing discrimination cases and likely to dissuade someone from bringing forth such a case. Furthermore, lawyers engaged in general practice were likely to have the community's employers and landlords as their primary clients and would therefore not want to antagonize these clients with claims of sexual orientation discrimination. Thus, charges may not have been brought in smaller communities because of the lack of competent counsel.

Informal pressures may also discourage complaints. A degree of social opprobrium attached to filing a discrimination charge against an upstanding member of society (a public official or an employer) in a small city or town likely operated as a deterrent to filing charges. Even if the complaint was successful, the problem of dealing with the neighbors would persist, unlike in the more anonymous big cities.[18]

Although the nature of the enforcement mechanism was important in the implementation process, there proved to be a host of problems commonly plaguing attempts fully to enforce legislation prohibiting discrimination against lesbians and gay men. Lack of funds was an issue that confronted many enforcement agencies. In 1975 not one of the fifteen cities that had adopted some kind of gay rights law within the previous three years had yet authorized additional funds to ensure enforcement.[19] As the *Portland Oregonian,* Portland's major newspaper, commented after the city passed its legislation: "The ordinance requires no implementation . . . or compliance monitoring. . . . [I]t (in effect) does not establish homosexuals as a minority group to be included in affirmative action hiring programs."[20]

By the 1980s many American cities were facing severe budget problems, and regulatory agencies in general often suffered cutbacks. Even Philadelphia's well-established Commission on Human Relations saw its personnel reduced little by little from seventy-five in 1975 to forty-four in 1994. Reflecting on the effect of these major cuts, a commission official lamented, "We were able to do a lot more affirmative action work in the 1970s . . . and more enforcement then." Partly as a result of these staff reductions, the number of complaints of alleged discrimination accepted by PCHR plummeted from 695 in 1986, to 327, or less than half that number, in 1993.[21]

Our survey of communities with gay rights statutes or policies also indicated the paucity of resources devoted to the enforcement of these provisions. Only 15 of the 126 communities declared that they had increased the staff size of the enforcement agency since enactment of the legislation protecting gays. Of these 15 cities and counties, only 4 could claim an addition of more than two staff members. In regard to the cost of enforcement, we asked public officials to estimate the expense of administering the gay rights measure for 1992, the year prior to our survey. Admittedly such an estimate is often difficult to make, given that the enforcement of all human rights provisions is usually under the umbrella of one agency. Thus 43 percent of officials did not respond to this question. Nonetheless, of the 72 respondents who were able to estimate costs, 48 of them (67 percent) stated that *no additional funds* had been allocated for the enforcement of this provision. Of those listing some costs, only 13 officials estimated expenses of $10,000 or more for the year. In contrast, the PCHR, certainly one of the largest enforcement agencies, had a total budget of $1.96 million to cover all enforcement responsibilities in 1992.[22]

The implementation and enforcement of legislation has also been greatly influenced by the attitudes of political and administrative leaders. In Duane Lockard's study of the enforcement of state Fair Employment Practice (FEP) laws, he found that the "foremost obstacle to more effective FEP action has been the lack of strong political support."[23] Lockard concluded that FEP laws were not "taken seriously" by many executive and legislative leaders, and that the problems of minorities generally did not command the time or attention devoted to major building projects, tax measures, or other important programs.[24] Protective legislation for gays and lesbians often lacked significant political support as well. For example, not only were Raleigh city officials the last among the Research Triangle city leaders to adopt an ordinance, but the law, when it was finally enacted, was very limited in scope, covering only city employees and businesses with city contracts. The attempt in 1993 to extend coverage to the private sector failed to gain majority support among council members. Political analysts, moreover, predicted that such an extension would not have been approved by the state legislature, which is required to vote on such local legislation. The legislature, located in Raleigh, had never passed gay-friendly legislation and had repeatedly rejected attempts to repeal the state's antisodomy law. Given this political atmosphere and general lack of supportive public officials, it is not surprising that not one formal complaint of discrimination based on sexual orientation was filed in the six years following the adoption of the Raleigh legislation.

Cincinnati, well known for its political conservatism, did not offer antidiscrimination protection *to any group* until passage of its human rights law in 1992. Immediately after its adoption, several council members and other local leaders initiated efforts to repeal by referendum (Issue 3) the portion of the law protecting homosexuals. Less than a year later, Issue 3 won voter approval to rescind gay rights, and while Issue 3 was under court appeal, the city council itself voted in early 1995 to remove gays from legal protection. Clearly lacking political support, the gay rights measure was not well enforced. The city's Office of Consumer Services, not an independent agency or a human rights commission, was charged with implementing the law. Gay leaders claimed this office was "not qualified" to play this role, that its director "did not even understand the ordinance well," and that it "did not investigate complaints thoroughly." In a city with a large, mobilized lesbian and gay population, Cincinnati's legislation produced only nine formal complaints based on sexual orientation in its first two years.[25] As a result, one gay activist asserted that the law "may do more harm than good because it doesn't find discrimination and therefore it looks like there is no discrimination."

Formal Complaints of Discrimination

Another frequently used indicator of the nature and degree of enforcement is the number of formal complaints based on the ordinance as it pertains to sexual orientation. Most gays and lesbians are closeted and often unwilling to file a complaint even when they believe they have been victimized. Indeed, filing a formal grievance typically requires gays to come out publicly, an action that is difficult and risky for many. Nevertheless, formal charges are at least suggestive of not only the amount of discrimination faced by homosexuals but also the level of understanding and trust lesbians and gay men have toward the legislation and the process of enforcement. In our survey of gay rights communities, we requested information on formal complaints for 1992, and the results are summarized in Table 4-3. Almost 40 percent of these communities reported no official complaints, and another 21 percent indicated five or fewer such charges. Only fourteen cities or counties, all much larger communities, listed more than ten formal charges of discrimination based on sexual orientation.[26] Controlling for population size, however, the rate of complaints was not significantly greater in the larger

TABLE 4-3   FORMAL COMPLAINTS OF ANTIGAY
             DISCRIMINATION, 1992

Number of complaints	Percentage of communities	Number of communities	Average population size	Complaint rate [a]
0	39	49	171,891	0.000
1–5	21	26	175,514	0.046
6–10	8	10	472,238	0.054
11 or more	11	14	1,505,808	0.050
Information missing or don't know	21	27	589,675	—
Total	100	126		

Source: Data are from U.S. Department of Commerce, Bureau of the Census, *1990 Census of Population: Social and Economic Characteristics* (Washington, D.C.: GPO, 1993), and authors' national survey.

[a] The complaint rate is the number of formal complaints of discrimination based on sexual orientation divided by population size (per thousand).

communities. Yet, as we have seen, many of the smaller cities and counties (less than 171,000 in population), which tend to have little or no formal enforcement mechanisms, had relatively few complaints. Charges of discrimination because of race and gender were by far the most common kinds of complaints filed under local human rights laws. Discrimination complaints based on sexual orientation were typically about as frequent as charges of discrimination based on national origin or handicap/disability.

Complaint information from Iowa City and Philadelphia tends to corroborate these findings. Both of these cities have had comprehensive gay rights legislation in place for more than a decade, and both showed relatively detailed complaint records. In Iowa City, the Human Rights Commission received an average of twenty-five formal discrimination complaints a year from 1988 through 1992. Most of these charges involved employment issues. Sexual orientation was the basis of complaint in only 8 percent of the cases during this period. Race was the primary basis for complaints (29 percent) with gender and disability next (totaling approximately 15 percent each). Sexual orientation rivaled age, national origin, and family status in the proportion of formal charges.[27] Complaint data for Philadelphia, a much larger city with a more diverse population, were similar. Between 1991 and 1993 an average of 560 charges of discrimination, the majority pertaining to employment, were filed with the PCHR. Antigay allegations accounted for no more than 3 percent of these complaints. Race, gender, and here, national origin, were the most frequent bases of discrimination.[28] A 1993 survey of states having civil rights laws that include sexual orientation depicted similar find-ings, with complaints of antigay discrimination typically making up less than 5 percent of all complaints.[29]

Opponents of protective legislation for gays contend that the low number of formal charges indicates that discrimination against lesbians and gays is not a serious issue and therefore legislation is unnecessary. In contrast, many gays argue that subtle and more blatant forms of discrimination are problems for homosexuals almost everywhere but that coming out to file a formal charge is too risky even in jurisdictions with protective ordinances. Whatev-er the reality, and it most likely varies from one community to another, it does appear that the enforcement process itself often plays an important role in either encouraging or discouraging formal complaints of discrimination. In Iowa City, for example, where the proportion of charges of antigay discrim-ination was somewhat higher than in many other cities, the gay rights mea-sure was seen by at least one city official as one "that could work." Shortly after amending its human rights ordinance to include gays, the city revised its law to meet state guidelines and to improve its enforcement. The revi-sions included granting the city authority to revoke licenses (like rental or liquor permits) from businesses found guilty of discrimination; giving the Human Rights Commission authority to order actions such as hiring, rein-statement, or promotion in order to remedy acts of discrimination; providing for court action against persons or businesses failing to fulfill conciliation agreements negotiated by the city; and extending the deadline for filing com-plaints from 120 to 180 days after the alleged act.[30]

Most of the people interviewed in Iowa City, including gays, believed that the city's ordinance was well designed and effectively enforced. Although the law was not used formally as much as some had thought it might be, it was widely understood that the human rights measure was important and that, in the words of one city official, "employers can't fire you for your sexual orientation, or landlords kick you out of your apartment." Many respondents referred to a well-publicized case in the early 1990s in which a gay employ-ee of Holiday Inn filed a formal complaint of sexual and religious harassment by co-workers and supervisors. The employee claimed that he was called "faggot" and "Jew boy," made to do extra work, and eventually fired. The case went to a public hearing, and the city's Human Rights Commission ruled in favor of the gay employee, awarding him $20,000 in damages.[31] This case, one of the few involving gays to go to public hearing, proved significant. Many respondents felt it had a chilling effect on those who might discrimi-nate, and believed it convinced many gays and lesbians that the ordinance had "teeth" and was well enforced.

In numerous communities, however, the enforcement process tended to discourage complaints. A general lack of knowledge about the law and how to file a complaint were major obstacles, since typically little money was spent on educating the public. More than four years after Santa Cruz adopted its antibias law, no formal charges had yet been made. Although the city had distributed some four thousand posters describing the ordinance to local businesses and had asked them to display the posters publicly, the local newspaper opined that the law was "being virtually ignored by a community that vehemently battled for its passage."[32] One lesbian activist claimed that many people did not understand the law, especially what was considered legal and what was not, and others did not know how to file a complaint. She also stated that the cost of mediation was a deterrent to some potential complainants. The Santa Cruz ordinance requires mediation, the expense of which is to be shared evenly by the private parties involved with no contribution by the city. As a result of these limitations of the local law, some gays chose to pursue their grievances at the state level (California adopted a statewide gay rights law in 1992), where enforcement was perceived as more effective and less costly.[33]

In Philadelphia many respondents evaluated the commission's enforcement efforts as less effective more recently. Gay and lesbian leaders in particular charged that the PCHR was understaffed and underfunded. They claimed that there were relatively few formal complaints by gays because the "message never got out" about the ordinance or how to file a complaint. In addition, a commission official admitted that the number of complaints had dropped over the years because "we had a reputation. . . . [B]lacks, gays, and Hispanics thought we didn't care, and we're located out of the way, not near City Hall anymore." In fact, the location of the PCHR offices, which are relatively small, is not clearly marked, and thus they are difficult to find.

A deterrent to potential complaints in some localities was the requirement of proof in alleged discrimination cases. According to one gay activist in Philadelphia, many gays and lesbians perceived the commission as "demanding a high burden of proof" and the staff as commonly saying "you don't have a case." Indeed, PCHR staff often determined "no cause" in complaint cases; in 1993, for example, this was the judgment in 43 percent of all cases.[34] In Iowa City, too, "no probable cause" was the final determination of the Human Rights Commission in 40 percent of all formal complaint cases from 1988 through 1992.[35] Finding cause in discrimination, even in nonjudicial circumstances, is a demanding requirement to fulfill, and the burden of proof is on the complainant. In the words of a leading Iowa City official, "There are few complaints of discrimination because it's so difficult to prove." Informal charges were much more common than formal ones in this midwestern city, indicating that discrimination was still considered an issue by many gays and others.[36]

Another factor discouraging complainants and limiting enforcement has been the unevenness of gay rights protection. As of 1994, antigay bias legislation existed in only eight states—California, Connecticut, Hawaii, Massachusetts, Minnesota, New Jersey, Vermont, and Wisconsin—plus the District of Columbia and in about 130 cities and counties. With no federal law covering sexual orientation, many lesbians and gay men live in jurisdictions with no legal prohibitions on discrimination. In New York, where no state law offers protection, a survey showed the state to be a "legal patchwork when it comes to gay rights, a place where discrimination may be outlawed in one place but permissible just across the county line."[37] Since the early 1970s thirteen local governments in New York, representing 54 percent of the state's population, have passed gay rights measures, but the rest of the state has remained uncovered. A gay leader in New York declared that the "absence of a state law sends a message that discrimination will be tolerated, even in the jurisdictions that currently have local ordinances."[38] In other cases, state law may actually prevent significant enforcement of local antidiscrimination legislation. In politically conservative Indiana, for example, state law prohibits local human rights commissions from investigating antigay discrimination, unlike discrimination based on race, gender, religion, and other classifications. Thus, when the cities of Lafayette and Bloomington approved ordinances banning discrimination based on sexual orientation, their authority to enforce these laws was seriously limited. According to Bloomington officials, only "voluntary" investigations by the city's human rights commission were acceptable under state law.[39]

The Effects of Antidiscrimination Legislation on Lesbians and Gay Men

The nature and scope of gay rights legislation, as well as its implementation and enforcement, have much to do with the consequences such laws or policies may have. Despite a good deal of popular and scholarly discussion of this issue, remarkably little research has been done on the effect of such legislation on society. The reason for this is that the "sociology of law" discipline is relatively new.[40] It is important, however, to explore the behavioral and institutional effects of antidiscrimination legislation for lesbians and gays because they have made up a prime part of the debate between gay rights proponents and opponents. Those supportive of civil rights protections have argued that such legislation is necessary to curb various forms of pernicious discrimination against lesbians and gays and to promote more tolerant attitudes toward this unpopular and misunderstood minority. Opponents contend, to the contrary, that legal protections for gays are unwarranted because they face little discrimination and because such protections are often burdensome and costly to other members of society. Opponents also argue that "special rights" for gays lends legitimacy to a group they consider deviant or sinful.

TABLE 4-4   POSITIVE EFFECTS OF LOCAL GAY RIGHTS
LEGISLATION (*N*=126)

Most important positive effects	Number of respondents	Percentage of respondents
Reduced discrimination based on sexual orientation in public employment and other covered institutions	34	27
Recognition that discrimination based on sexual orientation is legally wrong and not permissible	28	22
Shows progressive nature of community's policies	24	19
Gay men and lesbians feel more safe and comfortable in being open	23	18
Creates greater awareness and discussion of the issue	21	17
None; no positive effects	21	17
Lesbians and gay men feel more free to seek employment and housing	13	10

Source: Data are from authors' national survey.

Note: Question asked of survey respondents: "What do you think have been the two most important positive effects (if any) of the passage of this ordinance?" Effects mentioned by seven or more respondents are listed.

First we examine the impact of these laws and policies on lesbians and gay men themselves, the individuals to whom the legislation was directed. A full accounting of the effect of such laws would require community surveys and the interviewing of a larger group of gays than our resources can cover. We did, however, pose several questions concerning this issue in our nationwide survey of officials charged with enforcement of this legislation. The results of the first general, open-ended question are summarized in Table 4-4. We also asked a similar question of all sixty-five people whom we interviewed in our case study communities.[41]

The effect mentioned most frequently in Table 4-4, and commonly by community interviewees as well, was that such legislation has reduced discrimination against gays and lesbians in public employment and other institutions covered by the law. Furthermore, the recognition that such discrimination is illegal and not permissible was listed second most frequently. Thus, combining these responses, virtually half (49 percent) of the surveyed officials identified the antidiscriminatory effects of these local statutes.[42] Certainly the intended effect of gay rights legislation, according to advocates, was to lessen or eliminate discrimination, especially in public employment, the most commonly covered institution. Moreover, these indications that the human rights laws were successful in reducing antigay discrimination undercut the contention that the lack of large numbers of formal complaints from gays demonstrates that such legislation does not work well to protect this class of citizens. It seems that the laws or policies have a significant chilling effect on employers and others, thus serving to deter or prevent discrimination. According to a Michigan city official responding to our survey, "It [the legislation] put on notice members of our community who would be disposed to engage in discrimination that the city did have a means to combat this type of behavior." Another survey respondent from a suburban New York community put it more succinctly: "The law sends a message that no kind or type of harassment or hiring discrimination against gays will be tolerated."

The deterrent effect of nondiscrimination legislation is difficult to document, but our study offered other indications of this consequence. The first reported effect of the 1974 Minneapolis gay rights ordinance, for example, was to persuade Northwestern Bell Telephone to drop its no-gays-hired policy in the five midwestern states it served. The company changed its policy without first being asked to do so by city officials.[43] Because of its hiring policies, the Bell Telephone system was also an early priority for investigation by Detroit officials after adoption of gay rights provisions in that city.[44] Active and effective enforcement of the law has meant greater compliance. As a Philadelphia gay activist put it, "The law helps curb discrimination. Litigation and the assessment of damages makes it clear it is unacceptable. Some people who discriminate are more clever about it, but others have stopped doing it."

The recognition that discrimination based on sexual orientation is illegal and therefore impermissible aided the prophylactic function of the law. It suggests the widespread understanding that lesbians and gays are a "protected class," and that local government will take action against those who might refuse to employ or rent a home to persons because of their sexual orientation. It also indicates the respect and legitimacy afforded government law and policy. In the words of a Philadelphia city official, "Legislation makes discrimination a legal matter. You can be held accountable. It's no longer an acceptable community practice to discriminate against gays. . . . It's no longer a personal preference (whether one discriminates)."

Another important effect of the legislation and its ability to curb antigay discrimination has been that lesbians and gay men feel more comfortable, safe, secure, and generally more accepted in the community. As a result of this, gays were more likely to come out, or express their sexual identity. To a lesser extent, they also enjoyed greater opportunity to seek employment and housing, knowing that legislation provided an element of protection. These effects were mentioned by both interviewees and survey respondents (see Table 4-4). Responses to an additional, close-ended question asked of public officials in our survey further confirmed this finding about willingness to come out. Because government employment was covered in virtually all ordinances or policies, we asked, "Is there any evidence that since the enactment of the ordinance, lesbians and gay men who had already been employed in your city/county feel freer to be openly gay or lesbian?" We believed that the perceptions of public officials on this issue would be most accurate when the officials judged the impact on employees in their own domain. Forty percent of officials answered this question in the affirmative, indicating their belief that legislation had encouraged gays to come out. (Twenty-eight percent reported that they did not perceive such an effect, and the remaining 32 percent either did not respond to the question or said they did not know.)

It is most meaningful and interesting to listen to how lesbians and gay men themselves have reacted to living in a community with gay rights legislation. In Santa Cruz, a city employee and open lesbian praised the city for passing an antibias ordinance. "I feel absolutely safe at work. I don't have to hide it," she asserted, and she keeps a picture of her lover posted on her bulletin board in her office.[45] She also maintained that many high-profile women in the city have become increasingly open about their homosexuality. Similarly a gay man in Iowa City, in response to our question about the effects of the ordinance, declared, "I feel more comfortable in the workplace. I know there is some recourse if I were to be fired for my sexual orientation." He went on to say, "I'm accepted in my department and so is my partner. We even go to office parties together." And finally, a longtime gay activist in Philadelphia reported, "The ordinance shows gays they can be more open, and they are valued. They can also work more freely in the city. We don't have to worry about covering up so much and can just do our work." Clearly, civil rights laws and policies have afforded gays a level of comfort and protection, particularly in the workplace, that they had not experienced before.

Antidiscrimination legislation had other consequences for gays as well, although these effects were less commonly mentioned by survey respondents and interviewees. The political push to gain passage of such laws served to mobilize gays further in some communities. According to a lesbian activist in Santa Cruz, the adoption effort "got gays politically involved, some for the first time. . . . [I]t really helped to organize gays politically." It also galvanized other minorities such as women and African Americans as supporters of gay rights. The political mobilization for civil rights, moreover, indicated to some that gay activists were a political factor to be reckoned with. In the words of a survey respondent from a city in New York that had recently adopted protective legislation, "Politicians now saw the gay and lesbian community as an important political and social force."

The passage of gay rights legislation often opened the door to discussion of other policies affecting gays. In Philadelphia, for example, it made it easier to adopt a gay pride resolution subsequently, and in Iowa City it helped pave the way for serious consideration and ultimate passage of domestic partner insurance benefits for city employees. Evidence from our national survey of communities with gay antibias laws or policies confirmed this phenomenon. Almost half (48 percent) of these cities and counties had enacted or modified subsequent legislation relevant to lesbians and gays. The most common policies helpful to gays were those focusing on domestic partner benefits and AIDS programs and other health issues. Thus the adoption of a local ordinance seemed to "establish a climate that gays and lesbians are entitled to equal rights," as a Philadelphia official put it, and thereby facilitated the political acceptance of other policies and programs benefiting gays. Antidiscrimination legislation also established a legal basis for lesbians and gay men to seek access to other benefits, as administrative or court action has become a more common method of demanding employee privileges.[46]

Not all the effects of gay rights laws or policies, however, have been positive or beneficial to gays. In our nationwide survey we solicited views of the effects of legislation that would be interpreted as more negative for gays or for the community. We did so in the attempt to gain a more balanced perspective on the impact of this legislation. Responses are summarized in Table 4-5. As can be seen, a majority of respondents (51 percent) maintained that there had been no negative effects, and our case study interviews indicated a similar finding. Nevertheless, a modest number of surveyed public officials mentioned that the debate over and passage of legislation protecting gays resulted in divisions in the community, greater controversy or tension, or the increased mobilization of those opposed to gay rights. Clearly this issue has had a polarizing effect in some communities. In a large city in Florida, where gay rights generated intense conflict, our survey respondent contended, "It split this community apart at a time we could least afford it." In a similar fashion, a Pennsylvania city official asserted that the adoption of legislation "was a wedge driven into the community. . . . [I]t brought a lot of conflict and division." In Chapter 6 we further analyze the political opposition and conflict over this issue.

The Effects of Antidiscrimination Legislation on the Police

Many lesbians and gay men consider local police departments to be among the most antigay organizations in the country. This has been the case particularly since World War II, when homosexuals began to surface publicly and

TABLE 4-5   NEGATIVE EFFECTS OF LOCAL GAY RIGHTS
LEGISLATION (*N*=126)

Most important negative effects	Number of respondents	Percentage of respondents
None; no negative effects	64	51
Divided the community, created controversy or tension	13	10
Mobilized opposition to gay rights	12	10
Legislation is too limited in scope or jurisdiction, or inadequately enforced	9	7
Withdrawal of support for, or criticism of, local officials by conservative groups	6	5
Provides special rights not granted to others, or support for a different lifestyle	5	4

Source: Data are from authors' national survey.

Note: Question asked of survey respondents: "What do you think have been the two most important negative effects (if any) of the passage of this ordinance?" Effects mentioned by five or more respondents are listed.

the police responded by targeting them for harassment, arrest, and even violence. In many cities it was common for the police to carry out authorized (and unauthorized) raids on gay bars, bathhouses, and even social and political meetings. Although gay men were the focus of most of this police activity, lesbians were often included as well.[47] In John D'Emilio's words:

Throughout the 1950s gays suffered from unpredictable, brutal crackdowns. Men faced arrest primarily in bars and cruising areas such as parks, public restrooms, beaches, and transportation depots, while women generally encountered the police in and around lesbian bars. But even the homes of gay men and women lacked immunity from vice squads bent on increasing their arrest records.[48]

In states that maintained sodomy laws that declared sex between homosexuals as illegal, police harassment and violence were most frequent and virulent. Police officers almost everywhere, however, held an exaggerated hatred and intolerance of gays, whom they perceived to be "sexual deviants."[49] As a result, gays and lesbians feared the police intensely as perpetrators of violence and harassment. In addition, gay crime victims were reluctant to report such law-breaking because they felt the police would not take them seriously or might even abuse them. Many also feared that formally reporting a crime might lead to the public disclosure of their sexual orientation.[50]

Not surprisingly, post-Stonewall gay activists focused on municipal police as an institution most in need of reform.[51] They recognized that such change would not occur easily. Deemed potentially helpful, however, was the adoption of gay rights ordinances. Ideally, such laws would protect gays and lesbians in seeking employment in police departments, and thereby ultimately lead to internal changes in these departments. But more important, the inclusion of gays in civil rights codes would serve to lend greater legitimacy to this group and thereby provide notice that treating gays poorly was no longer acceptable. Given the history of police mistreatment of gays, and the general acceptance of this behavior, police reform was indeed a tall order for local legislation.

Many police departments were strongly opposed to gay rights laws for fear of having to hire lesbians and gay men as co-workers. In Portland, Oregon, for example, the president of the police association argued against applying such laws to the police because he thought it would lead to a decrease in public respect for police, a group he called a symbol of "legal and moral authority."[52] Even in gay-friendly San Francisco, the official publication of the police association stated in 1979 that "insisting on recruiting a certain percentage of homosexuals into the field of law enforcement is as reasonable as insisting on the same representation of diabetics, epileptics, child molesters, rapists."[53] In addition, the influential International Association of Chiefs of Police has long decried the hiring of gays in law enforcement, suggesting that gays are not stable, trustworthy, or morally principled. Voicing arguments similar to those opposed to gays in the military, many police contended that homosexuals were unreliable, that few officers would be willing to work with them, and their effect on morale would be disastrous.[54]

Despite this resistance from the police, gay activists staged protests, appealed directly to city officials, showed up at the ballot box, and sometimes took legal action to reduce discriminatory police actions and to open departments to lesbians and gay men. The adoption of gay rights legislation was often part of these political strategies. At the very least, legislation has made it less likely that gay cops are dismissed because of their sexual orientation. Nevertheless, few communities with legislation have policies that encourage the recruitment of gay police. Indeed, as of 1992, only an estimated ten police departments had made any direct attempts to hire gays.[55] Philadelphia's police force was one of these departments. In Philadelphia, however, it was almost a decade after the police commissioner ordered in 1980 the prohibition of discrimination within the department that the police actively began to recruit gay candidates. This response was due to pressure from lesbian and gay groups. Even then, active recruitment was limited to a relatively brief period of time and took place primarily near a gay bookstore.[56] According to city and police officials, as well as gay activists that we interviewed, the Philadelphia police force still has very few gay members, and none is known to be open about his or her sexual orientation. Despite having a mayor and police commissioner who are considered relatively tolerant, Philadelphia police are still viewed by many gays as being "generally homophobic and 'macho.'"

In addition to limited attempts to increase the number of gay police, the primary response of law enforcement agencies to gay political pressure was to introduce "sensitivity" programs in their departments. Interestingly, this response, along with recruitment, is reminiscent of the police reaction to increased racial conflicts and black political demands in the 1960s and 1970s.[57] Sensitivity programs that include sexual orientation are typically an extension of the cultural diversity or awareness programs that emphasized race and, to a lesser extent, ethnicity and gender. Sexual harassment is often included, but this does not always consider lesbian and gay harassment. Of the five communities we studied, all but Iowa City have cultural diversity programs that include sexual orientation for their police departments, although these programs have been in place for only a few years. The reason for the absence of such programs in Iowa City is that relations between gays and the police are generally quite good and city officials believe that the local police have more pressing educational needs.

Santa Cruz has the most comprehensive cultural diversity, or sensitivity, program for its police of any of our case study cities. Partly in response to a state mandate, the city carries out six days of diversity workshops annually with all police officers. Having been initiated in the early 1990s, before the city adopted its gay rights ordinance, the workshops focus on ethnicity and race (Latinos and African Americans), but a significant portion is devoted to sexual orientation as well. This training has typically included a discussion of gay and lesbian issues led by the city's gay former mayor. In addition, the police maintain a liaison with gay leaders and organizations, occasionally sending a representative to the Gay Community Center, a well-known gathering place, to listen to complaints. As a result, gay activists claim that the police have a good deal of credibility in their community and are generally sensitive to lesbian and gay concerns, especially those related to hate crimes.

Clearly, changes in relations between gay communities and the police have occurred in many cities in recent years. Reduced police abuse and harassment, increased implementation of cultural awareness programs, more police liaisons with the gay community, and more active recruitment of gay police are the most significant and apparent changes. These improvements have taken place primarily because of the increased political power of lesbians and gay men.[58] Gay rights laws and policies have played a contributing role, but their influence on these changes has been mostly indirect in nature.

Indications of progress in law enforcement, however, seem fragile and incomplete. Changes in police-gay relations have been generally modest and have taken place only within particular communities. Police raids on gay gatherings still occur, often with violence and abuse. In Cincinnati, for example, incidents of gays being treated poorly by police are not uncommon. According to one city official, "There's still real prejudice here against gays, and intolerance among police on the street. . . . Gay jokes are still common. The police don't treat gays well generally." Police officers themselves, moreover, admit that openly gay males would not be accepted on the force. Although the political mobilization of gays and the adoption of legal protections for gays may have improved police relations in Cincinnati, changes have been limited and much police animosity toward gays remains.

Even in Philadelphia, where a protective ordinance has been in place for more than a decade, and where police have made modest efforts at gay recruitment and instituted cultural diversity training, relations between the police and gays are still less than positive. A 1995–1996 survey of gay Philadelphians showed that 4 percent of lesbians and 7 percent of gay men reported abuse by the police within the previous year.[59] These figures were somewhat lower than those for 1991–1992 but higher than those for surrounding counties and for the rest of the state. The Lesbian and Gay Task Force, which carried out the survey, concluded that "our survey and other studies found many cases where law enforcement officers were unsympathetic to lesbian and gay victims."[60] Still in the minds of many Philadelphia gays and public officials was the police beating and mistreatment of gays who were peacefully demonstrating when President George Bush visited the city in 1991. A police advisory group investigating the incident reported that some officers called demonstrators "faggots," asked some of the people arrested if they had AIDS, used nightsticks on nonviolent ACT-UP protesters, and ignored pleas for medical assistance.[61] The advisory group concluded that the inappropriate behavior by police was primarily due to "AIDS-phobia, homophobia, and pressures associated with the presence of a high-ranking dignitary."[62]

The Impact of Gay Rights Legislation on Business

Many business owners and corporate leaders have adamantly opposed civil rights protection for gays and lesbians. From a business perspective, capitalist development is considered most successful when unencumbered by state regulations, civil rights, or unnecessary laws. As a longtime businessman in Cincinnati expressed it, "The gay rights ordinance raised concern about too much regulation and bureaucracy, and about business owners' rights being sacrificed, especially the right to hire or rent as they wished." Protective legislation also raised the fear of lawsuits that would be lodged against employers who fired or refused to hire homosexuals, regardless of the reasons for such decisions. According to business owners, the expense of litigating these suits would be unduly burdensome, particularly for small firms.[63]

Given the nature and significance of business opposition to gay rights, it is not surprising that a relatively small number of communities provide such legal protection. Moreover, as reported earlier, among those jurisdictions that do have antidiscrimination legislation that includes sexual orientation, only a little more than half (58 percent) of such ordinances or policies cover private employment, and only two-thirds (66 percent) provide protection in private rental housing. In contrast, more than 90 percent of gay rights laws cover public employment positions. As explained in Chapter 6, business leaders have been a force in limiting the scope of private sector protection for lesbians and gay men.

Among the most basic concerns of business owners is the fear that granting civil rights protections to homosexual workers would discourage the development of new businesses in the community and even drive out some established firms. The specter of increased government regulations, more employee lawsuits, and greater hassles over hiring and firing decisions has prompted some business leaders to predict dire economic consequences.[64] Public officials and others who view economic growth as essential to community prosperity and even fiscal survival consider new business development a key ingredient.

Despite these economic fears and concerns, our research indicates that gay rights legislation has had little or no effect on business growth and development. The most conclusive evidence comes from our survey of officials in communities with ordinances, where 86 percent indicated that the legislation had not discouraged new businesses from locating in the area (only one respondent perceived such a deterrent effect).[65] In contrast, when asked if such civil rights legislation had perhaps encouraged business development, only ten officials (8 percent) answered affirmatively and a majority of 60 percent indicated no such impact.[66] Our interviews tended to confirm these findings. Rather typical was the comment by a longtime official in Iowa City: "There's no evidence that the ordinance has hurt business or hiring in this city . . . nor housing either. There's been no effect, either negative or positive. In fact, I've never had any business person tell me it was any kind of problem to them."

Another belief of some businesspersons is that protective legislation for gays is unnecessary because there is so little clear-cut discrimination against homosexuals. Available evidence, however, indicates that such discrimination is not uncommon in the workplace. Results of surveys of homosexuals show that approximately one in three gays and lesbians has faced discrimination in employment.[67] Gays report having been fired when their sexual orientation became known, claim sexual and physical harassment, and report unfair practices such as the denial of promotion or pay raises.[68] Many gays and lesbians who have not directly experienced discrimination themselves can name friends or peers who have, or very much fear the possibility of discrimination against them at some time in the future.[69] Although some gays have taken action against their employers for alleged mistreatment, many others have not because they lacked legal recourse or because they feared further stigmatization if they revealed their sexual identity.

Etched in the memories of many gays is the well-publicized case of Cracker Barrel restaurants, a sizable business chain with nearly 14,000 employees in sixteen states. In 1991 the company summarily fired at least eleven gay and lesbian workers under a new corporate policy. In a public notice, Cracker Barrel stated that it would refuse employment to people "whose sexual preferences fail to demonstrate normal heterosexual values which have been the foundation of families in our society."[70] Despite national media attention and even some protests, the company remained relatively intractable and refused to rehire the dismissed employees, although it did formally rescind the policy. The gays and lesbians who were fired, moreover, had no legal recourse because they were not included under any local, state, or national civil rights law.[71]

Clearly, employment discrimination is a primary fear of gays. Yet mistreatment at work does more than influence the career plans of some lesbians and gay men. Many gays expend great amounts of time, money, and energy hiding their private lives and managing their sexual identity. This protective preoccupation at work has the effect of reducing productivity and hindering effective communication and good rapport with co-workers.[72] By the 1990s some employers had begun to understand these issues as serious problems affecting their firms.

The most important step toward reducing inequities in the workplace is a company policy that prohibits discrimination based on sexual orientation. Since most gays and lesbians are not protected by state or local laws, antidiscrimination policies at places of employment are vital for reducing job-related bias. By the early 1990s nondiscrimination policies had become standard in at least many of the high-technology industries that employed a sizable number of gays. A 1993 National Gay and Lesbian Task Force survey, for example, of Fortune 1000 companies (relatively large industrial and service firms) indicated that 72 percent had a nondiscrimination policy that included sexual orientation.[73] Trendsetters among these firms included Lotus, Digital, Microsoft, Apple Computer, Oracle, American Telephone and Telegraph

(AT&T), International Business Machines (IBM), Xerox, Kodak, and many smaller software companies. High-tech firms, as well as other large corporations like Walt Disney, Chase Manhattan Bank, and Procter and Gamble, became aware that many of their most talented employees might leave if they did not provide a more tolerant setting. There was also the recognition that such policies would help to make gay and lesbian workers more productive, as well as put companies in good standing with gay consumers, who were perceived to have above-average incomes and therefore considerable buying power.[74]

This shift in antidiscrimination policies in corporate America has no doubt been influenced by progress in the political arena. As we have seen, by the early 1990s more than one hundred local governments and seven states offered legislation protecting gays and lesbians in various institutions. More important, homosexuals were increasingly perceived as meriting minority status that placed them in the same category as African Americans, women, and other groups that were commonly granted civil rights protections through the law. Business leaders, too, began making this conceptual shift, which resulted in a new standard of treatment for lesbian and gay employees.[75]

Corporate policy has also been affected by lesbian and gay workers who have been mobilized through employee associations. In the mid-1980s gay employee groups first organized at Apple and Digital Equipment, and similar groups soon developed at several other major firms. Beginning in the 1990s, the National Gay and Lesbian Task Force focused attention on the workplace as a strategic site of gay rights organizing. By 1993 the task force survey of Fortune 1000 companies showed that 21 percent of the participating firms recognized gay and lesbian employee groups.[76] These organizations of gays have provided invaluable group support, networking, and socializing functions that help to counter the negative effects of discrimination and isolation on the job. In addition, gay and lesbian employee groups have served as advocates for issues of concern to their members. Of particular importance has been an emphasis on antidiscrimination policies in the workplace.[77] The Lambda Network at Eastman Kodak in Rochester, New York, is typical of such gay and lesbian grass-roots organizations. The Network operates with the full endorsement of Kodak and provides education, information, and support. The organization also hosts workshops and distributes information through electronic mail, an ideal technique because employees can remain invisible while accessing this material. In addition to making gay and lesbian employees feel more comfortable on the job, the Network has played a key role in educating Kodak workers and executives about the issues that gays face.[78]

Despite the pioneering efforts of high-tech industries and some larger corporations, most U.S. businesses still do not have written policies prohibiting discrimination against lesbians and gay men. This is especially the case for smaller firms, where, according to a Cincinnati public official, "discrimination against gays is rampant." A 1993 national survey of businesses, for example, reported that only 38 percent had such a protective policy in writing (another 25 percent claimed informal, unwritten policies).[79] Similarly, a 1993 random survey of twenty-eight relatively large private firms in the Raleigh metropolitan area showed that 46 percent had a stated nondiscrimination plan that included sexual orientation.[80] Some businesses that did not have written policies maintained that such statements were unnecessary because they did not discriminate against gays and lesbians, or because sexual orientation was already covered in state or local legislation. Many gay workers, however, believe that a written company policy is still essential in order to make the firm's intentions and norms clear to all employees as well as to prospective gay and lesbian workers.[81]

Although various forms of discrimination may be the foremost problem affecting gays in the workplace, another relatively recent and important equity issue involves domestic partner benefits. The partners of lesbian and gay employees normally do not receive the same medical, pension, and other benefits from the company that are provided to spouses of married workers. Because they cannot legally marry, this practice deprives many homosexuals of sometimes large economic dividends. The issue is also a matter of fairness and feeling valued. Many gays view the granting of company benefit packages to married, heterosexual employees only as a basic denial of "equal pay for equal work." Since the early 1990s lesbian and gay workers have increasingly clamored for such domestic partner benefits. In 1991 the progressive Lotus Development Corporation became the first major American firm to extend these benefits to gay employees. A year later Levi Strauss, which employed 23,000 workers, followed suit. In 1996 IBM became the nation's largest company (110,000 U.S. employees) to provide health benefits to partners of homosexual employees. By that year more than three hundred private firms had extended medical and often other benefits to gay and lesbian domestic partners.[82] Yet a deterrent to the provision of health benefits for same-sex partners is typically the anticipated expense, a concern that is exacerbated by fears of the possible cost of AIDS cases.[83]

Some companies have gone well beyond antidiscrimination policies and domestic partner benefits to respond to other needs of lesbian and gay workers. Many (58 percent of larger firms, according to the Fortune 1000 survey) have added sexual orientation issues to diversity training programs that already include race, gender, and ethnicity. A small but growing percentage of businesses offer AIDS education. A few firms have even declared a "lesbian and gay awareness week" or donated to charities that are connected with gays or AIDS. In other instances, companies have taken well-publicized political action in support of homosexuals. Levi Strauss, for example, withdrew its financial contribution to the Boy Scouts of America, publicly condemning that organization's policy of barring gay scouts.[84] Following voters' repeal of gay rights in Colorado in 1992, several companies joined a boycott of the state's convention and tourism industries that within two years cost the state an estimated $40 million in lost business.[85] While the boycott meant that some companies acted in a way that was economically harmful to other businesses, it was also an indication of the level of commitment of a portion of corporate America to the cause of lesbian and gay rights.

Despite progress on gay and lesbian employment issues, many businesses are still reluctant to confront problems associated with cultural diversity, especially those related to sexual identity. A large number of employers continue to insist that sexual orientation has nothing to do with work or job performance, despite mounting evidence to the contrary. Others express discomfort at the mere thought of gay workers with same-sex partners at company social events. More conservative business leaders believe that the gay and lesbian movement, along with recent antidiscrimination policies, may result in the overhiring of homosexuals and reverse discrimination against heterosexuals.

Clearly, "dismantling the corporate closet" will be no easy task. Nonetheless, the workplace has emerged as one of the frontiers of gay and lesbian activism in the 1990s.[86] Local politics, especially the battles over gay rights, have energized gays and helped to provide the experience, skills, and supportive milieu necessary to forge changes in the corporate world. The growth of grass-roots homosexual groups has spread to businesses, and these groups will continue to press for greater acceptance.

Educational, Legitimation, and Attitudinal Influences

Gay rights legislation has had a tangible effect on numerous lesbians and gay men, as well as on several institutions, including the police and businesses. Such legislation has also had less-clear-cut but nonetheless significant effects that go well beyond the protection of gays and institutions that provide services to these minorities. Indeed, proponents of law and social reform contend that a primary function of law is to educate, or perhaps reeducate, thereby altering behavior and, ultimately, attitudes. Implicit in this assumption is the idea that "law can educate men to new beliefs, that is, it can 'legislate morality.'"[87] Although basic beliefs or attitudes do not change easily or quickly, education may facilitate this process of change by encouraging a greater consciousness, and often skepticism. To the extent that law is a reflection of societal norms, new laws and even the process of forging innovative legislation create an educational and legitimation experience that is often transformative.

Early on it was apparent that the quest for civil rights legislation for gay and lesbian people was generating a public debate that was unusually informative. In 1975, and after only a dozen or so cities had even considered gay rights laws, Bruce Voeller of the National Gay Task Force (now known as the National Gay and Lesbian Task Force) commented, "Public discussion of equal employment opportunities for gays is almost as important in the long-run as the legislation itself. Without such public discussion, the legislators and the general population have no awareness of the gay lifestyle that must also be protected."[88] In public hearings and through the publicity surrounding the local struggles for legislation, gay and lesbian groups were able to describe various forms of discrimination by employers, landlords, the police, and others. With many Americans expressing ignorance and confusion about the degree to which gays are stigmatized and faced with discrimination, these public messages provided an invaluable means by which to educate the public.[89] In the words of a church leader in Raleigh, "Political discussions about legislation brought the gay issue into the open. . . . [M]ost people hadn't thought much about the need for protection for gays. It [the discussion] made them more aware of discrimination and persecution of gays."

The actual adoption of laws or policies protecting gay rights was important beyond its substantive effect on preventing discrimination. Civil rights legislation provided greater legitimacy for gays and lesbians. According to the legal historian Kimberle Williams Crenshaw, most people "act out their lives, mediate conflicts, and even perceive themselves with reference to the law."[90] In this sense, peoples' view of the world is shaped by law. Thus, giving legal force or status to gays has created a more positive image of that group in society. "It's a statement by government that these are valued relationships," stated a public official in Iowa City. This official went on to say that since the legislation was sanctioned by government, it extended to the entire community and had a moral authority that exceeded other pronouncements.

The passage of civil rights laws inclusive of sexual orientation has created a sense of legitimacy within the gay community as well. According to a gay leader in Cincinnati, self-hatred among homosexuals is great and "discrimination is looked on as a personalized failing," a form of "internalized homophobia." An ordinance focusing on societal discrimination and the illegality of antigay actions signals to gays that they are not paranoid and should not blame themselves. Gay rights laws have also provided a clear indication that homosexuality is a protected classification under civil rights legislation. This minority status, similar to that afforded blacks and women, is a political achievement with psychological significance in that it gives greater feelings of legitimacy and security to many lesbians and gay men.

Antidiscrimination legislation is also considered, in the words of a Santa Cruz city official, "a formal articulation of the community's standards . . . a statement of what the community will or will not tolerate." In this manner, protective legal codes reinforce more progressive values in many cities and counties. These progressive standards, moreover, often influence other communities. In Chapter 3 we discussed the diffusion-of-innovation process, whereby suburban and other outlying communities accepted new legislation from larger, more dominant cities. Major cities with diverse populations and sizable gay constituents were most likely to be the first communities to adopt gay rights legislation. In the 1980s and 1990s suburban cities and counties, following the pattern set by central cities, also moved to pass ordinances protecting sexual orientation. Once the new legislation gained a degree of approval and initial fears were alleviated, such laws were accepted more readily elsewhere. This "contagion effect" was very apparent by the 1990s. Our 1993 survey, for example, indicated that 65 percent of respondents in communities with gay rights laws or policies were aware of other nearby cities or counties with similar legislation. Moreover, many public officials in our case study cities stated that the most important source of information about policies protective of sexual orientation came from officials in adjacent or other jurisdictions with such laws. As a politically influential gay activist in Raleigh stated it, "The adoption of an ordinance here was an education for state legislators and showed other cities they can do it. It planted seeds of courage for others . . . and created a ripple effect."

Education and legitimation are more direct approaches by which civil rights laws influence beliefs. Attitudes, however, may be altered in more indirect ways as well. The primary focus here is on behavior and the theory that changes in behavior ultimately may produce changes in attitudes. Thus, to the degree that laws are enforced and able to regulate behavior, attitudes are adjusted to conform to new behavioral patterns. In this manner civil rights legislation that served to bring blacks and whites together in conditions of nondiscrimination and equality produced less prejudice.[91] Likewise, laws protective of gay and lesbian rights have also modified behavior in ways that have ultimately affected attitudes toward gays.

As noted earlier, a significant effect of gay rights legislation has been to reduce antigay discrimination in employment and other institutions. To the extent that such discrimination is curbed, gays and lesbians have felt more secure and safe in their jobs and elsewhere. As their comfort level has increased, gays have been more likely to express openly their sexual identity. Coming out of the closet, in turn, has meant that more straight Americans have come to know personally someone who is openly gay. Finally, evidence indicates that personal knowledge, at least among those who are relatively tolerant in general, has translated into greater acceptance of homosexuals.[92]

Thus the ability of civil rights laws to deter discrimination against gays has changed the behavior not only of those who discriminate, but of lesbians and gay men as well. Those who would discriminate against gays are forced to develop a more benevolent (or at least less malevolent) approach, and often, modified attitudes correspond to their changed behavior. The altered behavior of gays—coming out more completely—has also had the effect ultimately of influencing attitudes toward gays. Philadelphia exemplified this transformation in attitudes. As a high-level city official put it, "Mention 'gay' or 'lesbian' before the ordinance and it would close you out. But the last twelve years [since adoption of the law] have been an evolution for gays and lesbians in this city. It's no longer fashionable to be homophobic." In Cincinnati, even some antigay religious leaders expressed a similar appreciation of the influence of law on society. One religious leader stated, "Civil rights legislation began to change the attitudes of society. It legitimized the group that is seen as needing protection. . . . Attitudes are changing towards gays, they are more accepting."

Limitations of the Law

Although civil rights law inclusive of sexual orientation promotes social change in many ways, it also has its inherent constraints. Conventional wisdom and much experience suggest that one cannot "legislate morality," at least not very easily. The failure of Prohibition to limit the production and sale of alcoholic beverages is often cited as the best evidence for this claim. According to this view, law *reflects* dominant values, it does not create them, and therefore legislation cannot change the way people act or think. In this sense, "the state is a reflector, not a maker, of social change." [93]

Law is least effective when it runs contrary to peoples' beliefs and therefore lacks popular support. As we have mentioned, many Americans view homosexuality as a choice that is undesirable and thus oppose civil rights protections for gay men and lesbians. Under these circumstances, laws have limited usefulness. As a civil rights leader in Raleigh put it, "Many people still don't accept gays. They object to who they are and how they act. Law cannot change attitudes." A common contention is that attitudes must be altered first, before legislation is adopted or before it can be effectual. This is suggested by the words of a Philadelphia religious leader: "There is still some discrimination against gays . . . housing, for example. We need to attack the basic problem of discrimination through education, not through passing a law. Education about human dignity and respect for all."

Gay rights law has also been limited by its lack of enforcement and narrow scope. As we have seen, most communities put few resources, either in the form of money or staff, into the implementation of this legislation. This fact alone has discouraged the filing of formal complaints of discrimination by lesbians and gay men. Even when well enforced, however, legislation does not protect gays completely from acts of abuse and discrimination. Much of the private sector, including housing and employment, is often not included in gay rights measures. Statutes relating to family law, tax codes, pension provisions, and property rights always ignore gays and protect heterosexuals. These are the institutions that affect most citizens, including gays and lesbians, on a daily basis and are the arenas in which antigay actions are relatively common.

Even when lesbian and gay rights are enshrined in law, subtle and extralegal forms of discrimination persist. According to a gay businessman in Philadelphia, "The ordinance hasn't made much difference to the common gay on the street. He still can't be open . . . he may lose his job . . . and he is still called a 'faggot' and faces lots of hate crimes." Other lesbians and gays agreed. "There still is a bias here against gays," stated a lesbian leader in politically liberal Iowa City. "It's more subtle and insidious now. You won't be fired because you're gay, but your job evaluations will be poor or worsen, or you will hear gossip that you're not wanted. Most gays leave or are fired" for allegedly poor job performance. Moreover, she went on to say, even under these conditions most gays will not file a formal charge under the law. "People who file complaints are seen as 'troublemakers' and are labeled as 'gays' and won't be hired elsewhere."

In other places, antigay reaction to civil rights protections based on sexual orientation was more open and virulent. Several communities reported an increase in gay bashing and other hate crimes against homosexuals. This antigay backlash was most evident where the debate over gay rights generated intense political conflict. Violence sometimes occurred in communities where legislation was perceived as an act that encouraged the gay subculture, and in these settings some citizens contended that gays and lesbians needed to be "put back in their place."[94]

Ultimately, gay antidiscrimination law can provide more equal treatment, but it cannot go further to influence equality of outcome or results.[95] Thus, gay rights legislation serves to prevent certain discriminatory actions against individuals rather than redress directly more basic societal or institutional policies that oppress an entire group. Moreover, when injustices against individual gays are found, efforts to compensate these victims are limited by the competing interests of heterosexuals. In this sense, antidiscrimination law "seeks to proscribe only certain kinds of subordinating acts, and then only when other interests are not overly burdened."[96]

Conclusion

A great deal of heated debate has taken place about the effects of gay rights measures. Opponents have argued that such legislation is unnecessary because most gays remain closeted and therefore do not confront discrimination. An indicator of this, they contend, is the fact that homosexuals file few formal complaints of discrimination. Thus, not only are the laws superfluous but they tend to regulate and burden businesses, governments, and other institutions unduly. Opponents' gravest fear, however, is that legal protection will serve to legitimize and win greater popular acceptance for a "lifestyle" considered immoral and deviant. Lesbians, gay men, and their supporters counter these claims by asserting that well-enforced protective legislation is necessary and appropriate state action to prevent unjustified discrimination against homosexuals. Such government measures, moreover, are seen as an essential step toward changing general behavior and, ultimately, attitudes toward gays in the larger process of cultural transformation.

In regard to formal legal protection, our findings show that most gay rights laws or policies cover the public sector much more completely than the nongovernmental private sector. Private employment and most housing, for example, are protected in just half or less of all communities with ordinances. Extending civil rights codes to the private sector has always been more strongly resisted politically.

We also found that enforcement of gay antidiscrimination measures varied a great deal from one community to another. Larger cities and counties, like Philadelphia, tended to have independent, well-funded, and specialized administrative agencies. Human relations or human rights agencies proved to be particularly effective enforcement bodies. Such mechanisms served to encourage formal complaints of discrimination as well as the investigation and resolution of charges. Medium-sized and certainly most smaller communities were much less likely to have formalized routines, specialized bureaucracies, or lawyers skilled in litigating discrimination cases. Lack of proper enforcement in these communities discouraged formal complaints of discrimination and reduced the effectiveness of legislation. Thus the urbanism/social diversity theory is helpful in explaining the nature and degree of enforcement.

Although measuring the effects of civil rights legislation is no easy task, several indicators clearly demonstrate that such laws have reduced discrimination against lesbians and gay men. This is especially the case for those institutions, like public employment, that are most likely to be included in legislation. There is also substantial evidence that gays feel more safe and secure, particularly in the workplace, because of these measures. As a result, they are more likely to disclose their sexual orientation. For the gay proponents of legislation, protection from antigay discrimination and the creation of an atmosphere more conducive to proclaiming their sexual identity freely have been primary objectives.

Legislation has also benefited lesbians and gay men in other ways. The political push for local civil rights ordinances proved to be an effective mobilizing strategy for both gays and their allies. Furthermore, it often paved the way politically for consideration and sometimes adoption of other gay-supportive policies, such as domestic partner benefits. Although local police traditionally have been abusive of homosexuals, gay rights laws and significant political action by gays have helped to ameliorate such animosities. In many communities the introduction of cultural awareness programs, increased police liaisons with the gay community, and limited recruitment of lesbian and gay police have improved relations between homosexuals and law enforcement officials. Additionally, the adoption of antidiscrimination legislation has not proved harmful to business development, as some employers had feared. In fact, gay-friendly policies in the corporate and business community have been encouraged by the forging of gay civil rights in the public sector. By the mid-1990s, the business world has become the focal point of much gay political activity.

Finally, laws protecting gays and lesbians have influenced a social transformation that moves beyond these institutions and even gays themselves. Legislation often has provided educational and legitimation functions that have ultimately resulted in some modification of public attitudes toward gays. Furthermore, by reducing antigay discrimination, legal measures have encouraged homosexuals to become more open about their sexual identity.[97] As a result, more Americans have come to know and accept them. Although gay rights laws have inherent limitations and certainly have not totally eliminated homophobic attitudes and actions, they have significantly promoted an increased understanding of and tolerance for lesbians and gay men.

NOTES

Because of the controversial nature of this study, we promised the persons we interviewed that they would not be identified by name. Unless otherwise noted, all interviews pertaining to Iowa City took place in Iowa City in June 1994; all those pertaining to Philadelphia took place in Philadelphia in July 1994; all those pertaining to Raleigh took place either in Raleigh or Chapel Hill, N.C., in May 1994; all those pertaining to Santa Cruz took place in Santa Cruz in June 1994, and all those pertaining to Cincinnati took place in Cincinnati in November 1994. All quotations and information not otherwise documented are from these interviews.

1. Frederick M. Wirt, *Politics of Southern Equality: Law and Social Change in a Mississippi County* (Chicago: Aldine, 1970), 5–8.
2. Harrell R. Rodgers Jr. and Charles S. Bullock III, *Law and Social Change: Civil Rights Laws and Their Consequences* (New York: McGraw-Hill, 1972), 204.
3. Ibid., 1–4. See also Duane Lockard, *Toward Equal Opportunity: A Study of State and Local Antidiscrimination Laws* (New York: Macmillan, 1968), 141–143.
4. "Detroit Is No. 1 on Gay Rights," *Advocate*, July 17, 1974, 15.
5. William R. Keech, *The Impact of Negro Voting: The Role of the Vote in the Quest for Equality* (Chicago: Rand McNally, 1968), 96; Rodgers and Bullock, *Law and Social Change*, 150–151.

6. Jane Stancill, "Gay Rights Proposal Sparks Hot Debate," *Raleigh News and Observer,* January 27, 1993.
7. Mark F. Rohner, "Protection for Homosexuals Changed," *Iowa City Press-Citizen,* March 22, 1977.
8. Mark F. Rohner, "City Rights Ordinance Discussed," *Iowa City Press-Citizen,* February 15, 1977.
9. John Campbell, "Council Clears Rights Compromise," *Iowa City Press-Citizen,* April 24, 1984; John Campbell, "Apartment Owners Question Need for More Rules on Discrimination," *Iowa City Press-Citizen,* March 1, 1984.
10. Jack Greenberg, *Race Relations and American Law* (New York: Columbia University Press, 1959), 194–195; Lockard, *Toward Equal Opportunity,* 82.
11. Eighteen communities (14 percent) also specifically exempted certain geographical jurisdictions, typically cities, counties, or universities, that wanted to opt out or were outside the boundaries of local coverage.
12. Daniel A. Mazmanian and Paul A. Sabatier, eds., *Effective Policy Implementation* (Lexington, Mass.: Lexington Books, 1981), 3.
13. Charles S. Bullock III and Charles M. Lamb, eds., *Implementation of Civil Rights Policy* (Monterey, Calif.: Brooks/Cole, 1984), 2–16.
14. Lockard, *Toward Equal Opportunity,* 144–145.
15. City of Philadelphia, Commission on Human Relations/Fair Housing Commission, *Annual Report, 1993–1994* (Philadelphia: Commission on Human Relations/Fair Housing Commission, 1994), 4–10.
16. Greenberg, *Race Relations and American Law,* 201–202; Lockard, *Toward Equal Opportunity,* 126, 147–148.
17. Greenberg, *Race Relations and American Law,* 15–17.
18. Our appreciation to Kenneth Sherrill for the useful insights discussed within these two paragraphs.
19. "Employment Rights Roundup—Where We Are, Where We're Going," *Advocate,* January 29, 1975, 8.
20. As quoted in ibid., 8.
21. Philadelphia Commission on Human Relations, *1991 State of Intergroup Harmony, "Bridging the Old . . . with the New"* (Philadelphia: Philadelphia Commission on Human Relations, 1991), 28; City of Philadelphia, *Annual Report, 1993–1994,* 43.
22. City of Philadelphia, *Annual Report, 1993–1994,* 50.
23. Lockard, *Toward Equal Opportunity,* 83.
24. Ibid., 84.
25. "No on Cincinnati Issue 3," *Cincinnati Post,* October 27, 1993.
26. Our survey results indicated that the most common types of formal complaints based on sexual orientation were, in order of frequency, employment, housing, and public accommodations. These results were as expected, since these are the most common institutions covered by the ordinances. The small number of formal complaints filed by gays conforms to the results of another recent study of the enforcement of gay rights legislation at the state and local level. See Norma M. Riccucci and Charles W. Gossett, "Employment Discrimination in State and Local Government: The Lesbian and Gay Male Experience," *American Review of Public Administration* 26 (June 1996): 182–185.
27. Iowa City Human Rights Commission, *Annual Report, 1988–1992* (Iowa City: Human Rights Commission, 1989–1993).
28. City of Philadelphia, Commission on Human Relations/Fair Housing Commission, *Annual Report, 1992* (Philadelphia: Commission on Human Relations/Fair Housing Commission, 1992), 5; City of Philadelphia, *Annual Report, 1993–1994,* 43–47.
29. Kevin Sack, "Gay Rights Hurt by Lack of Uniform Protections," *New York Times,* March 28, 1993.
30. "City Revises Rights Ordinance," *Iowa City Press-Citizen,* April 11, 1979.
31. Marge Gasnick, "Fired Man Blames Gay Slurs," *Iowa City Press-Citizen,* August 16, 1990; Mindy Mozer, "Panel Rules Holiday Inn Worker Was Harassed," *Iowa City Press-Citizen,* March 12, 1991.
32. Martha Mendoza, "'Low-Key' Beginning for City's Bias Law," *Santa Cruz Sentinel,* December 13, 1992.
33. Ibid.

34. City of Philadelphia, *Annual Report, 1993–1994*, 47–48.
35. Iowa City Human Rights Commission, *Annual Report*, 1988–1992. See also Riccucci and Gossett, "Employment Discrimination," 183–186, a study of gay and lesbian employment discrimination complaints at the city and county level that found few successful claims.
36. Shawn Hubbell, "Some Shut Out of Housing," *Iowa City Press-Citizen*, July 17, 1989.
37. Sack, "Gay Rights Hurt."
38. Ibid.
39. People for the American Way, "Hostile Climate: A State-by-State Report on Anti-Gay Activity," Washington, D.C., 1993, 29–30.
40. Wirt, *Politics of Southern Equality*, 10–11.
41. The question, asked of each interviewee, was as follows: "What do you think have been the most important effects of this ordinance?"
42. The fact that open-ended questions do not suggest responses, and are more likely to be left unanswered in written surveys, lends additional credence to these responses. In addition, according to written comments and telephone interviews, survey respondents in general were supportive of human rights but were not necessarily advocates for gay rights.
43. "Unusual Support for a Rights Bill in St. Paul," *Advocate*, July 31, 1974, 12.
44. "Detroit is No. 1 on Gay Rights," *Advocate*, July 17, 1974, 15.
45. Tracie White, "Lesbian Community Has Become an Established Part of Santa Cruz," *Santa Cruz Sentinel*, September 12, 1993.
46. Riccucci and Gossett, "Employment Discrimination," 186–195.
47. Gary David Comstock, *Violence against Lesbians and Gay Men* (New York: Columbia University Press, 1991), 152–158; Lillian Faderman, *Odd Girls and Twilight Lovers: A History of Lesbian Life in Twentieth Century America* (New York: Columbia University Press, 1991), 164–165, 191.
48. John D'Emilio, *Sexual Politics, Sexual Communities: The Making of a Homosexual Minority in the United States, 1940–1970* (Chicago: University of Chicago Press, 1983), 49.
49. Comstock, *Violence against Lesbians and Gay Men*, 154.
50. Gregory M. Herek and Kevin T. Berrill, eds., *Hate Crimes: Confronting Violence against Lesbians and Gay Men*, (Newbury Park, Calif.: Sage, 1992), 235, 294.
51. As an example, see the case of Atlanta in "Necks Out for Gay Rights Support," *Advocate*, May 22, 1974, 2. See also Comstock, *Violence against Lesbians and Gay Men*, 160–161.
52. "Victory in Portland," *Advocate*, January 15, 1975, 1.
53. As quoted in Comstock, *Violence against Lesbians and Gay Men*, 157.
54. Stephen Leinen, *Gay Cops* (New Brunswick, N.J.: Rutgers University Press, 1993), 8–10.
55. Ibid., 11.
56. Ibid., 12.
57. Ibid., 7–8.
58. Comstock, *Violence against Lesbians and Gay Men*, 160–161; Leinen, *Gay Cops*, 7–8.
59. Larry Gross and Steven K. Aurand, *Discrimination and Violence against Lesbian Women and Gay Men in Philadelphia and the Commonwealth of Pennsylvania: A Study by the Philadelphia Lesbian and Gay Task Force* (Philadelphia: Philadelphia Lesbian and Gay Task Force, 1996), Table 8-B.1.
60. Ibid., 23.
61. Joseph A. Slobodzian and Fredrick N. Tulsky, "AIDS Fears and Homophobia Led City Police to Abuse Protesters," *Philadelphia Inquirer*, March 19, 1992. See also "Philadelphia Police Attack," *New York Times*, March 20, 1992.
62. Slobodzian and Tulsky, "AIDS Fears and Homophobia."
63. Mary Shedden, "Businesses Criticize Anti-Gay Effort," *Gainesville Sun*, October 20, 1994.
64. Ibid.
65. The question posed in the national survey was, "Is there any evidence that the enactment of the ordinance has *discouraged* new businesses from locating in your city/county?" Sixteen respondents indicated "Don't Know," and one did not answer.
66. The survey question asked was, "Is there any evidence that the enactment of the ordinance has *encouraged* new businesses to locate in your city/county?" Thirty-nine respondents indicated "Don't Know," and one did not answer.
67. James D. Woods, *The Corporate Closet: The Professional Lives of Gay Men in America* (New York: Free Press, 1993), 200, 271.
68. Urvashi Vaid, *Virtual Equality: The Mainstreaming of Gay and Lesbian Liberation* (New York: Doubleday, Anchor, 1995), 10.

69. Woods, *Corporate Closet*, 200–201.

70. Brian McNaught, *Gay Issues in the Workplace* (New York: St. Martin's Press, 1993), 85n.; Peter T. Kilborn, "Gay Rights Groups Take Aim at Restaurant Chain That's Hot on Wall Street," *New York Times*, April 9, 1992.

71. Vaid, *Virtual Equality*, 10.

72. Woods, *Corporate Closet*, 234–236.

73. National Gay and Lesbian Task Force, "Fortune 1000 Survey," preliminary results, National Gay and Lesbian Task Force, Washington, D.C., October 15, 1993.

74. McNaught, *Gay Issues*, 66–67; Thomas A. Stewart, "Gay in Corporate America," *Fortune*, December 16, 1991, 54, 56; Woods, *Corporate Closet*, 237–241. The alleged wealth of the gay community is contradicted by several recent surveys. See Kenneth Sherrill, "The Political Power of Lesbians, Gays, and Bisexuals," *PS: Political Science and Politics* 29 (September 1996): 471–472.

75. Sack, "Gay Rights Hurt"; Woods, *Corporate Closet*, 238–240.

76. National Gay and Lesbian Task Force, "Fortune 1000 Survey."

77. McNaught, *Gay Issues*, 82–84; Vaid, *Virtual Equality*, 10.

78. Kathleen Driscoll, "Gays Opening the Door," *Rochester Democrat and Chronicle*, October 23, 1994.

79. This survey was carried out by the Society for Human Resource Management and reported in McNaught, *Gay Issues*, 68.

80. Willie D. Pilkington, "Equal Employment Opportunity Policy Survey, Raleigh Metropolitan Area Employers," report presented to the Raleigh City Council's Law and Finance Committee, February 23, 1993.

81. McNaught, *Gay Issues*, 68–69.

82. Ibid.; "Benefits for Gays," *Gainesville Sun*, August 21, 1995 (Worklife Supplement); David W. Dunlap, "Gay Partners of I.B.M. Workers to Get Benefits," *New York Times*, September 20, 1996.

83. "Benefits for Gays," 13. This article notes that the average cost of treating an AIDS case is less than the cost of treating a premature infant.

84. Woods, *Corporate Closet*, 237–238.

85. Ibid.; Dirk Johnson, "Colorado Court Nullifies a Ban on Gay Rights," *New York Times*, October 12, 1994.

86. Woods, *Corporate Closet*, 241–246.

87. Wirt, *Politics of Southern Equality*, 8.

88. "Employment Rights Roundup," *Advocate*, January 29, 1975, 14.

89. Vaid, *Virtual Equality*, 21.

90. Kimberle Williams Crenshaw, "Race, Reform, and Retrenchment: Transformation and Legitimation in Antidiscrimination Law," *Harvard Law Review*, 101 (May 1988): 1352.

91. Wirt, *Politics of Southern Equality*, 8–10.

92. Shapiro, "Straight Talk about Gays," 46.

93. Wirt, *Politics of Southern Equality*, 4.

94. This trend was apparent in the written responses to an item in our national survey in which we asked, "What do you think have been the two *most important negative effects* (if any) of the passage of this ordinance?"

95. Crenshaw, "Race, Reform, and Retrenchment," 1331–1387.

96. Ibid., 1342.

97. Other laws, policies, and court decisions, in addition to antidiscrimination legislation, have also been protective and supportive of lesbians and gays. These laws include recent federal and state hate crimes legislation inclusive of sexual orientation and domestic partner legislation. Furthermore, the repeal of state antisodomy laws decriminalizes homosexual conduct and therefore provides greater legitimacy to gays. Most of these laws are not local in origin, but their effect is noticeable at the city and county level and is therefore sometimes difficult to disentangle from that of local gay rights laws.

CHAPTER 5

The Schools and Gay and Lesbian Youth

High schools may be the most homophobic institutions in American society, and woe be to anyone who would challenge the heterosexist premises on which they operate.
—Gerald Unks, "Thinking about the Homosexual Adolescent," *The High School Journal*, in its first volume devoted to gay and lesbian youth issues (1994)

We don't have any gay or lesbian students.
—Statement made to teachers by Cincinnati school counselors

T raditionally, schools have been entrusted with the responsibility for the moral development of youth. The primary mission of schools involves inculcating students with the norms and duties of society, another way of saying that schools impart the values of the dominant social identity.[1] Thus, it is not surprising that schools tend to deny the existence of homosexuality and reinforce society's heterosexism and antihomosexual bias. Such bias emerges in numerous ways, such as the omission of homosexuality in formal curricula, tolerance of antigay jokes and harassment, social events that affirm only heterosexual couples, and strong negative reinforcement of behavior or attitudes outside traditional gender roles.[2]

Most city or county gay rights ordinances and policies typically do not cover educational institutions because school districts are almost always run as separate entities from other local governments. Nonetheless, it was inevitable that schools would become an arena for the politics of gay rights. Schools typically represent the largest and most important institutions of local government. It seemed likely, therefore, that the same forces that encouraged local government sensitivity to gays and lesbians would be manifest in school policy and programs. Thus, we compared programs related to sexual orientation in school districts located in jurisdictions that had local antidiscrimination legislation with a control group of districts that did not. We also looked intensively at school efforts in our five case study communities. In this chapter we examine the basis for attempts to develop school programs that address gay and lesbian concerns, discuss the components of such programs, and identify barriers to program development. In addition, we determine what factors support school-based policies and programs that include sexual orientation issues.

Why Address Sexual Orientation Issues in School?

Health and education professionals concur that schools represent appropriate sites for programs dealing with sexual orientation. Schools offer access to the majority of youth, and many problems for gay and lesbian youth occur unmitigated in the school setting.[3] Institutionalized bias against homosexuality occurs in numerous ways in schools, and representatives from the school districts we studied provided explicit illustrations of it. Moreover, by not contributing to a complete understanding of human sexuality and by reinforcing traditional sex roles, schools are considered antithetical not only to the healthy development of gay and lesbian youth but to the optimal well-being of all youth.[4]

Students tend to share the antihomosexual bias of adults. Nine in ten (89 percent) heterosexual adolescent males in a recent national study considered sexual behavior between two men "disgusting," and 59 percent reported they could not be friends with a gay person.[5] Youth who are known or perceived as homosexual often experience serious verbal and physical abuse at schools.[6] A survey of high school students conducted by the Massachusetts Governor's Commission on Gay and Lesbian Youth in 1993 found that 97.5 percent of respondents had heard homophobic remarks made at their school, and 49 percent said these comments occurred "very often."[7] A recent national study of sexual harassment found that over 85 percent of both males and females considered "being called gay or lesbian" the most distressing type of harassment.[8] Testimony given by gay youth before the Philadelphia Board of Education on April 25–26, 1994, documented their experiences with such harassment:

In my current school, many assume that I am gay. Some of them humiliate me daily. In my language class two students call me "faggot" or act "gay" with me. [Male, 16 years old]

In my case, I was repeatedly tripped—everyday—in my classrooms. When students tripped me, they would call me "faggot," "pussy," etc. Nearly every day, someone would push up against me. Out of 8 teachers, I had only one teacher who would intervene in these anti-gay incidents. [Male, 16 years old]

As this statement indicates, teachers often ignore such abusive behavior. School teachers and counselors are typically ignorant about and biased against homosexuality.[9] Some even participate in the harassment. Philadelphia's gay youth provided poignant testimony about this situation:

I had a history teacher tell me that I couldn't come to class because I was gay. . . . She wanted me out of there. Teachers would often gossip and make anti-gay hand motions. . . . I expected teachers to help me and to protect me—not to be the main ones to ridicule me. [Male, 17 years old]

One health teacher tells her students that homosexuality is wrong and evil. The other health teachers avoid the subject when teaching sex education. Almost all of my teachers have at one point in the year made some kind of joke about homosexuals or have made a derogatory comment. Some do it on a regular basis. [Female high school student]

Students' perceptions are substantiated by gay and lesbian teachers. Because of fear of discrimination and retribution by their administrators and colleagues, most gay and lesbian educators are often unwilling to be open about their sexual identity.[10]

A recent study revealed that inadequate knowledge about homosexuality and bisexuality was a common characteristic among education professionals and was a source of significant discomfort in teaching.[11] Research also documents that instruction about homosexuality is inadequate—the topic of sexual orientation and identification is either omitted or only briefly addressed in the classroom and remains controversial.[12] Students report that the instruction they receive about homosexuality tends to be negative in tone.[13] Teachers may avoid discussing AIDS because they do not wish to discuss attitudes and beliefs about homosexuality.[14]

School experiences leave most gay youth unsupported, without healthy role models and confidants. Gay and lesbian students "hide their true self [and] constantly monitor their behaviors."[15] Again, the 1994 testimony of Philadelphia youth offers vivid accounts of these effects:

In my school, out of 2000 students, I only knew five other gay students. I felt very isolated, very alone, and I had no one I could turn to for support. [Female, 18 years old]

I felt like I didn't belong anymore. I felt like I was a small child in a sea of hate and that people didn't know me; they only knew of my sexual preference for women. [Female, 18 years old]

Parents typically are unprepared to cope with a son or daughter who is homosexual. As the Massachusetts' Governor's Commission documented, parents' angry reactions can lead to adolescents being "thrown out of their homes or driven to run away."[16] Because support is also missing from within their families and their larger communities, gay and lesbian youth typically feel isolated, alienated, and inferior.[17] Some youth resort to potentially high-risk and exploitative situations (such as bars) to seek social support.[18] Consequently, gay and lesbian youth are more vulnerable to such health-threatening problems as substance abuse, sexually transmitted diseases and HIV/AIDS, truancy, dropping out of school, homelessness, and suicide.[19] These problems, as the American Academy of Pediatrics and others are careful to note, are attributable to internalization of the antigay bias and prejudice surrounding them.

Recommendations for School-Based Intervention

Professionals and gay advocates propose several school programs and policies that could ameliorate the difficulties faced by youth. School-based programs are justified by two core convictions: students' right to an education that will enable them to achieve their potential, and students' right to a safe school environment.[20] Furthermore, proponents contend that addressing these issues will benefit all students by increasing tolerance for differences and enabling them more fully to understand human sexuality.[21] The sociologist William Marsiglio emphasizes that this approach will especially assist males whose "ability to develop male friendships characterized by emotional intimacy and physical affection is often hindered as a result of their disdain for homosexuals."[22]

Establishing and enforcing a policy that thwarts antihomosexual behavior is considered critical and is probably the least controversial action schools can take. Justification for such policies is based on protecting the safety of youths, whether self-identified or perceived as homosexual or both. The most prominent example of this intervention is the Massachusetts state legislation, passed in 1994, that prohibits discrimination against gay and lesbian students in public schools. This law permits students who have suffered harassment and violence (and who were not protected by the administration) to bring lawsuits against their schools.[23]

Developing a support group for gay, lesbian, bisexual, and questioning youth is also considered worthwhile. As the Minnesota Department of Education explains,

A support group shows that the school climate is one where diversity is respected and protected [and] says to all students and staff that gay, lesbian, and bisexual students and staff are present and valued by [the] school system. It increases the awareness and visibility of gay, lesbian, and bisexual individuals and assures that their issues will be addressed.[24]

These groups optimally should have male and female co-leaders, one of whom is officially connected to the school and would serve as a crucial catalyst for resolving problems within the system.[25] Groups can assist students through increasing their self-esteem, overcoming their sense of isolation, developing their social skills in a nonsexual setting, identifying their needs for information and resources, and providing a resource for their parents. These groups may decrease mental health problems, health-compromising behaviors, and the need for individual mental health services.[26] If instituting school-based groups is inhibited, referral to community support groups should be offered.[27]

In addition, many experts recommend that schools hire school counselors trained and willing to work with these youth. Support services include edu-

EXAMPLES OF DEVELOPMENTALLY APPROPRIATE
SUBCONCEPTS RELATED TO SEXUAL IDENTITY AND
ORIENTATION ACCORDING TO THE NATIONAL
GUIDELINES TASK FORCE

Early elementary:	Some men and women are homosexual, which means they will be attracted to and fall in love with someone of the same gender.
Later elementary:	Homosexual and bisexual people are often mistreated, called hurtful names, or denied their rights because of their sexual orientation.
Middle/junior high:	Theories about what determines sexual orientation include physical factors such as genetics and prenatal influences, sociocultural influence, psychosocial factors, and a combination of all these factors.
High school:	One's understanding and identification of one's sexual orientation may change during life.

cating colleagues, parents, and students, as well as helping students contend with the societal presumption of heterosexuality. This assumption or expectation that all relationships are heterosexual is one of the first issues gay and lesbian youth need assistance in challenging.[28] Counselors should also attempt to dispel myths about homosexuality and help youth, parents, and others identify community resources.[29] School counseling services should be confidential to ensure the psychological safety that youth need in order to use the services. Likewise, the youth should decide when and with whom they will disclose their sexual identity.[30]

Providing in-service education for teachers and other staff is also crucial. Training should include examining the effects of antihomosexual and heterosexual bias and the relation of these attitudes to other forms of discrimination. In-service and preservice training should help school personnel develop strategies to produce a more inclusive environment and to incorporate these issues into the curriculum, not only through health education but also through other subjects, such as English literature and social studies.[31] Instruction should include developmentally appropriate content from elementary school through grade twelve. The National Guidelines Task Force of the Sex Information and Education Council of the U.S. identified concepts appropriate for education about sexual identity and orientation (see box).[32]

The employment of openly gay and lesbian teachers and counselors in schools is recommended because they can provide students with important, positive role models. Gary Remafedi, a medical scholar who has studied gay and lesbian youth extensively, contends that two factors help youth develop self-acceptance as gay or lesbian: first, meeting other young lesbians and gay men, and second, beginning to recognize that they are part of a larger gay and lesbian community.[33] Role models also enable students to observe successful adults leading productive and ethical lives, resolving problems of identity disclosure, obtaining support, managing a career, and building relationships.[34] Gay and lesbian students claim they are more likely to confide in and receive assistance from teachers and counselors they know share their orientation.[35] The provision of openly gay and lesbian role models, however, tends to be a controversial suggestion because of the fear that such adults will "recruit" youth into homosexuality.[36] This concern, however, was rejected in a legal case that thoroughly explored the influence of various adults on the development of homosexual orientation. It concluded that "the danger was minimal in terms of school-related influences" and asserted that "young children who are gay, lesbian, or bisexual would probably benefit from access to information and role models in order to facilitate their optimal development."[37]

Finally, it is recommended that schools enact changes to become more inclusive and sensitive to gay and lesbian youth, such as modifying social functions (proms and dances) and athletic programs. Such extracurricular offerings often do not attempt to recognize or include homosexual individuals or couples, and tend to have leaders who contribute to the abuse of homosexuals through their verbal and nonverbal behavior.[38] The goals of such strategies are to ensure that school-sponsored events are open to all students and that leaders are enabled to recognize and eliminate antihomosexual language and behavior. The Massachusetts antidiscrimination law was designed to address this concern as well, as reflected in the legislature's stated intention: "to affirm the rights of openly gay students to many rituals of adolescence: to form alliances and clubs, to take a date to the prom, to participate freely in sports."[39]

Three prominent school-based programs have been instituted to meet the needs of gay and lesbian youth: the Harvey Milk School in New York City, Project 10 in Los Angeles, and the San Francisco Unified School District's Support Services for Gay and Lesbian Youth. The Harvey Milk School was named after San Francisco's first openly gay supervisor. The school was approved as an alternative high school by the New York City Board of Education in 1985 so as not to "abandon" homosexual students who "would never have been allowed to remain in a high school setting previously" because of the severe harassment they faced.[40] Housed in a church, the school served approximately twenty students that year and consisted of one teacher, supervisory personnel, and curriculum material. It provided additional services such as counseling, special reading material, and transportation, designed to prevent students from dropping out or developing other problems.

By 1991, still headquartered in the same Greenwich Village facility, the Harvey Milk school had grown to two teachers and was featured in a *New York Times Magazine* story that described the school as a "safe haven" from the problems experienced by gay and lesbian youth in mainstream high schools. Although disagreement persists about the need for segregating these students, one gay youth expressed the dilemma faced by his (and other) marginalized groups: "Although having this school is fabulous, I hope there will be a day when there is no gay school. Because you know . . . there shouldn't have to be one."[41] The Eagles School in West Hollywood, California, was also designed as a separate school. It and the Harvey Milk School are probably the only such separate public schools in the United States.[42]

During the same time period of the mid-1980s, Virginia Uribe, an educator at Fairfax High School in Los Angeles, addressed similar problems in the school setting. Project 10, pilot tested in 1985–1986, was the first official school-based response to the physical and verbal abuse of an openly gay student by his teachers and peers. Uribe, with the support of some faculty, was appointed by her principal to create a program to provide emotional support, information, and referrals for self-identified gay, lesbian, and bisexual students. Beginning with informal, unstructured group sessions in which gay students disclosed problems they faced, the program expanded to include training for teachers, counselors, and administrators; counseling and educational services for students; incorporation of materials about sexual orientation in the school library; a hotline; and awards and scholarships. The distribution of brochures and newspaper coverage also increased the community's awareness and sensitivity to these students and their issues. By 1987–1988, Project 10 was expanded to include all junior and senior high schools in the Los Angeles Unified School District.[43] School systems in Cambridge, Massachusetts, and Santa Rosa, California, have emulated this model.[44]

In a similar vein, the San Francisco Unified School District hired its first coordinator for gay and lesbian youth support services in 1990. An openly gay psychologist provides counseling and referral services directly to students and parents, in-service workshops for staff, and curricular assistance for grades 6–12 during his twenty-hour work week for the district. Other accomplishments of the district include enactment and enforcement of an antislur policy and provision of "designated gay/lesbian sensitive adults" in each middle and high school.[45]

The Status of School-Based Programs

Despite the successful implementation of some model programs and appeals by health and education professionals and organizations, results from our national survey confirm a dearth of programmatic attention to the needs and issues raised by sexual orientation. This investigation of the major program areas outlined above revealed that most school districts (whether their communities had a gay rights ordinance or not) did not offer the recommended programs nor had they instituted suggested policies on behalf of gay and lesbian students and staff. However, we also found that school districts within cities and counties with protective legislation did offer significantly more programmatically than other districts (Table 5-1).

Half of the school districts in communities with gay rights measures and about one-third of those with no ordinances reported that they provided some instruction about sexual orientation. Most districts, however, offered such education only within health courses. In about half of the districts within ordinance communities, and in 38 percent of nonordinance districts, instruction was offered at both junior high school (or middle school) and senior high school levels. Very few (and none within the nonordinance communities) addressed the topic at the elementary level. Less than a third of all districts had offered in-service education to staff about sexual orientation within the past five years. Even fewer had attempted to educate parents, school board members, or citizens about the issue. Communities with legislation protective of gays, however, were more likely to have offered training and community education.

Similar results were found for school services and support. Support groups and special counseling services for gay and lesbian youth existed within only one-quarter of the ordinance community districts and in virtually none of the districts without legislation. Fewer than one in four districts had a policy prohibiting antigay language and behavior. Most such policies had been passed since 1990.

Our case study school districts reinforced these findings. Two (in Raleigh and Cincinnati) offered none of the recommended services, policies, or programs for students. The Philadelphia Board of Education adopted two policies (in 1991 and in 1994) that specifically included sexual orientation for program development. Implementation of programs addressing sexual orientation within those policies, however, had not yet taken place as of mid-1996. Iowa City and Santa Cruz have instituted some programs, such as incorporation of instruction about sexual orientation, training of administrators and staff, and adoption of policies that protect gay and lesbian students or staff. None of these districts had begun to address these issues prior to the early 1990s, although several of the cities had incorporated sexual orientation in their antidiscrimination legislation much earlier.

TABLE 5-1 DIFFERENCES IN SCHOOL SEXUAL ORIENTATION
PROGRAMS BETWEEN COMMUNITIES WITH AND
WITHOUT GAY RIGHTS LEGISLATION

Programs	Communities with gay rights ordinances or policies[a] (%)	Communities without gay rights ordinances or policies[b] (%)
Education, instruction		
School district offers sexual orientation education to students	50	34
School district offers sexual orientation education below high school	31	20
School district offers sexual orientation education to staff	43	22
School district offers sexual orientation education to parents, school board, community	29	13
Support and services		
School district offers support groups for gay, lesbian, and bisexual students	27	2
School district offers special counseling for gay, lesbian, and bisexual students	24	1
School district offers special counseling for parents of gay, lesbian, and bisexual students[c]	9	—
School district has specific policy prohibiting antigay language and behavior	23	14
School library presents information on sexual orientation[c]	24	—
School newspaper has published information on sexual orientation[c]	31	—
School district has instituted other changes in response to gay rights advocates[c]	14	—

Source: Data are from authors' national survey.

[a] N=123. Average number of student sexual orientation programs per school: 0.87.

[b] N=118. Average number of student sexual orientation programs per school: 0.44.

[c] Survey not taken of communities without ordinances or policies.

Barriers to the Development of School-Based Programs

To understand this level of inactivity we must explore the forces that operate to deter establishment of recommended school-based interventions. The
mere suggestion that schools actively address sexual orientation raises the
fear of intense controversy. According to Karen Harbeck, who is both a
lawyer and an educator, the combination of homosexuality and education
evokes "one of the most publicly volatile and personally threatening debates
in our national history."[46]

The most renowned example of such controversy occurred in 1992 over
New York City's Children of the Rainbow multicultural education curriculum. Although sexual orientation occupied a minor segment within the plan,
it aroused vehement protest. According to a *New York Times* report, "Critics
focused on two pages in the 443-page book, which is not distributed to students, that urged teachers to 'include references to lesbians and gays in all
curricular areas.' They also objected to a bibliography that included three
books . . . which they said promoted homosexuality."[47] School Chancellor
Joseph Fernandez lost his job not long after this conflict. The school board
members who voted to oust him cited his "neglect of basic problems of the
city's educational system like low reading and math scores and conditions in
the schools [while he] concentrated his energies on a controversial social
agenda."[48] During the board's five-hour public hearing on his continuation,
"talk of condoms and homosexuals . . . dominated many of the speakers'
comments."[49]

Interestingly, especially given the publicity generated by fundamentalist
religious groups, further analysis of our survey results suggested that religious opposition to school efforts was relatively ineffective.[50] There are several possible explanations for this finding. Perhaps the kinds of school activities we examined were relatively technical and professional in nature and
therefore escaped the scrutiny of community activists. In contrast to school
programs, local gay rights legislation is an uncomplicated but symbolic and
contentious matter. Thus, moral traditionalists might affect ordinance adoption or repeal, as discussed previously, but not a rather detailed or subtle
school-based program initiative.

Another explanation for the lack of effective opposition is that most school
districts in our survey were doing very little to start programs to meet the
needs of gay and lesbian youth. Thus, opponents may not have seen the need
to focus their political resources on the schools simply because school leaders were showing little inclination to develop such new and potentially controversial policies. Indeed, most survey respondents in districts without ordinances or policies indicated that neither gay rights supporters nor opponents
had made a difference in school board elections in the past five years.[51] Seem-

ingly, the issue simply has not been raised. As a long-term school board member from Raleigh explained,

Sexual orientation has never been discussed by the school board in all the years I have been on it—by proponents or opponents. No letters, no phone calls. Neither has the issue been brought up at the portion of school board meetings devoted to public [input]. . . . The issue has never been brought to the school board.

Similar views were expressed by a school board member in Cincinnati.

Other evidence provides further support for the claim that opponents have not needed to focus efforts on the schools. Fernandez's ordeal in New York City seemed to be heeded by school officials nationwide. Arthur Lipkin of Harvard University described this outcome in Massachusetts: "[D]uring the New York battle, the curriculum recommendations of the Governor's Commission on Gay and Lesbian Youth were quietly dropped from its report . . . and the governor was quoted as saying, 'I don't personally favor teaching a gay and lesbian curriculum in the schools.'" [52]

The widely publicized Fernandez case seemed to elicit a diffusion of "inhibition" (as opposed to innovation). Informants in every community we visited referred to the New York episode as having a chilling effect on their community's efforts to address sexual orientation issues and youth. The potential for controversy affected program implementation by discouraging administrative support. In accordance with the "non-decisionmaking hypothesis" noted in urban politics, school leaders used their power to determine the agenda and keep this issue off the table. [53] According to a Raleigh school official:

Controversy causes administration to go into denial—to pretend sexual orientation doesn't exist—and hope that nothing forces us to handle the issue. . . . I believe there are teachers who will talk with students one-on-one, but they don't feel like they can say anything about sexual orientation aloud in the classroom—they are out on a limb.

When we asked representatives in our communities to estimate, on a scale of 1 to 10 (low to high), the level of controversy elicited within their community by school-based programs addressing sexual orientation issues, their answers ranged from an average of 4.25 in Iowa City to averages of 9.0 in Raleigh and 9.8 in Cincinnati. In Cincinnati and Raleigh, opponents were viewed as so strong and pervasive that they were credited with having stifled school-based program development. Raleigh was the only site in which no school district administrators agreed to participate in the study, despite the promise of anonymity (one middle-level administrator later granted an interview by telephone). A Raleigh school official vividly explained the situation: "This is the South. . . . [W]e don't want newspapers to run a story about researchers asking about sexual orientation—it's too controversial." Although some school board members were interviewed, two declined, and both noted its controversial nature. As one of the two said, "I wouldn't want anyone misinterpreting my dialoging with someone on this topic. . . . [I]t's controversial . . . [and] could jeopardize other initiatives we have going." Cincinnati's school officials also attributed their lack of school-based programs to opposition and the potential for controversy. One Cincinnati school board member stated that "sexual orientation is not an issue raised in the schools here . . . like in New York. Whatever level of controversy happens in the community, multiply it in the schools—even close-by incidents raise all kinds of problems."

Significantly, program opponents, even when they were perceived as a minority of the general public, were considered to be vocal, angry, and disruptive. "Those who recoil at the mere mention of sexual orientation are adamantly opposed [to programs], even violently opposed," in the words of one Philadelphia school board member. Many had witnessed this wrath personally. For example, a school board member in Santa Cruz cited "unmerciful attacks" on a teacher who developed the district's curriculum that included sexual orientation. This board member also reported that opponents came to school board meetings in large numbers to complain. Opponents "hooted, hollered, were rude and willing to break ground rules that had been established, such as run over time limits and make personal attacks," affirmed a community activist present at those meetings. Respondents in every community described such behavior as a major deterrent to support for more comprehensive programming.

Administrators and elected school board members also believed their jobs would be threatened. In the words of a Raleigh school official, "We saw what happened to the superintendent in New York City—we don't need to know more than that!" A Philadelphia school board member deduced, "No issue is more contested [than gay rights], especially in education. . . . Joe Fernandez is not in New York today because of this in large measure." A Cincinnati school board member, who was supportive of some programming addressing sexual orientation, described being threatened by opponents who said they would withdraw their children from the schools and "beat us at the ballot box." He believed they had targeted certain school board members, including himself, for defeat in the next election.

Another fear was the threat to school funding. In Cincinnati, for example, one school official recalled that "in November 1993, the same people backing the repeal of the ordinance were against a school tax levy—both went down to defeat." That election campaign and its results served to "reinforce the perceived power of those conservatives—more power than they should have, given their numbers." Subsequently, the school district had become "more cautious" (for instance, in unveiling plans for sex education), and negotiating for domestic partner benefits on behalf of people with "nontraditional lifestyles" was considered untenable "because people will kill school levies" in response.

Furthermore, as respondents in all the communities we studied noted, no *incentives* exist for school administrators to address these issues. An Iowa City school official reasoned, "Administrators generally only get criticized for dealing with this issue. They receive very little praise. Therefore, we tend to stay away from it." A Philadelphia community agency representative described the pressure of public opinion on administrators: "Administrators and school board members want to please the public—and the public is saying they don't want kids to be gay and to have gay teachers."

A related constraint involves lack of organized support for such school-based programs. The inactivity of districts may be attributed to the reluctance of advocates to pressure schools directly for programmatic change. Gay and lesbian organizations have been wary of raising issues related to youth because of their fears of being accused of "recruiting." In addition, other teachers and potential allies face the fear of being stigmatized by being labeled homosexual themselves as a result of advocating for such programs.[54] Therefore, the collective support necessary to initiate school-based programs has been inadequate in most communities.

Representatives from both Cincinnati and Raleigh consistently depicted local lesbian and gay organizations and their allies as inactive on youth issues and cited this as a significant barrier to addressing sexual orientation issues within their schools. For example, teachers and administrators in Cincinnati believed that its gay and lesbian educators' organization, Gays and Lesbians United in Education, was "not doing much," did not have "much teeth," and needed "to be more proactive." In Raleigh, a school official stated that while some "teachers would like to address (sexual orientation) issues, there is no unity in the community to stand behind." Likewise, a teacher there observed, "No one is on the bandwagon for sexual orientation [programming]. . . . The gay/lesbian community doesn't see that they have a vested interest in schools."

One significant factor underlying the lack of activity is the perception by gays and lesbians that important aspects of their lives would be threatened if their homosexual identity were known. The risks of unemployment, compromised collegial or student rapport, and threat of violence compel many gay educators to hide and deny their orientation.[55] All respondents in Raleigh, with the exception of school board members, echoed these concerns, particularly the fear of unemployment. Even in Cincinnati, where sexual orientation is specifically included in the school district's employment antidiscrimination statement, most gay and lesbian teachers still feel insecure. As one school official explained, "It's never been tested—we're not sure how effective the antidiscrimination protection is—and Cincinnati is not welcoming for gays and lesbians." Fear of disclosure and the subsequent necessity to maintain a dual identity to ensure acceptance form "the most pernicious problem facing lesbian and gay educators." Adverse consequences of "such enforced secrecy" include significant levels of stress for these educators, as well as deprivation of positive, healthy role models, the reinforcement of invisibility (and inauthentic relationships), and the perpetuation of stereotypes for students, colleagues, and the community.[56]

In addition, in every school district, several individuals reported that other issues, such as violence, drop-out rates, teen pregnancy, and race relations, compete for the time and attention of school officials. As one Cincinnati school administrator assessed the situation, "This is not a high priority issue—it's frosting on the cake," or, in a teacher's words, "a luxury." Race and ethnic concerns were considered higher priority issues by high-ranking school officials in both Philadelphia and Raleigh. In addition, some respondents felt that their ability to address these multicultural issues might well be damaged if they included sexual orientation.

Another quandary faced by school officials involved the breadth of services for which schools should assume responsibility. As one principal in Cincinnati asked, "Should schools respond to only academic needs or to the whole needs of students?" A Cincinnati school board member thought, like many others, that "schools have too much to do already." This dilemma seems especially significant in light of prevailing financial pressures challenging most public schools today.

In sum, the failure to secure administrative support was considered a key barrier to program development. A Cincinnati school official stated that attempting to initiate school-based programs to address sexual orientation issues "would hurt the furthering of my career because the ideas are not shared by most administrators." Representatives from both Raleigh and Cincinnati attributed the general aversion of their schools to addressing issues of sexual orientation to inadequate support from central administration.

Factors That Encourage School-Based Programs

Despite these significant barriers, school districts within communities with gay rights protection were doing significantly more to address these issues than those without such legislation (see Table 5-1). When we analyzed the underlying basis for this activity, we found that having city or county gay rights legislation per se was not what mattered most. By controlling for background factors that promoted gay rights ordinance adoption, we discovered that the ordinance itself lost predictive capacity. In other words, it was not the legal statute itself that seemed to encourage efforts to address sexual orientation issues in schools, but the factors that produced a gay movement strong

TABLE 5-2   DEMOGRAPHIC AND POLITICAL CHARACTERISTICS
OF SCHOOL DISTRICTS AND COMMUNITIES

Characteristic	Communities with gay rights ordinances or policies (N=123)	Communities without gay rights ordinances or policies (N=118)
Urbanism/social diversity		
Total student enrollment at all three levels of school district	46,971	8,296
African Americans in community (%)	15	8
Per capita income for community ($)	16,045	12,422
Nonfamily households in community (%)	40	30
Resource mobilization		
Gay rights supporters have made a difference in school board elections (% of respondents in agreement)	13	1
Number of openly gay elected public officials	0.33	0.24

Sources: Data for urbanism/social diversity variables are from U.S. Department of Commerce, Bureau of the Census, *1990 Census of the Population: Social and Economic Characteristics* (Washington, D.C.: Government Printing Office, 1993); other data are from authors' national survey of school districts.

Note: All figures are averages.

enough to get an ordinance passed. Thus the ordinance seemed to be symbolic of the social forces that influenced the school district.[57]

To discern what factors might explain the differences in district efforts, we further analyzed our survey results. This time we used characteristics within the four major theoretical models associated with public policy outcomes. Our findings affirmed the factors found to be important in the adoption of antidiscrimination ordinances. In addition, they corroborated the findings of other researchers.[58]

Urbanism/Social Diversity

Districts within larger communities (and therefore with higher student enrollments) and with higher income levels tended to have more sexual orientation programming. In accordance with the urbanism/social diversity model, large, diverse populations that are relatively more affluent are more likely to have gay rights legislation and to adopt innovative school programs (Table 5-2). African Americans, although in greater proportion in ordinance communities, tended to be less likely to support such school programs. A study of gay youth by the educator James Sears suggested that prejudice against homosexuality was stronger than racial bias in both the African-American and white populations.[59]

In Cincinnati, blacks—particularly African-American ministers—were considered formidable opponents of programs dealing with sexual orientation in the schools. As we have seen, African Americans were an important influence in the repeal of the sexual orientation provision in that city's antidiscrimination ordinance as well. The Philadelphia Board of Education recently considered two program policies (sexuality education and multicultural education) in which sexual orientation was explicitly included. It was the most highly contentious (indeed, the only) topic of debate in its public hearings. African-American members on the task force committees that developed the policies were openly supportive. Black clergy in the community generally, however, opposed the policies. Catholic priests and elected officials representing white ethnic groups of middle and lower socioeconomic status also joined in opposition. Both policies were passed, but it was clear that the component dealing with sexual orientation would not be implemented fully in the foreseeable future because of this considerable opposition. One school official expressed fear that Philadelphia had "been targeted by the right wing" for subsequent city elections in order to reverse these policies. Members of the Philadelphia Board of Education are appointed by its elected city council.

Political Opportunity

The political opportunity structure is important for successful program adoption and implementation. Our analysis showed that states that had enacted gay rights legislation had more gay and lesbian programming in the schools.[60] This fosters the contention that a politically supportive environment is necessary for program development. Yet, inclusion of sexual orientation in statewide guidelines for sexuality education was not significantly related to district program efforts. This finding implies that school officials respond more to local than to state climates for political cues before instituting program change. States encourage, but cannot require, schools to implement policy.

Massachusetts provides insight as to how a supportive state-level structure can facilitate change in schools. In 1992 Gov. William Weld convened the nation's first Governor's Commission on Gay and Lesbian Youth "in response to the epidemic of suicide by young gays and lesbians" as disclosed in a 1989 report by the U.S. Department of Health and Human Services. The commission gathered information through five public hearings held around the state.

Its report, *Making Schools Safe for Gay and Lesbian Youth,* presented the evidence of problems encountered by such youth (including harassment, isolation and suicide, dropping out of school and poor school performance, need for adult role models, and problems with families). The report made eight specific recommendations for schools and families:

1. School policies protecting gay and lesbian students from harassment, violence, and discrimination;
2. Training for teachers, counselors, and school staff in crisis intervention and violence prevention;
3. School-based support groups for gay and straight students;
4. Information in school libraries for gay and lesbian adolescents;
5. Curriculum which includes gay and lesbian issues;
6. Peer counseling in the P-FLAG (Parents and Friends of Lesbians and Gays) model and family counseling in school;
7. Education of families through information in public libraries;
8. Parent speakers bureaus to advocate for fair treatment of gay and lesbian youth in schools.[61]

The commission also made recommendations for the state's Department of Education, Executive Office of Education, Commission against Discrimination, and legislature that related to promoting its recommendations. The state board of education subsequently adopted the first four recommendations for Massachusetts schools.

Massachusetts illustrates the effectiveness of providing follow-up support to largely symbolic decrees in affecting district-level program implementation. The governor convened the "first-ever statewide effort to train teachers about lesbian and gay issues." In addition, the state legislature committed $450,000 to the Department of Education for AIDS training and education. Through that program, twenty-five staff members conducted workshops on violence prevention, focusing on gay and lesbian youth issues. In another aspect of that program, every high school was invited to appoint one liaison to the commission, and these liaisons were asked to develop school teams to attend regional workshops. About half the schools with liaisons formed these teams.[62]

Such comprehensive state-level support, however, is rare. Iowa and Pennsylvania both passed state initiatives that encouraged their schools to address these issues but did not provide the same level of follow-up support to implement them. Iowa mandates that school districts have an Equity Committee with membership that reflects community diversity. Iowa City's committee stands apart from most in its receptivity to including sexual orientation concerns as part of its agenda. The Philadelphia Lesbian and Gay Task Force lobbied the Pennsylvania State Board of Education for inclusion of gay and lesbian issues in education beginning in 1989. In 1992 the board passed a policy to "prohibit discrimination in educational programs on the basis of sexual orientation and disability." The Pennsylvania secretary of education subsequently issued a Statement of Equity Principles to support a multiracial, multicultural, and nonsexist curriculum, and amended the state's Equity Statement to call for "maximizing the potential of all students regardless of race, cultural heritage, religion, gender, sexual orientation or disability." These nonbinding guidelines were approved by the Pennsylvania Board of Education in 1993, despite opposition by the governor and state legislature.[63]

Representatives from all five cities in our study could list national-level resources, such as conferences and publications of the National Education Association, the American Federation of Teachers, and the National Association of School Administrators, from which they garnered information about sexual orientation and schools. Only in Iowa City, however, was there a state-sponsored effort (a conference held several years earlier) to assist districts with developing such programs.

The importance of creating a political opportunity structure at the local level that supported addressing sexual orientation was also evident. A school official in Santa Cruz summarized the confluence of conditions that typically enabled district personnel to begin to address the issue, and substantiated the importance of a political opportunity structure:

Gays and others carry this fear of losing our jobs, parental reaction, etc. We just came together for the first time on this issue. The previous Superintendent—who was not supportive, not one to make controversial stands—left two years ago. The new one is more supportive—a big influence. . . . One other key factor is that gays and sympathizers are in key [central administration] positions now. They have more power and influence, and they are district-wide positions—they get around to all schools. In the past, individual gay and lesbian advocates were isolated—not as much opportunity to talk with others. It's taken a "critical mass" and increased discussion, especially with issues like gays in the military, [to get to the point that] the time has come to address sexual orientation [in these schools].

Furthermore, it was clear that developing a supportive political opportunity structure within local government as well as within the school system was important. As we explain more thoroughly in the section below on resource mobilization, in each of the communities, gay and lesbian community organizations had made a concerted effort to influence local elections, including some school board races. Although sexual orientation per se was not typically raised as an issue, gays and lesbians supported "liberal" or "progressive" candidates. Electing these supportive high-level officials was important to their subsequently feeling empowered to organize ways to influence school district programming directly. Thus, many program supporters actively participated in school board and city council elections, waited until lesbian or gay men were in significant school administration positions, and secured the support of government officials and community leaders prior to initiating school efforts.

Another significant factor supportive of school programming in the political opportunity structure was the contribution of "nonfamily households." Higher numbers of nonfamily households are typically found in communities with colleges and universities. In our analysis, this variable marked a cluster of college towns that had gay rights laws (such as Ann Arbor, Michigan; Berkeley, California; Columbus, Ohio; East Lansing, Michigan; and Iowa City). Such college communities tended to be relatively liberal on social issues. Thus, school districts in these communities are typically more open to policy innovation.

Iowa City was our representative college community, and virtually all respondents there credited the university with creating a climate supportive of equality and of gays and lesbians. Iowa City is a liberal and highly educated community, where openly gay candidates have run for public office. We found that lesbians and gay men actively supported these and other candidates—mainly Democrats—who, although they did not specifically address sexual orientation issues, did focus on youth problems such as gangs and violence. A variety of community leaders, including city elected officials, chamber of commerce members, school board members, community organizers, and the district superintendent, supported sexual orientation programming within schools. Gay and lesbian parents and teachers, more open as a result of the city's antidiscrimination ordinance, began to push the issue in the schools as well. School-based program efforts were initiated with the support of a representative school-community committee. As of mid-1996, their efforts had not elicited any organized opposition.

In Iowa City and Santa Cruz, university policies and programs that directly addressed sexual orientation also influenced school district programming. Universities in these cities offered workshops, conferences, and courses on sexual orientation, which school district employees attended or at least read about in the local newspaper. In Iowa City, the school district's domestic partner insurance benefit, approved in 1994 (an uncommon benefit for school-based employees), was a replica of the University of Iowa plan passed previously.

Many of the school personnel we interviewed in the five cities perceived that city or county gay rights legislation served to increase awareness and sensitivity to gay and lesbian issues. Furthermore, they said, it incited public discussion, which created an educational experience for their students (and others). In every community except Raleigh, ordinances were credited with another significant effect—the increased legal protection that encouraged gay and lesbian school personnel to feel safer and to be more open. Some gay and lesbian personnel acknowledged that they had sought to work in these communities because of the protection afforded them by the city statute or school district policy. Some consequently felt enabled to engage in further efforts. As a Santa Cruz school employee recounted, "The city ordinance gave us more protection. We feel more empowered to take the next step—to get schools to serve gay and lesbian kids. It still is controversial, but the city took the first heat. The ordinance was an important first step."

The inclusion of sexual orientation in antidiscrimination policies adopted by the school districts themselves gave lesbian and gay employees added feelings of security. Sometimes such district protection followed the city's ordinance, and sometimes it preceded it. Presently, the Cincinnati, Iowa City, Philadelphia, and Santa Cruz school districts have such policies. Nevertheless, in each city it was also acknowledged that most gay and lesbian school personnel remained in the closet to a great degree—that not even these explicit policies assured most that they were truly protected against discrimination. According to a gay activist in Santa Cruz in 1994, "The ordinance lays the foundation for teachers and staff to be more open . . . but not many are out." The reasons underlying the decision by gays to remain hidden echoed those stated previously. Their freedom to be open is curtailed by fears—of job loss, of losing respect, of harming relations with students or their parents, of harassment, and of physical violence.

An important factor in determining the institutionalization of new school programs, according to scholars Goodman and Steckler, is "the extent to which an innovative program fits into an organization's mission and operations."[64] They contend that if the fit is perceived to be poor, institutionalization is unlikely. Sometimes, as in Massachusetts and Pennsylvania, the state initiated the support and maintained that it was the responsibility of the schools to provide a safe environment in which all youth could learn. This factor was validated when school officials articulated their underlying beliefs about why schools should address sexual orientation issues. Many stated that their programs would increase students' ability to function within an increasingly diverse society, identified as an important mission of schools. Such justification also serves to clarify how these programs will assist *all* students, thus increasing perceived benefits and forming a basis for gaining more broadly based community support. As a Santa Cruz school official explained it, "The mission of the public school is to prepare students to be life-long learners and productive, accepting citizens. We're helping to teach tolerance and accepting diverse peoples. We share this responsibility with parents and others in the community."

Another determinant of program implementation within the political opportunity structure is the existence of avenues or organizations within which advocates can furnish information about needs and programs.[65] Each school district in our study that had initiated some programming had a structure within its bureaucracy in which sexual orientation issues could be addressed. In Santa Cruz, for example, the Substance Abuse/Student Assistance Advisory Committee created a Task Force for Support Services for Gay, Lesbian, and Bisexual Students and Families. In Iowa City, the district's first openly gay teacher worked through the Equity Committee. The teacher secured the support of the equity coordinator, who had a strong commitment to multicultural concerns and fairness for all minorities, as did the district superintendent. The teacher developed local documentation by holding confidential meetings with gay and lesbian students and staff to develop a list of their concerns to present to the committee. This list enumerated the problems gay and lesbian students faced and specified requests that would affect all facets of school life—from use of school facilities to social events to curriculum. The Equity Committee spent the better part of 1994 planning ways to address the requests. Its work continued through 1996 and included conducting teacher in-service workshops based on *Coming Out of the Classroom Closet,* a comprehensive book about school programs to address sexual orientation. In addition, the Philadelphia Board of Education, following its established procedures, developed community-school task forces. These groups included parents and students, sought to represent the whole community, and held many meetings in developing policies that included sexual orientation issues.

Parents often played an important role within these committees. School officials tend to be particularly sensitive to the needs and concerns of parents. Supporters felt that the public, particularly parents, should become educated on issues related to sexual orientation and become involved in program development, an approach found successful in establishing other potentially controversial school-based programs.[66] It was considered crucial to give parents an opportunity to remove their children from these programs (the right to "opt out"). Although rarely used, this privilege provided an important point of conciliation to opponents and left no room for anyone to argue that their religious beliefs were being violated by mandated programs. The P-FLAG organization had active chapters in three of the communities we visited (Raleigh, Philadelphia, and Cincinnati). Although potentially useful to school programs, none of the chapters has been directly involved in the schools.

Support groups or alliances that encourage student involvement represent another helpful internal structure. Project 10 East in Cambridge, Massachusetts, under the leadership of an openly gay teacher, began as a support group for gay and lesbian students but expanded to include "straight" students. This opening up was significant in that it "made it safe for questioning kids to come and for kids who are straight, and who come because they're interested in these issues—they see it in social justice or civil rights terms."[67]

Finally, all school districts mentioned their city or county's gay and lesbian youth group as a supportive local resource. These groups were typically affiliated with their community's gay and lesbian organizations and provided education and social support networks, as well as hotline or counseling services for youth. Educators and counselors within schools were able to refer gay, lesbian, and questioning students to these organizations. Some respondents noted that these groups provided valuable services to their schools through guest speakers in certain classes. In Philadelphia, for example, Voyage House—a community agency for at-risk youth—has a Sexual Minority Youth Services component, which provides educational outreach to the high schools and receives referrals from the schools' counselors.

Resource Mobilization

According to resource mobilization theory, a politically engaged gay constituency is another factor that made a significant difference in school district efforts to provide programs and policies for gay and lesbian students and staff. In analyzing the results of our survey, we found that educational programs and policies were greater when gays and lesbians served in local public office and mobilized to influence school elections (see Table 5-2). Political scientists Kenneth J. Meier, Joseph Stewart, and Robert E. England, in their empirical study of major urban schools, identified political mobilization as a major determinant influencing second-generation discrimination against African Americans. They found that supporters could accrue benefits for black students through a three-step process: first, gaining representation on the school board, the policymaking body; second, obtaining school administrative positions to implement those policies in ways that were supportive and not detrimental; and, most important, increasing the representation of minority teachers, those most directly responsible for carrying out established rules and procedures. They concluded that "without the political action that results in more black school board members, which in turn produces more black administrators, who in turn hire more black teachers, second-generation discrimination against black students would be significantly worse."[68]

The importance of efforts by gay and lesbian organizations to stimulate the establishment of school-based interventions were confirmed in our case studies. As one Philadelphia school board member said, "Change in education is a direct consequence of political movement. The ability of gay and lesbian political organizations and their allies to rally affects education." Philadelphia's Lesbian and Gay Task Force was consistently identified as the "driving force" behind getting the schools to address sexual orientation issues.

Once mobilized, the gay and lesbian community and their allies must work to effect change in the schools. Program planners in our case study communities and some of the literature in this area revealed effective strategies for doing so.

MOBILIZING PIONEERS. The organized effort to plan and implement programs is often initiated by a highly motivated individual. As Woog asserts, one person can "turn the tide."[69] A prominent example of these leaders is Virginia Uribe, the Los Angeles earth science teacher who founded Project 10 in the mid-1980s. Another is Gov. William Weld of Massachusetts, who launched the first statewide effort to protect gay and lesbian youth through legislation. Several others were featured in *School's Out: The Impact of Gay and Lesbian Issues in America's Schools,* by the journalist Dan Woog. We also found that in districts that had incorporated some gay and lesbian programming, proposals for change often originated with one person who then organized and activated others. The feelings of anger, fear, and determination held by many of these individuals are reflected in Virginia Uribe's recollection: "It [the antigay violence] was outright bigotry. . . . I knew I had to talk to the principal. . . . I was very nervous—it was almost like coming out for me. I screwed up my courage, told him . . . and held my breath."[70] Underlying their efforts is hope, captured in a statement by a Philadelphia advocate: "If schools taught about gay/lesbian issues when our parents were young, we wouldn't go through all this suffering."

Rita Addessa, mentioned previously as head of Philadelphia's Gay and Lesbian Task Force, clearly qualifies as a motivated pioneer. As one local agency representative summarized, "Schools are her mission." She personally lobbied city and school leaders, assisted with task force studies, wrote major reports, prepared and delivered testimony on behalf of the task force to the board of education, and assisted Philadelphia gay and lesbian youth to testify before the board during its public hearings on policy implementation. Her lobbying efforts on behalf of Philadelphia's Lesbian and Gay Task Force subsequently persuaded the board of education to include sexual orientation in two recently adopted education policies. Policy 123, Adolescent Sexuality, includes ensuring a "safe, equitable and positive school experience for lesbian and gay students" and was adopted in June 1991.[71] Policy 102, Multicultural-Multiracial-Gender Education, was adopted in January 1994 and is intended to promote "an educational process designed to foster knowledge about and respect for those of all races, ethnic groups, social classes, genders, religions, disabilities, and sexual orientations." Its purpose is to "ensure equity and justice for all members of the school community, and society as a whole, and to give those members the skills and knowledge they need to understand and overcome individual biases and institutional barriers to full equality."[72] Efforts by the task force continued in 1994, focusing on support of gay and lesbian youth in their testimony to the board at public hearings on implementation of Policy 102.

Another example of a highly motivated individual who made a difference was a teacher from Iowa City. In the district for twenty-five years, he became its first openly gay teacher. His decision to come out in 1992 was the result of a national event, the Republican National Convention, which he perceived as "anti-gay and anti-women—which made me so angry." He also responded to a local stimulus—observing his principal placate parents who objected to a school assembly on homosexuality by referring to gays and lesbians as "different from us." Among other important accomplishments, the district's passage in 1994 of domestic partner insurance benefits for its employees was directly attributed by a member of the school board to this gay teacher's efforts.

PROBLEM RECOGNITION.   Increasing official awareness and acceptance of the need to address problems are two of the "critical precursor conditions" for institutionalizing school-based programs.[73] The first step taken by many advocates within the schools was to document the problems gay and lesbian youth face, particularly as they were encountered by youth within the schools and community. Such documentation would constitute what political scientists Frederick M. Wirt and Michael W. Kirst termed "crystallizing events," one of the most powerful forces that instigate change within schools.[74]

The *Report on Youth Suicide,* published by the U.S. Department of Health and Human Services, served as a crystallizing event for Gov. William Weld to take action on the issue. His commission's initial activity involved documenting gay youth problems by conducting surveys and holding public hearings. These efforts resulted in Massachusetts becoming the first state to enact legislation that banned discrimination against gay and lesbian students in public schools.

Similarly, in 1991 the Philadelphia Lesbian and Gay Task Force initiated its third, and most comprehensive, survey of antilesbian and antigay discrimination and violence and included questions concerning school peers and officials. The task force reported that between one-quarter and one-third of lesbian women and about three of five gay men had experienced harassment, mostly by peers, while in school. About 15 percent of gay men reported that they had been abused by teachers or school officials. The more recent task force survey (1995–1996) revealed similar findings.[75] Furthermore, analysis of other local data showed that teenage and young adult males accounted for the majority of perpetrators of antigay and antilesbian violence. The task force cited the schools for inadequately protecting young gays and lesbians; for not providing accurate, comprehensive education about sexual orientation; and for neglecting to condemn violence. The reported findings and recommendations were used by the task force to lobby effectively in support of the Multicultural-Multiracial-Gender Education policy approved by the Philadelphia Board of Education in 1994.

Conversely, most school board members in Raleigh and Cincinnati could not identify any needs of gay or lesbian youth, and many said they did not know of school programs that addressed sexual orientation. No efforts to provide programming had been made in either district, thus affirming the importance of problem recognition.

PROGRAM ADVOCATES.   Another condition conducive to the institutionalization of school programs identified by Goodman and Steckler is "receptivity to change," or support for a programmatic solution to the problem. Administrative proponents within the system proved to be crucial to institutionalizing health promotion programs.[76] Activists for sexual orientation programming sought to obtain school board and high-level administrative support. According to a Santa Cruz school official, program planners "started from the top—and worked down from there." They strongly believed that they initially had to secure the support of central administration in order to proceed further in their efforts. Training for administrators—in workshops or through other modes of presenting information on sexual orientation—was viewed as a key factor in building awareness and gaining this support. Such workshops were implemented and proved useful in Iowa City and Santa Cruz.

Students are increasingly perceived as powerful advocates who can influence high-level officials.[77] Gay and lesbian advocates often asserted that their activism was inspired by the suffering (including suicide) of students. Several respondents indicated that their motivation stemmed from general knowledge; sometimes students (or their families) had confided their experiences to a trusted teacher, nurse, or school board member directly. The successful passage of the Massachusetts bill in 1995, which had been held up in senate committee for the two previous years, is illustrative of students' power to increase awareness and concern for the problem as well as inspire support for school-based remedies. "What made the difference this year," according to the chief secretary to Governor Weld, "were the students—the extraordinary lobbying campaign by hundreds of high school students—gay and lesbian, as well as heterosexual [who] were able to persuade members of the Legislature that the problem was real and that the solution was reasonable." [78]

In another example, students in Philadelphia testified before the board of education in April 1994 to recommend that sexual orientation be included in the multicultural education policy. They graphically described the verbal and physical harassment they received, with no authoritative intervention and assistance, while in school. They conveyed feelings of isolation, rejection, loneliness, fear, and self-hatred, as well as their hopes and dreams:

I want all students to be able to live and learn together in peace. Peace is only possible when fear is gone, and fear is gone only when ignorance has been eliminated. The only way to eliminate ignorance and fear is through knowledge. . . . That is why it is so important to me, to everyone, that Policy 102 be implemented in its entirety. It ensures us that learning will start, that peace will happen. [Female, 18 years old]

Some youth appeared on television during press coverage of the hearings. One student was "outed" and experienced painful harassment at school during the following few days. On the whole, however, the media coverage was considered helpful, and the students felt "very good" about having testified. In addition, as a representative from a community agency put it, "The gay/lesbian community, including its publications, has ignored youth. Our kids have pushed themselves on these publications—forced them to cover youth issues." As a result, everyone we interviewed in Philadelphia could identify specific problems experienced by gay and lesbian youth in their schools.

In each community except Cincinnati some students had become actively involved with gay issues. A school official in Iowa City explained that Iowa City's high school group Students against Intolerance and Discrimination was "formed in response to homophobia—by students—and has broadened to address all kinds of discrimination." Gay or lesbian students were members of the school committees addressing sexual orientation issues in both Iowa City and Santa Cruz. Even high school students in Raleigh were inspired to take action on such an issue in 1994. Six students, known as the Enloe 6, created a leaflet in response to a poster with "homophobic content" put up by other students. "Their pamphlet was a call for tolerance," explained one school board member. The incident attracted newspaper attention when both sets of students were suspended by the principal, and hundreds of students signed petitions in support of the Enloe 6. The six protested their punishment to the school board, which changed the suspension to detention. The controversy quickly became focused on the issue of free speech. "No one ever dealt with the underlying issue of tolerance," according to one high-level school official.[79] Nonetheless, one teacher noted, the Enloe 6 and the media coverage made students (and others) more aware of gay issues.

PROGRAM EFFECTIVENESS.   Goodman and Steckler contend that accessibility to a program that can successfully address identified needs is required for program initiation. Moreover, program "adequacy" (sufficiency of its theory, structure, design; staff expertise and effort; resources and supervision) is necessary for implementation. In a similar vein, Wirt and Kirst refer to "new concepts" as a second force critical for change in the schools. New concepts represent "someone's notion of the preferable, the efficient, the humane, the inexpensive, and the just in matters of schooling."[80]

Our findings corroborated the importance of these two factors. Proponents in all five of the communities we studied used recommendations found within the Department of Health and Human Services report and in books, such as *Coming Out of the Classroom Closet,* as the basis for new program plans. Training for teachers and other personnel to build staff expertise was seen as crucial. An official in Iowa City explained, "Not everyone is capable of teaching the curriculum, and they need to be comfortable. We have talked a lot about this issue—and how to develop comfort in teachers." A related staff issue, voiced by several school officials in Iowa City, Santa Cruz, and Philadelphia, is the need to provide training for responsiveness to gay and lesbian parents, who are increasingly revealing their sexual orientation to school personnel.

As stated previously, sometimes resources outside the schools developed quality programs and made them accessible. For instance, lesbians and gay men in Santa Cruz formed a speakers' bureau called Triangle Speakers which, with the approval of various principals, began to offer presentations for high school health classes in 1989–1990. They suffered one setback initially when a few ultra-conservative parents became alarmed and were joined by a local conservative organization in what one teacher called a "very loud, ugly protest at the school board." Nonetheless, Triangle Speakers received endorsement from the school board to continue to provide such services to the district's high schools. Members of Triangle Speakers had investigated prominent school-based programs, including personal visits to Project 10 and the San Francisco Unified School District, and had shared their findings with the district's Task Force for Support Services for Gay, Lesbian, and Bisexual Students and Families. In 1993 Triangle Speakers participated in the task force's sensitivity training for administrators, which was viewed as a major first step in institutionalizing future curricular offerings on sexual orientation.

COST-BENEFIT ANALYSIS.   Goodman and Steckler argue that the most important condition for the institutionalization of new school programs is that the innovative program be perceived as conferring benefits that outweigh the costs. These benefits tend to accumulate when all the other conditions are met. Thus the final task for program advocates is to build conditions that increase perceived benefits and decrease costs.

One important cost, as described earlier, is the potential for sexual orientation programs to create controversy and incite opposition. Program planners from the cities we studied sought to assuage potential controversy. Those we interviewed stressed that planning was deliberate and carefully conceived, more than that for other programs. Even in Iowa City, where opposition forces were viewed as a definitive minority, a school official described program planning in this area as necessitating slow, "whispering" change. In Santa Cruz, the committee "has been quiet, careful, logical, planned. We're trying not to raise red flags." Many school officials argued that their plans needed to be made in public, albeit carefully. They did not want to be seen as planning without public input. Significant time was spent discussing issues in committees that were representative of the school community. Leaders employed well-developed communication and negotiation skills in order to secure consensus among the broadest possible audience. These findings provide further support to previous research, which concluded that eliciting community-wide support was a critical strategy for establishing controversial school programs.[81]

Proponents also sought to increase perceived benefits by identifying ways the program could affect a wider range of students and problems. Toward that end, proponents in Philadelphia, Iowa City, and Santa Cruz contended that identifying gay and lesbian education needs as "equity" issues, not as a health issue, was extremely important to the institutionalization of programs. A Santa Cruz school official, for instance, stated that support from central administration for a program was grounded in its strong support for "diversity education." An Iowa City school official explained that the program process in that city was supported by "the nature of this community that supports *equality* strongly." Thus, the Iowa City School District plans were developed through its established Equity Committee. Statements by Philadelphia school officials also reflected the importance of program support based on equality and justice: one asserted, "Schools cannot deal with multiculturalism without dealing with everyone," and noted that "the superintendent is very supportive and has publicly stated that it's discrimination that's immoral." Similarly, a Philadelphia school board member claimed, "It's a matter of basic rights for all people." An African-American school official in Cincinnati who was willing to support sexual orientation programming declared, "I am a person of integrity. I couldn't look myself in the mirror if I didn't tackle these issues. There are many of us out there. If you're doing the right thing, nothing's going to happen of consequence."

In sum, successful implementation occurs when policymakers become program advocates because they are convinced that programs will yield positive benefit-to-cost assessments. These "program champions" have been found to be important to implementation because they can gain approval from the highest levels of school administration, facilitate successful implementation within the school system, and build supportive school-community coalitions.[82] In accordance with these findings, school officials in each of the communities we studied described efforts to build strong coalitions that would provide visible support for sexual orientation programs. In Philadelphia, Iowa City, and Santa Cruz—school districts that have incorporated programmatic change to some degree—these collaborations consisted of groups that supported equality and justice issues.

The Santa Cruz school district exemplifies a community in which these supportive factors have converged decisively. Commitment to program development has been sustained by increasingly open gay and lesbian parents and community members. Strong administrative support, even through a change in personnel, has been critical for the inception of program efforts. Equally important, programs are based on students' right to a safe, equitable learning environment. In the words of a school official:

They [the administrators] are caring, fair-minded, and all straight except one. They care for kids, and we have, from the beginning, approached this as a kids issue—their learning, safety, and self-esteem. This approach has been successful in maintaining support, especially at the elementary level, where many wonder why we should address sexual orientation issues. The task force points out that there are many children with gay and lesbian parents and the [negative] effects of having them hear terms such as *fag* when it pertains to their parents.

Since 1994, most of the staff in the Santa Cruz schools have attended training sessions sponsored by its Task Force for Support Services for Gay, Lesbian, and Bisexual Students and Families. Instruction has been incorporated in health courses and in some history and English curricula. Gay and lesbian teachers are increasingly open and thus approachable and sensitive to gay and lesbian students. Domestic partner benefits were passed for school personnel in July 1995, with the support of both the teachers' union and the administration.

Conclusion

Schools are the focus of contentious political battles over sexual orientation issues. Proponents of including sexual orientation in the school agenda assert that education is critical for social transformation and changes in attitudes toward lesbians and gay men. They maintain that this education needs to begin early and that schools provide the best environment for such activity because of their accessibility to youth. Such proponents contend that schools also need reform because of their general intolerance and hostility toward homosexuality. Opponents of this view argue that youth should not be exposed to any influences that would make them more accepting of homosexuality, a condition they regard as immoral and unhealthy. As John D'Emilio argues, "the right wing is choosing its targets shrewdly . . . attempting to construct a barbed-wire fence of law and public policy. Its purpose: to keep lesbians, gay men and bisexuals out of the territory marked 'children and family.'"[83] In analyzing state legislative efforts made in 1994, the majority of which focused on prohibiting or eliminating positive or neutral references to homosexuality in the schools, People for the American Way concluded, "Religious Right activists are well aware that if they can control the images of gay men and lesbians projected onto the public consciousness, they will to a large extent control the debate over gay rights."[84]

We found a paucity of programs addressing sexual orientation currently offered through schools. This finding can be understood to reflect the two factors Goodman and Steckler cited as most important to program institutionalization. First, in the minds of decision makers, costs outweigh benefits. Most school officials are reluctant to initiate efforts on a topic so fraught with controversy, with so little public support, and with an abundance of vociferous opposition. Second, programs addressing sexual orientation issues are not considered central to the mission of schools.

The Philadelphia schools provide an example of these significant barriers to program development. The superintendent, hired in 1994, introduced his school reform plan, Children Achieving Agenda. Because it did not incorporate sexual orientation issues or other specific components from the Multicultural-Multiracial-Gender Education policy (Policy 102) passed earlier that year, seventy members of the policy-planning committee signed a petition asking that the superintendent do so. The requested changes had not been made as of mid-1996, however, and the committee has been "virtually disbanded," another illustration of the non-decision-making political strategy. Its members have not been involved on the committees established to plan school reform, and two strong advocates of Policy 102 no longer serve on the board of education.

School programs to address the needs of lesbian and gay youth, still relatively infrequent, were more likely to be found in larger, more diverse and affluent communities. This finding supports our urbanism/social diversity model of policy development. State gay rights legislation and a college community environment were important aspects of the political opportunity structure necessary for program innovation. In addition, we found that a politically mobilized gay constituency proved vital to school district efforts, thus confirming the significance of the resource mobilization theory. These findings also attest to the potency of communal protest. It was not so much that formal movements of opposition to the initiatives emerged but rather that fear of such protest prompted school officials to censor themselves. Communal protest, even if only anticipated, thus seems to be a powerful inhibiting factor.

The extent to which recommended programs develop in schools will likely depend on how the cost-benefit factor and the school mission are assessed. Will proponents or opponents be more convincing when explaining how addressing sexual orientation issues will affect race relations, violence, dropout prevention, and other high-priority problems in the schools? Which side can muster the better argument about whether new programs should be implemented in these times of fiscal constraints? Can proponents argue persuasively about how programs can be instituted with public support? And can new agendas be carried out with minimal controversy and opposition? The answers to these questions will determine whether schools become a key institution in the process of transforming societal views about sexual orientation, or whether they remain a reflection of society's antigay bias and defenders of the status quo.

NOTES

Because of the controversial nature of this study, we promised the persons we interviewed that they would not be identified by name. Unless otherwise noted, all interviews pertaining to Iowa City took place in Iowa City in June 1994; all those pertaining to Philadelphia took place in Philadelphia in July 1994; all those pertaining to Raleigh took place either in Raleigh or Chapel Hill, N.C., in May 1994; all those pertaining to Santa Cruz took place in Santa Cruz in June 1994, and all those pertaining to Cincinnati took place in Cincinnati in November 1994. All quotations and information not otherwise documented are from these interviews.

1. Ruth E. Fassinger, "And Gladly Teach: Lesbian and Gay Issues in Education," in *Homosexual Issues in the Workplace,* ed. Louis Diamant (Washington, D.C.: Taylor and Francis, 1993), 119–142.
2. Susan K. Telljohann and James H. Price, "A Qualitative Examination of Adolescent Homosexuals' Life Experiences: Ramifications for Secondary School Personnel," *Journal of Homosexuality* 26 (January 1993): 41–56; Susan K. Telljohann, James H. Price, Mohammad Poureslam, and Alyssa Easton, "Teaching about Sexual Orientation by Secondary School Teachers," *Journal of School Health* 65 (January 1995): 18–22; Gerald Unks, "Thinking about the Homosexual Adolescent," *High School Journal* 77 (October–November 1993/December 1993–January 1994): 1–6.
3. Telljohann and Price, "A Qualitative Examination," 41–56; Telljohann et al., "Teaching about Sexual Orientation," 18–22.
4. William Marsiglio, "Attitudes toward Homosexual Activity and Gays as Friends: A National Survey of Heterosexual 15-to-19-Year-Old Males," *Journal of Sex Research* 30 (February 1993): 12–17; James T. Sears, "Educators, Homosexuality, and Homosexual Students: Are Personal Feelings Related to Professional Beliefs?" in *Coming Out of the Classroom Closet: Gay and Lesbian Students, Teachers, and Curricula,* ed. Karen M. Harbeck (Binghamton, N.Y.: Harrington Park Press, 1992), 29–79; and Unks, "Thinking about the Homosexual Adolescent," 1–6.
5. Marsiglio, "Attitudes toward Homosexual Activity," 12–17.
6. Ritch C. Savin-Williams, "Verbal and Physical Abuse as Stressors in the Lives of Lesbians, Gay Males, and Bisexual Youths: Associations with School Problems, Running Away, Substance Abuse, Prostitution, and Suicide," *Journal of Consulting Clinical Psychology* 62 (April 1994): 262–269; Telljohann and Price, "A Qualitative Examination," 41–56.
7. Governor's Commission on Gay and Lesbian Youth, *Making Schools Safe for Gay and Lesbian Youth: Breaking the Silence in Schools and in Families* (Boston: State House, 1993), 9.
8. American Association of University Women Educational Foundation, *Hostile Hallways: The AAUW Survey on Sexual Harassment in America's Schools* (Washington, D.C.: AAUW Educational Foundation, 1993), 20.
9. Andi O'Conor, "Who Gets Called Queer in School? Lesbian, Gay and Bisexual Teenagers, Homophobia, and High School," *High School Journal* 77 (October–November 1993/December 1993–January 1994): 7–12; Eric E. Rofes, "Making Our Schools Safe for Sissies," *High School Journal* 77 (October–November 1993/December 1993–January 1994): 37–40; Telljohann and Price, "A Qualitative Examination," 41–56.
10. Karen M. Harbeck, "Introduction," in Harbeck, *Coming Out of the Classroom Closet,* 2; Karen M. Harbeck, "Gay and Lesbian Educators: Past History/Future Prospects," in Harbeck, *Coming Out of the Classroom Closet,* 121–140.
11. Diane L. Kerr, Diane D. Allensworth, and Jacob L. Gayle, "The ASHA National HIV Education Needs Assessment of Health and Education Professionals," *Journal of School Health* 59 (September 1989): 301–307.
12. Alan E. Gambrell and Debra W. Haffner, *Unfinished Business: A SIECUS Assessment of State Sexuality Education Programs* (New York: Sex Information and Education Council of the U.S., 1993); Arthur Lipkin, "The Case for a Gay and Lesbian Curriculum," *High School Journal* 77 (October–November 1993/December 1993–January 1994): 95–107.
13. James H. Price and Susan K. Telljohann, "School Counselors' Perceptions of Adolescent Homosexuals," *Journal of School Health* 61 (December 1991): 433–438; Sears, "Educators, Homosexuality, and Homosexual Students," 29–79; Telljohann and Price, "A Qualitative Examination," 41–56; Telljohann, "Teaching about Sexual Orientation," 18–22.

14. James H. Price, Sharon Desmond, and Gary Kukulka, "High School Students' Perceptions and Misperceptions of AIDS," *Journal of School Health* 55 (March 1985): 107–109.
15. Telljohann and Price, "A Qualitative Examination," 42.
16. Governor's Commission on Gay and Lesbian Youth, *Making Schools Safe*, 26.
17. American Academy of Pediatrics Committee on Adolescence, "Homosexuality and Adolescence," *Pediatrics* 92 (October 1993): 631–634; William P. McFarland, "A Developmental Approach to Gay and Lesbian Youth," *Journal of Humanistic Education and Development* 32 (September 1993): 17–29.
18. John C. Gonsiorek, "Mental Health Issues of Gay and Lesbian Adolescents," *Journal of Adolescent Health Care* 9 (March 1988): 114–122; Virginia Uribe and Karen M. Harbeck, "Addressing the Needs of Lesbian, Gay and Bisexual Youth: The Origins of PROJECT 10 and School-Based Intervention," in Harbeck, *Coming Out of the Classroom Closet*, 9–28.
19. Paul Gibson, "Gay and Lesbian Youth Suicide," in *Report of the Secretary's Task Force on Youth Suicide*, vol. 3, *Prevention and Intervention in Youth Suicide*, no. (ADM)89-1623 (Washington, D.C.: U.S. Department of Health and Human Services, 1989); Gary Remafedi, James A. Farrow, and Robert W. Deisher, "Risk Factors for Attempted Suicide in Gay and Bisexual Youth," *Pediatrics* 87 (June 1991): 869–875; Savin-Williams, "Verbal and Physical Abuse," 262–269.
20. Richard A. Friend, "Undoing Homophobia in Schools," *Education Digest* 58 (February 1993): 62–66.
21. Lipkin, "The Case for a Gay and Lesbian Curriculum," 95–107.
22. Marsiglio, "Attitudes toward Homosexual Activity," 16.
23. Sara Rimer, "Gay Rights Law for Schools Advances in Massachusetts," *New York Times,* December 8, 1995.
24. Minnesota Department of Education, *Alone No More: Developing a School Support System for Gay, Lesbian, and Bisexual Youth* (St. Paul: Minnesota Department of Education, 1994), 25.
25. Gonsiorek, "Mental Health Issues"; Minnesota Department of Education, *Alone No More,* 27.
26. Gonsiorek, "Mental Health Issues."
27. Telljohann and Price, "A Qualitative Examination," 41–56.
28. McFarland, "A Developmental Approach," 17–29.
29. John P. Elia, "Homophobia in the High School: A Problem in Need of a Resolution," *High School Journal* 77 (October–November 1993/December 1993–January 1994): 177–185; McFarland, "A Developmental Approach," 17–29; Del Stover, "The At-Risk Kids Schools Ignore," *Executive Educator* 14 (May 1992): 28–31.
30. Leo Treadway and John Yoakam, "Creating a Safer School Environment for Lesbian and Gay Students," *Journal of School Health* 62 (September 1992): 352–357.
31. Warren J. Blumenfeld, "Gay, Lesbian, Bisexual, and Questioning Youth," in *The Sexuality Education Challenge: Promoting Healthy Sexuality in Young People*, ed. Judy C. Drolet and Kay Clark (Santa Cruz, Calif.: ETR Associates, 1994), 321–341. See also Friend, "Undoing Homophobia in Schools," 62–66; Treadway and Yoakam, "Creating a Safer School Environment," 352–357; American School Health Association, *Position Statement on Gay and Lesbian Youth and the Schools,* (Kent, Ohio: ASHA, 1990); Stover, "At-Risk Kids Schools Ignore," 28–31; Telljohann, "Teaching about Sexual Orientation," 18–22.
32. National Guidelines Task Force, *Guidelines for Comprehensive Sexuality Education: Kindergarten–12th Grade* (New York: Sex Information and Education Council of the U.S., 1991).
33. Gary Remafedi, "Fundamental Issues in the Care of Homosexual Youth," *Medical Clinics of North America* 74 (September 1990): 1169–1179.
34. Gonsiorek, "Mental Health Issues."
35. Telljohann and Price, "A Qualitative Examination," 41–56.
36. Gibson, "Gay and Lesbian Youth Suicide," 3–122.
37. Uribe and Harbeck, "Addressing the Needs of Lesbian, Gay, and Bisexual Youth," 12.
38. Elia, "Homophobia in the High School," 177–185; Pat Griffin, "Homophobia in Sport: Addressing the Needs of Lesbian and Gay High School Athletes," *High School Journal* 77 (October–November 1993/December 1993–January 1994): 80–87; "Homosexuals Make Social History at Sioux Falls Prom," *New York Times,* May 24, 1979; Eric E. Rofes, "Making Our Schools Safe for Sissies," *High School Journal* 77 (October–November 1993/December 1993–January 1994): 37–40; Unks, "Thinking about the Homosexual Adolescent," 1–6.
39. Rimer, "Gay Rights Law."

40. Larry Rohter, "New York Offering Public School Geared to Homosexual Students," *New York Times*, June 6, 1985.
41. Quoted by Jesse Green, "The School Is Out," *New York Times Magazine*, October 13, 1991, 68.
42. Dan Woog, *School's Out: The Impact of Gay and Lesbian Issues on America's Schools* (Boston: Alyson, 1995).
43. Uribe and Harbeck, "Addressing the Needs of Lesbian, Gay, and Bisexual Youth," 9–28.
44. Woog, *School's Out*.
45. Kevin Grogin, "Support Services for Gay, Lesbian, and Bisexual Youth, San Francisco Unified School District" (paper delivered at the annual meeting of the American School Health Association Convention, Houston, October 6, 1994).
46. Harbeck, "Introduction," *Coming Out of the Classroom Closet*, 2.
47. Steven L. Myers, "Values in Conflict: Schools Diversify the Golden Rule," *New York Times*, October 6, 1992.
48. Sam Dillon, "Board Removes Fernandez as New York Schools Chief after Stormy 3-Year Term: Social Issues Cited," *New York Times*, February 11, 1993.
49. Ibid.
50. Barbara A. Rienzo, James Button, Kenneth D. Wald, "The Politics of School-Based Programs Which Address Sexual Orientation," *Journal of School Health* 66 (January 1996): 33–40.
51. Ibid., 38.
52. Lipkin, "The Case for a Gay and Lesbian Curriculum," 99.
53. Peter Bachrach and Morton S. Baratz, *Power and Poverty: Theory and Practice* (New York: Oxford University Press, 1970), 43–46.
54. Stover, "At-Risk Kids Schools Ignore," 28–31; Treadway and Yoakam, "Creating a Safer School Environment," 352–357; Woog, *School's Out*.
55. Fassinger, "And Gladly Teach," 119–142.
56. Ibid., 130–131.
57. Rienzo, Button, and Wald, "Politics of School-Based Programs," 39.
58. Robert M. Goodman and Alan Steckler, "A Model for the Institutionalization of Health Promotion Programs," *Family and Community Health* 11 (February 1989): 63–78.
59. James T. Sears, *Growing Up Gay in the South: Race, Gender, and Journeys of the Spirit* (New York: Harrington Park Press, 1991), 322–323.
60. Rienzo, Button, and Wald, "Politics of School-Based Programs," 36.
61. Governor's Commission on Gay and Lesbian Youth, *Making Schools Safe*, 2; see also Gibson, "Gay and Lesbian Youth Suicide."
62. Woog, *School's Out*, 363.
63. *Philadelphia Lesbian and Gay Task Force Bulletin* (Philadelphia: Philadelphia Lesbian and Gay Task Force, 1993), 1.
64. Goodman and Steckler, "Model for the Institutionalization of Health Promotion Programs," 76.
65. Ibid., 69–70.
66. Barbara A. Rienzo, "Factors in the Successful Establishment of School-Based Clinics," *Clearing House* 67 (July–August 1994): 356–362; Barbara A. Rienzo and James Button, "The Politics of School-Based Clinics: A Community-Level Analysis," *Journal of School Health* 63 (August 1993): 266–272.
67. Woog, *School's Out*, 328.
68. Kenneth J. Meier, Joseph Stewart, Robert E. England, *Race, Class, and Education: The Politics of Second-Generation Discrimination* (Madison: University of Wisconsin Press, 1989), 141.
69. Woog, *School's Out*, 22.
70. As quoted in ibid., 321.
71. School District of Philadelphia Board of Education, *Policy 123: Adolescent Sexuality* (1991), 2.
72. School District of Philadelphia Board of Education, *Policy 102: Multicultural-Multiracial-Gender Education* (1994), 1.
73. Goodman and Steckler, "Model for the Institutionalization of Health Promotion Programs," 74.
74. Frederick M. Wirt and Michael W. Kirst, *The Politics of Education: Schools in Conflict* (Berkeley, Calif.: McCutchen, 1982), 20.
75. Larry Gross and Steven K. Aurand, *Discrimination and Violence against Lesbian Women and Gay Men in Philadelphia and The Commonwealth of Pennsylvania: A Study by the Philadelphia Lesbian*

and Gay Task Force (Philadelphia: Philadelphia Lesbian and Gay Task Force, 1992), 8; Larry Gross and Steven K. Aurand, *Discrimination and Violence against Lesbian Women and Gay Men in Philadelphia and The Commonwealth of Pennsylvania: A Study by the Philadelphia Lesbian and Gay Task Force* (Philadelphia: Philadelphia Lesbian and Gay Task Force, 1996), 20.

76. Goodman and Steckler, "Model for the Institutionalization of Health Promotion Programs," 74.
77. Woog, *School's Out*, 22.
78. Rimer, "Gay Rights Law."
79. See Todd Silberman, "Enloe Principal Upholds Students' Suspensions," *Raleigh News and Observer*, March 10, 1994.
80. Goodman and Steckler, "Model for the Institutionalization of Health Promotion Programs," 71; Wirt and Kirst, *Politics of Education*, 19.
81. Rienzo, "Factors in the Successful Establishment of School-Based Clinics," 356–362; Rienzo and Button, "The Politics of School-Based Clinics," 266–272.
82. Goodman and Steckler, "Model for the Institutionalization of Health Promotion Programs," 74.
83. John D'Emilio, "Where Have All the Homophobes Gone? State Politics in the Gingrich Era," *NGLTF Task Force Report*, fall/winter 1995, 6.
84. People for the American Way, *Hostile Climate: A State by State Report on Anti-Gay Activity* (Washington, D.C.: People for the American Way, 1994), 11.

CHAPTER 6

The Opposition:
Protectors of Traditional Values

No culture that has ever embraced homosexuality has ever survived.
—Rep. Steve Largent, U.S. Congress

s residents of one city prepared to vote on removing "sexual orientation" from their community's antidiscrimination ordinance, a news
commentator complained that the campaign posed the issue as a bizarre
choice: "Do you favor a takeover of Cincinnati by goose-stepping Nazis or child-
molesting drag queens?"[1] To the advocates and opponents of gay rights, the
people who try to "frame" the issue for the electorate, the conflict over
whether to cover sexual orientation in antidiscrimination laws represents a
fundamental clash of values. The protagonists use lurid stereotypes to associate the other side with unpopular groups and unacceptable social values.

Supporters argue that adoption of gay rights legislation gives the community a choice between embracing tolerance or succumbing to bigotry. To make
this point more vividly, they portray the opponents of gay rights as "bigots
and homophobes who belong in a post-office lineup with the KKK."[2] The
opponents, no less certain of the high stakes in the battle over gay rights,
perceive a choice between upholding divine morality or choosing the deca-
dent path of Sodom and Gomorrah. They routinely contend that the "gay
agenda" is not fundamentally a matter of civil rights but instead a far more
sinister plot to impose "pedophilia, incest, sadomasochism, and even bestial-
ity" as legitimate practices.[3] Such overheated rhetoric is not unknown in
American political life, but it seldom emerges in the context of local government policy. Recognizing that the gay rights issue has the potential to introduce new and intense lines of cleavage to American communities, we explore
in this chapter the nature and source of opposition to gay rights ordinances.

The Extent of Opposition and Controversy

First, let us assess the *level of community conflict* associated with the issue.
The simplest measure of community opposition is the report of efforts to
repeal or rescind ordinances or policies that provide legal protection based
on sexual orientation. Of the 126 communities with such protection in force

at the time of our survey, 35, or 1 in 4, reported local or state efforts to over-turn it.[4] Considering how strongly the norm of consensus operates in local government and how few government policies are overturned, this level of conflict is remarkable. Moreover, because our study was limited to communities that still had such protection in mid-1993, this figure significantly understates the magnitude of opposition. At the time we collected our data, gay rights measures had already been successfully repealed in Dade County (including Miami), Florida; Duluth, Minnesota; Houston, Texas; Tacoma, Washington; Wichita, Kansas; and other communities.[5] If we were to include these localities in the set of communities that had adopted gay rights laws, the percentage of repeal attempts would rise to more than one in three. Even this figure does not fully convey the level of controversy such legislation may inspire, for it does not count the number of communities that have chosen deliberately not to implement equal protection policies, often after acrimonious debate, nor does it consider the nearly thirty communities that have passed resolutions condemning the principle of protecting sexual orientation.

The extent of opposition can also be gauged by the reports of the local experts who supplied us with information about the gay rights ordinances and policies. We asked our survey respondents to assess the level of political controversy surrounding their communities' gay rights policy. They used a 10-point scale in which a value of 1 represented "no conflict" and 10 indicated "intense conflict." Although it is difficult to know how controversy on this question compared with conflict on more typical policies in these communities, the average of 4.1 suggests less intensity than we suspected. This average, however, may disguise the much higher passion associated with the issue of gay rights in recent years. Indeed, that is the case. The level of conflict reported by our community informants rose from 3.3 for localities with policies adopted before 1986 to 4.7 in cities and counties that adopted gay rights thereafter.[6]

Was opposition and controversy more common in some kinds of communities than others? Suspecting so, we created a scale of community conflict that incorporated four factors: the number of groups opposed to the ordinance or policy, whether a candidate had entered a recent election primarily to challenge the law, whether the law or policy had been the object of a repeal effort, and the subjective level of conflict reported by those surveyed. In an analysis reported elsewhere, we had found striking differences in size, social composition, size of the gay population, and degree of religious adherence between the communities with ordinances and jurisdictions that did not provide legal protection based on sexual orientation.[7] Looking at the vastly more homogeneous set of 126 communities with such protection, we found that some of the same factors that influenced whether or not such pro-

TABLE 6-1   FACTORS ASSOCIATED WITH COMMUNITY
CONFLICT OVER GAY RIGHTS ($N=126$)

Level of community conflict associated with gay rights[a]	Higher education enrollment as a percentage of population (%)	Conservative religious groups as a percentage of church adherents (%)
Low conflict (40)	21	12
Medium conflict (40)	15	15
High conflict (41)	16	17

Source: Data are from authors' national survey.

Note: All figures are averages.

[a] The numbers in parentheses refer to the number of cases; five of those surveyed did not respond. The communities were divided into equal thirds based on the score on the objective measure of community conflict.

tection was adopted also helped account for the level of conflict experienced in communities that embraced gay rights.

The two differences that stand out are reported in Table 6-1. The level of conflict was lower, relatively speaking, in communities with large concentrations of higher-educated citizens, and conflict was higher as the concentration of religious traditionalists grew. Both findings are consistent with our earlier suggestion that ordinances were most enthusiastically passed in college towns (because of a supportive political opportunity structure) and faced the greatest opposition from advocates of traditional religious values. Such ordinances would be least likely to face serious pressure for repeal in places where the population was thought to be supportive, such as college towns, but much more prone to engender serious resistance where a substantial population of religious traditionalists was available to be mobilized in opposition.

Who Opposed Gay Rights?

Experts have identified two main sources of opposition to gay rights, corresponding generally to the cultural-identity and self-interest models of political behavior.[8] In the first theory, religious conservatives occupy the center of the opposition to gay rights. Gay rights are seen as a threat to the social values and cultural dominance of people who are committed to a particular vision of an ideal society. This theory fits in well with the communal protest model of ordinance adoption, introduced in Chapter 1 and referred to in other chapters. The second theory regards gay rights legislation as principally offensive to certain segments of the business community. Antidiscrimination legislation potentially threatens to impose costs on employers in the form

TABLE 6-2   SOURCES OF OPPOSITION TO GAY RIGHTS POLICIES

Groups mentioned as actively opposed to gay rights policies or ordinances	Number of communities	Percentage of all groups mentioned
Church or religious group	41	53
Christian right organizations	10	13
Business group	5	6
Parent or women's group	2	3
Other	19	25
Total responses	77	100

Source: Data are from authors' national survey.

of lawsuits for wrongful dismissal, efforts to ensure compliance, and the potential extension of job benefits to same-sex partners. Beyond the immediate cost of such legislation, gay rights ordinances add another level of regulation on top of existing mandates. These two theories are not incompatible because both groups may oppose gay rights for different reasons and may rationalize their opposition in terms of both culture and economic interest.

We asked our survey respondents to tell us if any local groups had fought against gay rights and, if so, to identify them (Table 6-2). Fifty-six informants volunteered the names of opposition groups, and fully two-thirds of the groups mentioned had a clear religious connection. Most of those surveyed singled out either specific religious denominations (for example, Baptists or Catholics) or groups defined by broader labels such as "religious conservatives." We also observed the names of organizations generally associated with the Christian Right movement in the United States (Eagle Forum, Concerned Women for America, and so on). Nor is this necessarily the full extent of religious influence on the policy process because some of the other groups not identified explicitly may well have been associated with religious movements or campaigns.[9] The predominance of such organizations among the opposition further reinforces our judgment that the communal protest model best explains resistance to gay rights ordinances.

The findings in Table 6-2 are also interesting for what they do *not* reveal. Specifically, the business community was seldom identified as a source of opposition. There were just five such mentions, only 6 percent of the total, suggesting that businesses and business organizations did not play a prominent public role in the conflict over gay rights. Of course, it may be that the business community was involved in opposition but disguised its role as a major player, allowing others to take the lead in public opposition. But for reasons to be explained later, we accept this general impression that the primary contestants against gay rights were religious traditionalists. Business opposition was less general and more sporadic.

The Religious Community and Gay Rights

The opponents of gay rights frequently refer to homosexuality as a clear violation of something they call the Judeo-Christian tradition, implying that virtually all religious communities regard homosexuality as sinful. In truth, as noted in Chapter 3, America's diverse denominations hold a great variety of positions on homosexuality. At one extreme, some churches regard homosexuality as another of God's gifts to humanity, no less precious than heterosexuality. This perspective was nicely represented by an episode of the popular *Friends* television series in which the minister at a wedding ceremony for two women proclaimed, "God is happy when any two people come together in love." Armed with this view, such churches accept gays and lesbians as full members of the church, recognize and support gay caucuses, and emphasize services that address gay needs. Churches at the other extreme regard homosexuality as fundamentally incompatible with the core of Judeo-Christian tradition and impose severe restrictions on the ability of gays to join, lead, or pastor local congregations. To the extent such denominations reach out to gays, their ministries are intended to bring homosexuals to "repent" of their sins and adopt a heterosexual life. Most churches fit somewhere between the extremes, offering some services specially targeted to gays but stopping well short of endorsing homosexuality as the moral equivalent of male-female relationships. To undermine further the notion of a unitary antigay bias in organized religion, it is worth noting that some gays have formed their own denomination, the Metropolitan Community Churches, discussed in Chapter 3, whereas others worship in virtually all denominations or in gay caucuses within denominations. The myth of gays as people without religious faith is belied by the assessment of one well-informed activist that churches constitute "the largest grassroots organizations" in the gay community.[10]

Thus, rather than treat religion as an all-encompassing source of opposition to gay rights, we focus on the three distinct communities that have most often been implicated in resistance to the gay rights movement—white evangelical Protestants, Roman Catholics, and black evangelicals.

Protestant Fundamentalists

The most prominent opponents of the ordinances in the 126 communities surveyed, according to our informants, were members of conservative religious groups who argued on doctrinal grounds against giving legal recognition to what they regarded as sinful behavior. We use the term *fundamentalist* to refer to these Protestant opponents of gay rights, although we recognize that such a term is imprecise and both includes and excludes people who fall into the category of opponents of gay rights.

In practice, active opposition to the gay rights movement—as opposed to essentially passive rejection—shows up most commonly in a small set of Protestant churches. The twenty churches that signed an open letter against the proposed human rights legislation in Santa Cruz included virtually none of the historic mainline Protestant denominations—no Lutherans, Presbyterians, United Methodists, or Episcopalians and only one of the twelve Roman Catholic congregations in the community.[11] Instead, the public religious opponents were drawn from churches with three traits. Many of the signees were part of the diffuse traditions of a Pentecostal, charismatic character within Protestantism. This broad trend incorporates such denominations as the Assemblies of God, the Christian and Missionary Alliance, the Church of the Four Square Gospel, and the Seventh-Day Adventists, all of whom were prominently represented among the opponents to gay rights in Santa Cruz and elsewhere. In these traditions, people experience God directly through such manifestations of the holy spirit as speaking in tongues, spiritual healing, and other forms of joyful, emotional, active encounters with the divine. These churches as well as most of the Baptist signees and many other signees share another trait—congregational organization. These traditions grant considerable independence to individual congregations or, as in the case of independent Baptists, do not even maintain a central denominational structure. Such a system leaves the congregations free to pursue whatever objectives they deem important.

Finally, most of the signing churches were strongly centered on their pastors. Responsibility for interpreting the Scriptures, making sense of social trends, and a whole host of issues are generally lodged with the clergy who lead such congregations. The theological uniqueness of these churches may incline them to take very seriously state-sanctioned violations of biblical morality, and the lack of strong central coordination and pastoral independence permit the congregations to enter the political fray if there is consensus on an issue.

The creedal basis of fundamentalist opposition to homosexuality—which extends well beyond the circle of churches that have taken the lead in opposing gay rights—is rooted in biblical statements interpreted as prohibitions against homosexual conduct.[12] One Philadelphia church distributed to city council members a list of fifteen separate biblical passages condemning sodomy.[13] The most commonly cited passages include the story of Sodom and Gomorrah (Gen. 19), the discussion of the covenant in the nineteenth chapter of Leviticus, Paul's speech (Rom. 1), and the list of inheritors of the Kingdom of God (1 Cor. 6). Apart from these statements, most theological critics of homosexuality point to the second chapter of Genesis, which describes the relationship of Adam and Eve. One theologian interpreted the second chapter of Genesis as follows:

[T]he claim is that woman is taken out of man, that they are for each other, interdependent and made to be rejoined. This grounds heterosexual relationships, and only these, in God's very purposes for the being, growth and companionship of people. *This* is what the bible says about homosexuality as a natural sexual orientation: it leaves no room for it.[14]

To regard homosexual conduct as unbiblical does not necessarily imply that it should be subject to criminal penalties or even that it is a legitimate basis upon which to deny employment, housing, or other civil rights protection. One seldom finds conservative Christians calling for similar penalties or legal restrictions on other forms of conduct, sexual or otherwise, that are condemned with equal or greater vigor by the Bible. To understand why theologically conservative Christians have so enthusiastically embraced the antigay cause, it is essential to return to the concept of identity politics.

The leading edge of the evangelical antigay movement, religious fundamentalism, emerged early in the twentieth century as a revolt against many disturbing social trends. The eclipse of rural America and small towns by rapid urbanization, the immigration of Catholics and Jews, the erosion of various social norms regarding sexuality and social restraint—all these seemed, to traditionalists, to strike at the heart of a culture that had once dominated American society. Many responded by falling back on the fundamentals of the faith and taking a stand against what were perceived as destructive social changes. The process by which social identity leads to political mobilization was concisely reported by Debra Burrington:

[R]eligious fundamentalists have a long history of attention to what they consider "traditional moral values." At the center of these traditional moral values is bible-based religion. Around this core are related values about God-given "natural differences" between men and women, traditional gender roles, the nuclear family, and procreatively-focused sexuality, or what religious right activists recently have called the "heterosexual ethic." From these values emerge political interests in protecting the traditional family, preventing abortion, and prohibiting homosexuality.[15]

This comment captures two key aspects of the identity politics that drives fundamentalist opposition to gay rights—its belief in a threatened social order and its comprehensive social agenda.

The various efforts by gays to extend their social role—by military service, antidiscrimination laws, adoption, and marriage—constitute a direct challenge to what social conservatives regard as basic cultural norms. Consider the language of one Christian activist in defending heterosexual marriage:

[M]arriage is a covenant established by God wherein one man and one woman, united for life, are licensed by the State for the purpose of founding and maintaining a family. A family that follows biblical principles nourishes and cherishes its members. Spouses practice unconditional love toward each other and their children. Parents provide protection within a healthy physical and emotional environment. And children learn to respect authority—and develop self-discipline. Additionally, they learn from positive role models how to be good citizens.[16]

From this perspective, gay marriage is not simply bad, wrong, or inappropriate. Rather, it threatens virtually every social value cherished by religious traditionalists—role differences between men and women, the process of procreation, the raising of children, respect for authority, the practice of self-control, and the development of civic commitment. All these practices and values rest on a definition of marriage as a legitimate union of man and woman. Precisely because it targets the divinely ordained institution of the family, religious conservatives believe, the pursuit of gay rights threatens "the basic building block of a stable culture."[17] Society has traditionally defined marriage a certain way—with reference to God's law—and any change in the definition takes the institution of "marriage" away from those who legally monopolize it—heterosexual couples. To adopt policies of this nature is seen by religious traditionalists to undermine the essence of our cultural identity.

In this sense the opposition to gay rights was perceived by its leaders and much of its constituency as a profoundly religious crusade. At one level, this was evident from the reports of hymn singing, public prayer, and religious chants at public hearings on gay rights ordinances. We also heard repeatedly from local opponents that their efforts were a direct extension of their religious beliefs. In typical testimony before a city council committee, one Cincinnati minister said the ordinance was wrong because it defies the word of God "that the practice of homosexuality is wrong," and he lectured council members about their duty "to reward good conduct and to execute judgment upon evil." Lest anyone still miss the point, he concluded his testimony by admonishing the public officials, "If you pass the ordinance to give protection to homosexuals, you will be inviting the judgment of God upon our city."[18]

A Baptist minister in Cincinnati emphasized that the ordinance was wrong because it legitimized homosexuality, which, Scripture makes "plain and clear," God rejects. What was at stake, he insisted, was nothing less than the immortal souls of gays, who could not be saved from eternal damnation unless they repented of their sinful behavior. Yet another Baptist pastor, who achieved public prominence for his involvement in the referendum drive, indicated he had never taken a public role before this issue and preferred to work quietly within his own congregation. He now wondered if perhaps God had put him in a leadership position precisely so he could take a high-profile role in the repeal campaign. It is tempting to dismiss this as rationalization for ambition, but that does not seem to be the case. The minister in question has subsequently resisted invitations to run for the city council and seems genuinely committed to building his congregation rather than seeking public office. Except for one black minister who did capitalize on his public prominence to gain a city council seat, the opponents seem to have been motivated by their deep-felt convictions rather than any potential benefits such participation may have conferred.

As Burrington also suggests, opposition to gay rights is just one of a whole packet of priorities that drives Christian conservatives. The "threat" to traditional identity does not begin or end with political mobilization by homosexuals, as serious as that threat is seen to be. From the fundamentalist perspective, our culture has been under assault from all manner of pernicious trends and movements. The rise of feminism undermined the traditional basis of male authority. The ability of women to control their reproductive systems—by birth control and abortion—seemed to raise questions about the sacredness of procreation. No-fault divorce further eroded the notion of marriage as an eternal union prescribed by God. The elimination of government-sponsored prayer in public schools was yet another social change that seemed to undermine a traditional notion of who we are as a people and society. What we recognize today as the "religious right" came into being to fight these various social changes and to deflect the challenge to traditional identity.[19] It took on these threats by defeating the Equal Rights Amendment and, with less success, by trying repeatedly to limit abortion, regulate access to birth control, make divorce harder to obtain, and restore state-supported prayer in schools. The resistance to gay rights may have been an attractive issue precisely because public opinion, so profoundly hostile to gays and lesbians, is more equally divided on the merits of feminism, reproductive rights, and other concerns.

Although they might agree that homosexuality is sinful conduct that threatens the salvation of gays and lesbians, all fundamentalist churches do not become active in the campaign against gay rights. Many fundamentalists remain persuaded that their urgent task is saving souls, not entering political combat. Moreover, to engage in open political action is to raise the possibility that congregations will split over the issue and thus that parishioners will be driven away from the church. There is also the personal cost in becoming publicly identified as a sworn opponent of gay rights, a description that frequently produces charges of bigotry and homophobia. Those local clergy in the five cities we studied who did become involved frequently mentioned that they had to persuade their congregants that such activity was not "political" but was instead "moral" and thus within the minister's appropriate role. They were also contemptuous of those ministers who shared their theological beliefs but were reluctant to get involved because it would threaten the harmony of the church or ministry. Thus, fundamentalist theology is a necessary but not a sufficient basis to explain the antigay rights activism among conservative Protestants.

Roman Catholics

Roman Catholics present another religious constituency that has played an important role in the struggle over local gay rights. If for no other reason than sheer size—Catholicism is the largest Christian denomination in the United States—the position of the church on this issue would be important. But the case of Catholicism is interesting because it shows how a generally conservative and tradition-rich church can adapt to a controversial issue and stake out a distinctive position. Persons who associate the church primarily with the antiabortion movement suppose that it must therefore lead the fight to maintain a privileged position for heterosexuality. This expectation may be reasonable, but it overlooks the strong emphasis on social justice in the Catholic tradition. Influenced by that tradition, the leadership of American Catholicism has taken a strong position in behalf of antipoverty programs, the rights of immigrants, control of nuclear weapons, and other issues usually associated with a liberal agenda. By the same logic, although the church inherits the same religious texts that Protestant fundamentalists rely upon to argue against gay rights, it does not read them in quite the same manner. Because of these differences, we were not surprised to find that the Catholic response to the gay rights campaign was often different from that of fundamentalist Protestants.

Theologically, the contemporary Roman Catholic Church draws a sharp distinction between homosexual orientation, which is not considered sinful in and of itself, and homosexual behavior, which is regarded as contrary to God's law. Although it stops short of labeling homosexual orientation as intrinsically sinful, official church teaching does regard it as an "objective disorder" that "evokes moral concern."[20] Nonetheless, this distinction permits the church to take a more nuanced position toward questions of homosexuality. As long as they forswear sexual activity, gays may enter the priesthood on the same terms as celibate heterosexuals. The church maintains and supports many organizations that offer ministries to gays, the parents of gays and lesbians, and persons afflicted with AIDS. In larger communities that have gay and lesbian neighborhoods, some parishes are recognizably gay. Unlike the similar outreach efforts of Protestant fundamentalists, however, the Catholic mission to gays does not include efforts to "convert" gays to a heterosexual life. Rather, the church aims to enable gays to live within its umbrella.[21]

In practice, this difference does not always matter all that much. For example, the Catholic hierarchy in Philadelphia made essentially the same arguments as the fundamentalist Protestant leaders in other communities. The church could not support legal protection for a sinful behavior that was a matter of choice rather than involuntary. Passage of antidiscrimination laws based on sexual orientation would open the door for other disagreeable policies, such as domestic partner benefits or the like. Even on its own terms, the Philadelphia hierarchy contended, passage of such a law was bad public policy because it endorsed immorality and sent the wrong message about social norms. Even if the style of argument is less based on specific biblical injunctions than is true for fundamentalist Protestants, the content of these arguments has a familiar ring. For Catholic leaders, as for their Protestant counterparts, scriptural and philosophical arguments against homosexuality are available to be deployed if necessary.

Nonetheless, it seems clear that Catholic leaders have not regarded the issue as urgent or compelling as have their counterparts in fundamentalist Protestantism. The supporters of the gay rights ordinance proposed in Philadelphia in 1982 thought that church opposition was more a matter of show than a deep-felt conviction. Beyond issuing a mild statement against the bill, the Catholic Church did not mobilize its congregations nor testify against the proposal at a public hearing. The church's intervention was described as late and half-hearted. Despite the public opposition of Philadelphia's cardinal, several Catholic clergy from the area testified in favor of the bill, and several practicing Catholics on the city council voted for it.[22] In Iowa City, two priests testified in favor of the city's proposed human rights ordinance despite fears by critics that prohibiting discrimination based on sexual orientation and marital status condoned homosexuality and promiscuity.[23] The Catholic churches did not oppose the ordinance, it was argued by gay rights opponents, for fear of offending a parish that was relatively tolerant of gays and lesbians. In Santa Cruz, the church was not much in evidence, although one priest was identified as a supporter of the amendment, and the diocese had sponsored local workshops on combating homophobia in the church.

When the gay rights legislation was up for consideration in the Cincinnati City Council, the archbishop issued an elliptical statement that condemned "arbitrary discrimination and prejudice, violence and harassment against any person because of his or her sexual orientation" and simultaneously declared unacceptable "any legislation which explicitly or implicitly involves acceptance or approval of homosexual behavior, or directly or indirectly promotes a life style that encourages such behavior."[24] As we learned from numerous interviews in the city, that evenhandedness encouraged both advocates and opponents of the legislation to claim church support. Shortly before the 1993 referendum, the archbishop weighed in with a carefully worded statement that encouraged citizens to reject the proposed Issue 3, which prohibited legal protection based on homosexual orientation. Because Issue 3 did not distinguish between practicing homosexuals and people who were homosexually inclined but celibate, he found the amendment "as detrimental to the public good as is the . . . ordinance which it intends to invalidate."[25] Although consistent with the official position of the Roman Catholic Church, this stance drew criticism from conservative Catholics and others who opposed the original ordinance on religious grounds. No wonder that one advocate of the Cincinnati legislation perceived what amounted to "faint" support from the archdiocese.

Despite its reputation as a centralized church with a coherent theology, we found evidence of considerable variation in the Catholic role from one community to the next or even from one period of time to the next. To a degree, this variation seemed to depend on the views of local Catholic leadership and the aggressiveness with which the church pursued the issue. Cardinal John Krol of Philadelphia played a major role in killing the city's first attempt to enact a gay rights ordinance in 1974. By 1982, when public sentiment had moved to a more supportive position, Krol and the church were much less in evidence. When Cardinal Krol retired, his role was taken over by a much more conservative archbishop, who seems to have given the issue much higher priority. Cardinal Anthony Bevilacqua mobilized the church energetically against the 1993 proposal to provide domestic partner benefits. He testified personally against the measure, had a letter of opposition read to parishioners from the pulpit, and distributed postcards opposing the policy to members of the city council. These efforts were cited by a former public official of Philadelphia as the major reason domestic partner legislation did not pass. A year later, the cardinal deployed the same tactics in an attempt to defeat a new city charter, which differed from the gay rights ordinance in that it failed to exempt religious organizations from the sexual orientation provision of the ordinance. Of course, the more aggressive stance of the church in 1993 and 1994 was partly because domestic partner benefits and the new charter were recognized as more threatening to Catholic social policy and as more intrusive than a relatively benign policy of nondiscrimination in employment and hiring. But some of the difference in energy and involvement undoubtedly reflected the change in clerical leadership.

Black Evangelicals

The American civil rights movement is so strongly associated in the public mind with African Americans that it often shocks observers when black Americans oppose legislation to extend civil rights protections to gays and lesbians. Surely, it is believed, a people who have suffered so greatly from bigotry and have achieved a measure of deliverance from changes in the law would understand the attempt by another beleaguered minority to secure similar protection. When reality does not correspond to this expectation, gays, lesbians, and their allies are often bitterly disappointed.

Upon closer examination, the expectation of monolithic black support for gay rights overlooks many factors that potentially divide African Americans from the coalition that favors extending antidiscrimination protection. Local governments devote limited resources to probing complaints of discrimination based on race, ethnicity, gender, and other categories recognized in civil rights legislation. Accordingly, adding another category as a basis for legal complaints potentially dilutes the resources available to combat racial discrimination and may even threaten to produce a new class of people eligible for affirmative action. Thus, some blacks think about antidiscrimination efforts as a zero-sum game in which new claimants for legal protection reduce the resources available to assist their own community. As we have mentioned before, that dilution may be particularly galling when blacks perceive gays to be quite different from their own community. The most visible leaders of the gay rights movement are often perceived as affluent and privileged whites representing a constituency that simply cannot match the experience of the black community in suffering and discrimination. The claim that gays "choose" a lifestyle often resonates with black critics, who pointedly emphasize that they had no choice about their race or the way they were treated by the white majority.

Apart from competition for the antidiscrimination budget, a strong religious factor may also turn blacks against what some observers regard as their "natural" allies in the gay and lesbian community. The black community in the United States is much more church-based than its white counterpart, and black political leadership, today as in the civil rights period, is still drawn disproportionately from the ranks of the clergy. Although black religious commitment is as diverse as the community itself, most African Americans worship in churches that promote an evangelical theology. Refracted through the black experience of slavery and oppression, African-American evangelicalism both resembles and differs from its white counterpart in ways that affect black attitudes to gay rights.

On the one hand, black theology emphasizes what is called the "prophetic," a religious call to society to treat all its citizens justly. In the moving rhetoric of a Martin Luther King or a Ralph Abernathy, this impulse manifests itself as a divinely inspired demand for equality and human dignity. For blacks embedded in this tradition, adding sexual orientation as a protected category in antidiscrimination legislation is part and parcel of the civil rights agenda, and excluding gays is contrary to the entire spirit of the human rights movement. Both Jesse Jackson, King's heir as the preeminent black spokesman in America, and King's widow have embraced the gay rights movement and campaigned personally to encourage blacks to stand with the gay rights campaign. In many communities, black council members were instrumental in passing gay rights legislation.

On the other hand, black evangelicalism also emphasizes the moral traditionalism that has been a hallmark of white Protestant fundamentalism. Although it has seldom been noticed, African Americans are as a group considerably less liberal on social issues than white Americans.[26] This difference is apparent in regard to the abortion issue, on which black attitudes are much closer to that of white evangelicals than other religious groups. Moral traditionalism is also a basis for antigay attitudes. Thus an African-American minister in Cincinnati justified his objection to gay rights on the grounds that "[t]here's no place for homosexuals and lesbianism in Judeo-Christian teaching."[27] Another black minister in the city, when asked about the agenda of the gay movement, reduced it to a desire to "sodomize the kids."

Because of these conflicting forces, the position of the black community has varied enormously from one place to another. In Santa Cruz and Iowa City, neither of which has a large black community, the black church was not cited as a major player on this issue, and the local NAACP was described as uninvolved. In Raleigh, even though the black community was not organized in opposition, a black member of the city council had been severely criticized by African-American clergy for his support of the ordinance. Some black ministers registered public objections in Philadelphia but did not actively mobilize the African-American community to oppose the city's gay rights provision. The divergent perspectives of the black community were evident in the wildly conflicting estimates about black attitudes to the Philadelphia ordinance. We were told by three of the people we interviewed that the black community was, respectively, overwhelmingly supportive of the gay rights law, just supportive, and equally divided between supporters and opponents. By 1993, black ministers, with prodding from the new Catholic archbishop, were drawn into the alliance against domestic partner benefits, and ministers from the city's largest Muslim and black Baptist congregations joined the archbishop in testifying at a public hearing. Many of the black members of the city council who had voted for the gay rights ordinance in 1982 voted against domestic partner benefits as a result.

In Cincinnati, the power of church-based moral tradition was strong enough to push the majority of the black community into active opposition to gay rights. Indeed, it is not too much to say that inspiring black resistance to the sexual orientation provision of the city's new human rights ordinance was the centerpiece of the opposition campaign. Opponents of the Cincinnati repeal campaign recognized the value of splitting blacks from the liberal coalition that normally operates in urban affairs. Apart from producing black votes to repeal that provision, the open opposition of blacks would signal to moderate whites that one could support repeal without being a bigot. The way to send this message, to "frame" the issue so it was not a "civil rights" issue, was to feature black opposition to gay rights in the referendum campaign. The point man in these efforts was the Reverend K. Z. Smith, a young pastor who was serving as the head of the Baptist Ministers Conference when the ordinance was first proposed.[28] An able and articulate spokesperson, Smith appeared at numerous forums and churches throughout the city, was featured on billboards calling for repeal, and even appeared on national television talk shows as a representative of the anti–gay rights movement. The black leaders who joined Smith in the repeal campaign sent a message that gays were a "privileged group seeking special protection at the expense of the legitimate rights of the African-American community." If the ordinance stood as passed by the city council, black audiences were told, it would give businesses a green light to hire white gays—or whites who claimed to be gay—ahead of black heterosexuals. This fit in with the intent of repeal organizers to undermine the analogy between black and gay oppression by prompting voters to ask themselves, as one conservative activist put it, "Is committing homosexual sodomy the same thing as being black?"

The strategy evidently worked because a large majority—perhaps as high as three-fifths—of black voters endorsed the repeal of the sexual orientation provision of the human rights ordinance. The strong mobilization of black churchgoers overwhelmed the voices in the black community calling upon African-Americans to treat gays as an oppressed minority. During the campaign to repeal the sexual orientation provision of the human rights ordinance, the city's NAACP chapter remained conspicuously silent. Those black churches thought to be sympathetic to the gay community, principally the various Methodist denominations, did not take a public stand.

This strategy produced strange bedfellows indeed. None of the clergy we interviewed in Cincinnati, black or white, could recall a single instance before the Issue 3 referendum when black and white clergy had cooperated on a common political venture. Nor was there much evidence of subsequent activity. In Philadelphia, the cooperation of Roman Catholics and black ministers in the fight against domestic partner benefits did lead to further joint action in an attempt to ban handguns in the city.

The Business Community

Although it was not usually identified as a key source of opposition in our survey, the business community did play a role in restricting gay rights ordinances in many locales. In large measure, the tendency of informants not to identify this constituency as a primary opponent may reflect the style of opposition. Rather than oppose ordinances in their totality, the local business community often attempted to structure the protection in a way that would minimize its effect on business.

In Santa Cruz, for example, some local business owners focused their criticism not on the sexual orientation provision but rather on the phrase that prohibited discrimination based on "physical appearance." Complaining that this might force them to hire people with spiked purple hair, tattoos, nose rings, or pierced tongues, these business owners successfully prompted the council to redefine the provision so that it covered "physical characteristics" like weight and disabilities rather than matters of fashion and taste. In response to lobbying by landlords and small property owners, the Iowa City ordinance was amended by the council in 1977 to exempt landlords offering rental housing. Such property owners were included under the ordinance when it was amended again in 1984, and most of the debate focused on the desire of some landlords to preserve adult-only complexes. In Raleigh, businesses did not object to the original ordinance in 1988, which applied only to government agencies, but complained loudly in 1993 when gay rights advocates attempted, unsuccessfully, to extend the ordinance to the private sector. Working through the chamber of commerce and Better Business Bureau, business opponents encouraged ministers whose parishioners objected to testify against the extension.

In Cincinnati, the local chamber of commerce took a formal position of opposition to the ordinance on grounds of both necessity and the cost to small businesses. When the repeal effort began, some members of the business community worried that the city was vulnerable to a boycott by gay rights supporters and would suffer economically if the ordinance was overturned. We received information that some business leaders played an important role in the referendum campaign on Issue 3. One city council member argued that business was the key opponent of gay rights but that it preferred to work in the background through proxy organizations. This member attributed business opposition both to the ideological conservatism of corporate elites and, more tangibly, to fears that the ordinance would impose huge costs in the form of mandatory coverage for HIV-infected employees. While this version of events might be dismissed as the rumblings of a sore loser, we heard other comments from knowledgeable members of the business community that added credence to it. One businessperson we interviewed thought that much of a $390,000 contribution to the repeal effort from a Colorado pro-family organization actually originated as a donation from a conservative Cincinnati business leader that was laundered through the out-of-state source. The president of the city's Convention Bureau, who was particularly concerned about a boycott of Cincinnati by national organizations, initially advised the city council not to appeal the federal court ruling that invalidated the repeal referendum; he was overruled by the bureau's board of directors, however, after they met with business leaders active in the repeal campaign. To add further credence to these reports, one of the attorneys who helped argue the federal case against the Issue 3 repeal was fired shortly thereafter by his prestigious law firm, one of the city's oldest and best connected.[29] Cincinnati presents the strongest instance of business influence arrayed against the gay rights movement.

In large measure, the role of the business community depended on the size and scale of the businesses. Many large corporations already had nondiscrimination policies and active programs to combat sexual harassment. Such major Philadelphia employers as Cigna Insurance, Bell Telephone, the University of Pennsylvania, and Temple University had adopted nondiscrimination codes prior to adoption of the city ordinance. In Cincinnati the same was true of Federated Department Stores, Procter and Gamble, and the Hyatt Hotel chain, major corporations with headquarters in the city. After Raleigh failed to require local businesses to observe nondiscrimination against gays and lesbians, one of the largest local employers announced its decision to extend spousal benefits to the unmarried partners of gay employees. The University of Iowa, the dominant economic force in Iowa City, also adopted domestic partner benefits for its employees. As businesses compete fiercely to attract qualified employees, many have decided that nondiscrimination policies and spousal benefits offer a competitive advantage and regard homophobia as an inefficient business practice.

With the exception of the conservative corporate executives in Cincinnati, business opposition to gay rights legislation came mostly from small businesses and the self-employed.[30] Small business is often the source of resistance to proposals for government regulation both because such enterprises probably are more vulnerable to the costs of complying with regulation and because small business owners often subscribe to a strong free market ideology. In Raleigh, this resistance was further reinforced by the overlap between the owners of small businesses and the fundamentalist religious community.

The Organization of the Opposition

What did opponents of gay rights do as their communities considered and then passed antidiscrimination legislation that included sexual orientation as a basis for complaints? To a considerable degree, the nature of the opposition seemed to reflect the political culture and traditions of the community. In the progressive and left-leaning climates of Santa Cruz and Iowa City, it was difficult to find more than traces of opposition. Apart from an occasional letter to the editor, an angry speech to the city council, or a group presence at public hearings on the measures, the opposition barely constituted a "movement." In Philadelphia and Raleigh, two communities with a reputation for moderation rather than bold experimentation, proponents of gay rights moved cautiously lest they inspire intense opposition from the large and influential population of Catholics and evangelicals in their respective communities. The initial legislation in each city was narrowly drawn to avoid inflaming public opinion. These efforts succeeded initially, as strong opposition movements failed to crystallize in either city, but they undermined later attempts to expand the scope of the legal protection based on sexual orientation.

Cincinnati presented the most compelling evidence of a strong opposition movement. As noted elsewhere, the passage of the human rights legislation in Cincinnati was controversial from the beginning, passed amid considerable opposition, and produced a countermovement that succeeded in repealing the ordinance by popular vote. Not by coincidence, Cincinnati has long had a reputation as the censorship capital of America, a community that bans adult bookstores, indecent literature, sexually explicit businesses, and erotic art exhibits. The challenge to gay rights was just another incident in the community's long war in behalf of cultural conservatism.

As is common in social movements, the mobilization against gay rights drew on existing organizations. In Santa Cruz, what little opposition was apparent was coordinated by the Forum, an evangelical network that distributed a local newsletter and had a weekly talk show on local radio. Although principally devoted to the antiabortion cause, it quickly adopted an oppositional stance toward gay rights and became a major means of communication among conservative Christian opponents of the ordinance. When it came time for a public hearing on the proposed legislation, the Forum devoted most of its publication space and air time to the theme and drew on its associated congregations to promote attendance at the hearing. In Iowa City, such opposition as emerged seemed to be the product of individual clergy who essentially recruited themselves. The Raleigh opposition, mute in 1988, was larger and better prepared to contest attempts to broaden the ordinance in 1993. Opponents used in-home prayer meetings, a Christian businessmen's group, a Christian radio station, and a television talk show as their primary means to stoke opposition to the 1993 proposal. Fundamentalist churches supplemented these efforts with sermons and newsletter appeals to churchgoers, resulting in city officials' being hounded by telephone calls against the extension.

The most significant of all opposition campaigns, the repeal campaign in Cincinnati, was based on a broad coalition of thirty-two organizations under the banner of Equal Rights, Not Special Rights (ERNSR). The pro-family groups arrayed under this heading included local affiliates of national organizations (such as the American Family Association), local organizations devoted to various conservative causes (Citizens for Community Values), and special-purpose groups organized around particular issues such as abortion, pornography, public displays of "indecent" art, and sex education. Unlike the ad hoc coalitions in other cities, the Cincinnati movement persisted after the successful repeal. It targeted for defeat the city council members who had voted for the human rights ordinance with the sexual orientation clause, hired lawyers to defend the repeal in federal court, and generally kept up the pressure on the city to withhold support from homosexuality. By late 1994, ERNSR had raised and spent more than $800,000 in fighting the ordinance. The funds spent to elect repeal advocates to the city council raised the overall spending level of gay rights opponents to $2 million.

These opposition movements did not draw extensively on broadly based political organizations like political parties. In the Cincinnati referendum effort, the local Republican organization endorsed the repeal option, and many Republican activists were involved in the campaign; the party itself, however, did nothing beyond recommending a "yes" vote.[31] The Philadelphia archdiocese was careful not to appeal for Republican support in its campaign against domestic partner benefits for fear such action would threaten the church's nonpartisan reputation and make it difficult to appeal to Democratic council members on other issues. A conservative religious activist in Santa Cruz reported that the local Republican organization was split on the issue and stayed out of the public debate.

Despite these differences of organization from one community to another, we identified certain similarities in the opposition movements of the five communities. The most striking was the use of common arguments and evidence against the gay rights movement. Does this suggest that the local opponents of gay rights were part of a broader national movement of resistance to gay rights? That suspicion gains plausibility from the reports that national leaders of the "cultural conservatism" movement met privately in 1994 to chart a coherent plan of opposition to the extension of gay rights in the United States. According to a taped transcript of the meeting that was leaked to a sympathetic reporter, the leaders hoped to make the issue the centerpiece of grass-roots mobilization for Christian activists.[32]

Rather than regard the family resemblances among the local opposition movements as evidence of some national conspiracy, however, it seems more reasonable to suggest that they are a product both of coincidence and coordination. There is nothing particularly strange about finding similar objections to gay rights in different communities. The main opponents, the business community and Protestant fundamentalists, have clear interests in challenging the extension of gay rights legislation. The former fears legal penalties and, more generally, objects to government regulation of its enterprises. Under the circumstances, we would expect common arguments from businesspeople. The same is true for antigay religious activists for whom theological arguments against homosexuality are common staples of preaching and social activism. Seminary training, denominational conferences, national newsletters, and other mechanisms help to shape the rhetoric of the opposition. In much the same way, the fact that proponents of gay rights sound alike regardless of locale does not mean that local movements are the creation of a centralized drive directed from a national headquarters in New York or Washington.

Antigay activists, like their gay rights counterparts, can draw upon many national organizations that serve as clearinghouses for information and arguments. The most prominent of these organizations are California's Traditional Values Coalition; Colorado for Family Values; the Family Research Council of Washington, D.C.; and Focus on the Family in Colorado Springs. Local opposition groups often acquired material from these sources, reprinting it with adaptations to the local community.[33] It seems likely that these external organizations also provided the names of funding sources and political advice to local activists who sought help in resisting or repealing gay rights laws.

Reliance on these networks helps to account for the considerable overlap in the opposition literature around the country. For example, opponents often present statistical evidence that portrays "the gay lifestyle" as fundamentally unhealthy or that cites various information sources to establish the threat of "a gay agenda." We found opponents in all cities quite conversant with abstract legal doctrines regarding the conditions under which courts define a group of people as a "protected class" and thus submit legislation involving group members to what is known as "strict scrutiny." Further research revealed that these arguments originated in materials distributed by one or more of the national organizations. Most statistics on the health, demography, and alleged sexual practices of homosexuals can be traced back to the research of Paul Cameron's Institute for the Scientific Investigation of Sexuality. Despite Cameron's expulsion from the American Psychological Association and shoddy research practices, his materials are widely circulated among antigay activists.[34] Thus we found many references to "facts," such as the claim that the average life expectancy of gay males was just forty-one or that gays accounted for a third to one-half of the sexual assaults on children. Both of these claims originated in Cameron's various pamphlets and newsletters.

Another common source of mobilization, a staple of opposition tactics, was the use of videotapes prepared by national organizations. In all the communities we observed directly, the opponents of gay rights relied heavily on the *Gay Rights, Special Rights* video program that was produced and distributed by Lou Sheldon's Traditional Values Coalition. The video mixes on-camera interviews of such conservative luminaries as Sen. Trent Lott (R-Miss.)

and the Christian Coalition's Ralph Reed with highly inflammatory clips from gay rights demonstrations and marches. It also prominently features many black men and women who heatedly deny the status of gay people as a "legitimate" minority entitled to legal protection.

When Cincinnati's antigay movement organized to repeal the sexual orientation provision of the human rights ordinance, it drew much of its support from these networks, and leaders made no secret of their alliance with the national antigay campaign. Philip Burress, who headed Citizens for Community Values, described the Cincinnati repeal campaign as "part of a wave that is sweeping the country."[35] In the campaign itself, his organization drew considerable funding from outside the local community, although, as noted earlier, many of these funds appeared to have been transferred indirectly from Cincinnati business leaders who did not want to be identified publicly.

What can we conclude about the balance of organizational power between groups favoring and opposing gay rights ordinances? It probably depends on the arena of conflict. When the issue is fought out largely among decision makers with little public involvement, gays may face something close to an even playing field. Under such conditions a small group like the gay community can engage in discreet lobbying with some hope of success.[36] The application of local antidiscrimination laws to cover sexual orientation is likely to be a high priority for the organized gay community and can be portrayed to local legislators as an incremental extension of existing law. The prospects of success are improved if gays are perceived by public officials to have affected previous election outcomes in some way. Just such factors accounted for the success of ordinance passage in all our case study communities (see Chapter 3). Similarly, gays face a relatively promising environment when the issue of antidiscrimination protection reaches the courts. In the judicial setting, numbers of opponents count less than the content of the law, the views of a judge, and the quality of advocacy. Accordingly, gays have achieved some important courtroom successes that eluded them in open political combat.

When the issue captures public attention and significant opposition is mobilized, the gay community faces a severe organizational disadvantage. Its minority status, negative public evaluation, and limited organizational resources make it vulnerable to defeat by an aroused opposition. Reflecting this reality, gay activists in several of our case studies failed repeatedly in early attempts to pass antidiscrimination laws. This disadvantage intensifies when the issue comes to a public vote. In referendums, the local gay organization is typically no match for a network of opposition churches that possess such crucial organizational resources as public credibility, physical space, membership lists, professional staffs, ready access to volunteers, and a community-wide communication network. In some communities, church-based opposition movements can raise money from allied organizations in the political and business community and draw on the assistance of the national organizations devoted to moral traditionalism. The local gay movement, by contrast, seldom obtains much financial or organizational support from its allies—certainly nothing on the scale that opponents obtain from sympathetic elements in the business community—and it has a much smaller and appreciably less wealthy group of national organizations to assist in the battle. This characteristic imbalance of resources contributes to the overwhelming pattern of defeat for gay advocates in local referendums about gay rights legislation.[37]

Themes in the Opposition Campaign

The language and images used by political activists may both reveal and conceal true motives. In the case of the campaign against gay rights, the rhetoric used has been carefully crafted to avoid arguments that might alienate public opinion. This showed most clearly in the public referendums on gay rights laws passed by local governments. It was also apparent, however, when the issue was decided by local government officials. In these campaigns, the opponents of gay rights generally followed three principles: avoid "God talk," appear tolerant, and emphasize "rights talk."

Although the core of opposition to gay rights is located in traditionalist religious communities, many activists have come to understand that religiously motivated campaigns are often politically counterproductive. Claims that homosexuality is contrary to God's law or will bring down God's wrath might rally the faithful but will probably antagonize the numerous swing voters whose votes determine the outcome of referendums. Such voters may resent claims that their faith is associated with only one side in a political dispute or, more generally, may worry about breaching the wall of separation between church and state. This lesson was learned well by the Christian activists who watched the repeated national failures of the pioneering religious right movement in the 1980s. From that experience, most have learned to couch their proposals in language that does not rely on explicit religious appeals. Indeed, many religious conservatives prefer to be known as either "cultural" or "social" conservatives, terms that have no explicit reference to theology or creed. This explains why the Cincinnati repeal effort, motivated fundamentally by people who regard homosexuality as morally objectionable, a matter of "sin and damnation," scrupulously avoided such language in their public communication.

A second part of this rhetorical strategy is the appearance of open-mindedness and tolerance, or at least the avoidance of blatant homophobia. Again, the American public generally prides itself on tolerance and has shown an increasing openness to accept gays as members of the community. A repeal campaign that is understood to be a crusade against gays, incorporating harassment, violence, or overt discrimination as part of the agenda, could well rebound and push uncommitted voters to the side of the beleaguered minority. Thus, the opponents of gay rights have generally tried to appear calm and reasonable and to ground their differences with gays in a language of moderation. The organizers of the Cincinnati repeal campaign insisted they were not homophobic, called for a "clean, respectful" crusade, and disassociated themselves from strident visitors like the Reverend Lou Sheldon, the head of the California-based Traditional Values Coalition. Most have taken pains to emphasize that they do not want to encourage discrimination, they only want to build a "live and let live atmosphere." Indeed, the opponents often argue that the community had achieved a kind of peaceful resolution of the issue until "militant gays" destroyed public harmony by insisting on legal privileges. Then, reluctantly, the religious traditionalists felt compelled to react but always sorrowfully and in a spirit of compassion. In this effort, they assert, they are not "antigay" but are merely opposed to giving legal endorsement to gays.

Despite this concerted effort to appear free of religious prejudice and anti-gay bigotry, the opponents do not always succeed. As noted earlier, one can find in their language and signs lurid stereotypes of gays as child molesters, sources of disease, and an abomination in the eyes of God. In the more sophisticated campaigns, this theme is promoted by emphasizing the threat of gay school-based programs to children. A circular distributed by advocates of repeal in Alachua County, Florida, asked voters if they were concerned about:

- Who cares for your children or your grandchildren?
- Who teaches your child or grandchild?
- Who will teach your child what is normal sexual behavior?
- Who counsels your children with their personal problems in school?
- Who leads your child on camping trips in the Boy Scouts or Girl Scouts?[38]

These questions become relevant only if the reader assumes gays are prone to molest children entrusted to their care or will use their position to recruit children to the gay subculture.[39]

The third component of the anti–gay rights rhetoric, perhaps the most important, is the use of "rights talk."[40] American political language in the last half of the twentieth century has often been framed in terms of the human and political rights to which citizens are entitled. The case for extending antidiscrimination laws to cover sexual orientation is part of this process and makes a strong claim on public opinion precisely because the concept of equal rights is so central to our understanding of justice. With considerable sophistication, the opponents of gay rights have appropriated this language and turned it on its head. A veteran of the gay rights movement, Suzanne Pharr, has identified five steps by which this is accomplished. The opponents begin by defining civil rights as "a special category for 'minorities' such as people of color and women." These are not rights available to all citizens, it is suggested, but rights reserved specifically for minority groups that have suffered discrimination. Second, the legal protections associated with civil rights are further defined as "'Special Rights' that can be given or taken away by the majority, who have ordinary rights, not 'special rights.'" In the third step of this process, opponents of gay rights contend that such special rights are "earned" by people who "qualify" on the basis of various hardships. Special rights are deemed appropriate treatment for such suffering. Fourth, it is suggested that extending special rights does impose a cost on society. Specifically, the preferential policies enacted on behalf of minorities "have resulted in the loss of jobs for deserving, 'qualified' people through affirmative action and quotas."[41]

With the stage set by these four arguments, the anti–gay rights forces move to their central conclusion: gay people do not deserve special rights.[42] This crucial claim may be based on a belief that gays have simply not suffered discrimination on a scale anything like that of the other minorities society has justifiably decided to protect—principally, African Americans. Even more strongly, some opponents argue, gays are the polar opposite of blacks in terms of affluence and political power. Indeed, opponents contend, gays may simply avoid discrimination by concealing their sexual identity. Taking another tack, opponents may concede that gays do suffer from various forms of discrimination but argue that society has a right to show its disapproval of people who choose to behave in a certain way. "Deserving" minorities— African Americans and the physically disabled—have no choice in their condition and so are entitled to special rights. But gays, it is argued, make a conscious decision to embrace a "gay lifestyle" and so cannot qualify for the same minority status and the privileges that go with it. With civil rights defined as special privileges reserved for certain minorities, it is equally effective to argue that gays do not meet the standard either because of inadequate suffering or because their suffering results from voluntary choice.[43]

With this chain of reasoning, the opponents are able to describe the campaign for gay rights as a power grab by militant homosexuals. This image recurs frequently in the language of opposition, particularly in the title of organizations that challenge the gay rights movement. In both Cincinnati and Tampa the repeal movements appealed to voters to "take back" their cities. The suggestive language conveys an image that these communities have been overrun by alien forces and that local patriots must organize to regain control.

Conclusion

The opposition to the campaigns for gay rights was often intense, reflecting the strong views that animate social conservatives. It was also frequently well organized. Although the business community may have played an important role in challenging gay rights proposals, often behind the scenes, the more common pattern was for public leadership to be vested in religious groups in the evangelical, or fundamentalist, wing of American Protestantism. In their efforts to dramatize the issue and rally the community in behalf of repeal efforts, these groups often used the language and slogans of the culture war, implying that the conflict was a clash of moral absolutes with enormous consequences for society.

These findings generally support the communal protest model. Of the policy models used in this book, only the communal protest model devotes much attention to the forces and institutions that resist social movements, such as the campaign against gay rights ordinances. According to this perspective, the social changes associated with rapid urbanization, economic development, and declining religious authority are particularly unsettling to people who are deeply enmeshed in traditional institutions and committed to a particular way of life. The campaign by gay rights advocates to redefine sexual and social identity has predictably encountered its most severe challenge from people deeply rooted in fundamentalist religious networks who condemn homosexuality as contrary to Scripture, "natural law," and the family. Persons with this perspective see gay rights legislation as a pernicious policy that will further undermine social order, promote what they call "alternative lifestyle" choices, and diminish public respect for traditional values. As American politics increasingly confronts questions of social identity based on challenges to traditional ways of life and social norms, we can expect more frequent episodes of communal protest.

NOTES

Because of the controversial nature of this study, we promised the persons we interviewed that they would not be identified by name. Unless otherwise noted, all interviews pertaining to Iowa City took place in Iowa City in June 1994; all those pertaining to Philadelphia took place in Philadelphia in July 1994; all those pertaining to Raleigh took place either in Raleigh or Chapel Hill, N.C., in May 1994; all those pertaining to Santa Cruz took place in Santa Cruz in June 1994, and all those pertaining to Cincinnati took place in Cincinnati in November 1994. All quotations and information not otherwise documented are from these interviews.

1. Peter Bronson, "Nobody Will Win This Election," *Cincinnati Enquirer,* October 31, 1993.
2. Ibid.

3. Richard G. Howe, "Homosexuality in America: Exposing the Myths," World Wide Web site of the American Family Association (http://gocin.com/afa/toc.htm), June 1996.

4. Three of the jurisdictions in our sample—Alachua County, Florida; Cincinnati; and Tampa—repealed their ordinances by referendum, and those in Colorado were overturned by a statewide vote that was subsequently invalidated by the U.S. Supreme Court.

5. National Gay and Lesbian Task Force, "The Record on Gay-Related Referenda Questions," memorandum, May 20, 1996, National Gay and Lesbian Task Force, Washington, D.C.

6. It is difficult to tell how much of this pattern is due to memory and how much to real change. The survey was done in 1993, and those representing communities that passed ordinances twenty years ago may have forgotten how much conflict was aroused by gay rights policies. Yet it is also possible that such communities passed ordinances twenty years ago precisely because their communities were more open to nontraditional ideas and faced little opposition at the time.

7. Kenneth D. Wald, James W. Button, and Barbara A. Rienzo, "The Politics of Gay Rights in American Communities: Explaining Antidiscrimination Ordinances and Policies," *American Journal of Political Science* 40 (November 1996): 1152–1178.

8. It should be noted that these theories refer principally to the *leadership* of the campaign against gay rights. In most communities, neither business leaders nor religious conservatives are sufficiently numerous to defeat gay rights proposals in referendums. Nonetheless, these groups are most often identified as the key agents in defeating or repealing legislation that adds sexual orientation to antidiscrimination law.

9. A similar set of responses emerged when we asked school board administrators about the opponents of school-based programs concerning sexual orientation.

10. Urvashi Vaid, *Virtual Equality: The Mainstreaming of Gay and Lesbian Liberation* (New York: Doubleday, Anchor, 1995), 17.

11. "Open Letter to the Santa Cruz City Council," *Forum,* April 28, 1992, 1.

12. See Chapter 3 for the alternative scriptural understanding of homosexuality commonly endorsed by mainline Protestants and religious liberals.

13. Burholme Baptist Church, "Opposition to Bill No. 1358," memorandum to Philadelphia City Council Members, August 4, 1982, Burholme Baptist Church, Philadelphia.

14. John W. Espy, "Continuing the Discussion: 'Homosexuality and the Church,'" *Christianity and Crisis* 37 (May 30 and June 13, 1977): 116.

15. Debra Burrington, "Competing Visions of Community: The Religious Right and Gay Rights" (paper presented at the annual meeting of the American Political Science Association, Washington, D.C., 1993), 7.

16. Jim Woodall, "Lawfully Wedded?" *Family Voice* 18 (April 1996): 5.

17. Ibid. Reread the first sentence of the quotation but without the phrase "established by God." At first glance it seems quite plausible that a household unit headed by two people of the same sex with children could fulfill all the functions identified by this definition of marriage—nourishing one another emotionally, raising children in safety, providing a strong sense of discipline and social responsibility. Keep in mind, further, that the power to confer marital status does not by law require religious approval. The United States has a system of civil marriage. People may choose whether or not to consecrate their marriage with religious rites. Moreover, there is no compulsory childbearing in the United States. A married couple does not forfeit its legal status if it remains childless nor does the state forbid unmarried people from having and raising children. Thus the institution of marriage, in a legal sense, does not necessarily have a religious basis or involve the raising of children. So gay marriage threatens only a particular definition of what makes a marriage and family. Of course, it is undeniable that most people envision a "family" to be made up of a heterosexual couple with biological offspring.

18. Charles E. Sams, remarks made at the Public Hearing on Human Rights Ordinance before the Law and Public Safety Committee of City Council, Cincinnati, Ohio, October 13, 1992.

19. Alan Crawford, *Thunder on the Right* (New York: Pantheon, 1980).

20. Congregation for the Doctrine of the Faith, "Responding to Legislative Proposals on Discrimination Against Homosexuals," *Origins* (Catholic News Service Documentary Service) 22 (August 6, 1992): 176.

21. This difference between Catholicism and fundamentalist Protestantism is partially explained by the difference between churches and sects. *Churches,* as the term is used sociologically,

define themselves as inclusive communities open to all, whereas *sects* are exclusive religious organizations that restrict membership to people who are willing to accept a specific creed. Consistent with this differing emphasis, Catholicism stresses a search for ways to enable gays to remain within the fold, whereas the more sectlike Protestant fundamentalists regard homosexuality as grounds for expulsion.

22. Joseph Ryan, "Gay Rights Bill Passes Despite Archdiocesan Request," *Catholic Standard and Times,* August 12, 1982.
23. Larry Eckholt, "Iowa City Council Urged to Ban Bias toward Gays," *Des Moines Register,* March 16, 1977.
24. Daniel E. Pilarczyk, "Statement of Archbishop Pilarczyk on Possible Gay Rights Legislation in the City of Cincinnati," letter distributed by the Archdiocese of Cincinnati, Cincinnati, June 15, 1992.
25. Daniel E. Pilarczyk, "Statement of Archbishop Pilarczyk Concerning the Proposed Amendment to the Charter of the City of Cincinnati," letter distributed by the Archdiocese of Cincinnati, Cincinnati, September 13, 1993.
26. Kenneth D. Wald, *Religion and Politics in the United States,* 3d ed. (Washington, D.C.: CQ Press, 1997), 184–188.
27. Beth Menge, "Catholic Gays Begin to Seek Acceptance," *Cincinnati Enquirer,* November 16, 1992.
28. The Reverend Charles Winburn, another black clergyman, was the first prominent spokesman against the ordinance from the African-American community. Smith was tapped for his leadership role during the campaign to pass Issue 3.
29. Ben L. Kaufman, "Gay Lawyer Says Firm Forced Him to Quit," *Cincinnati Enquirer,* October 9, 1993.
30. One should bear in mind that some of the strongest public proponents of the legislation were gay business owners. Business owners who catered primarily to the gay community were freer than gays employed by others to stand up publicly for gay rights.
31. In the referendum, the Democrats and a local reform group known as the Charter Party also took formal positions—against the repeal of the sexual orientation provision—but do not seem to have played a large role in the campaign.
32. Tom Roberts, "Right Takes New Aim at Gays," *National Catholic Reporter,* September 2, 1994.
33. See, for example, Charles E. Winburn, "Should Heterosexuals, Gays or Lesbians be Granted Special Status and Privileges under Cincinnati 'Protected Class' Ordinances?" privately circulated paper, Cincinnati.
34. Mark E. Pietrzyk, *The Man behind the Myths: A Report on the Chief Anti-Gay Researcher of the Religious Right* (Washington, D.C.: Log Cabin Republicans, 1994).
35. Howard Wilkinson, "Gays, Religious Right Square Off," *Cincinnati Enquirer,* June 28, 1993.
36. Donald P. Haider-Markel and Kenneth J. Meier, "The Politics of Gay and Lesbian Rights: Expanding the Scope of the Conflict," *Journal of Politics* 58 (May 1996): 332–349.
37. National Gay and Lesbian Task Force, *The Record on Gay-Related Referenda Questions* (Washington, D.C.: National Gay and Lesbian Task Force, 1996).
38. Circular headed "Informed Choice," distributed as a political advertisement by the Concerned Citizens of Alachua County, in possession of the authors.
39. For evidence that these fears are misplaced, see Carole Jenny, Thomas A. Roesler, and Kimberly L. Poyer, "Are Children at Risk for Sexual Abuse by Homosexuals?" *Pediatrics* 94 (July 1994): 41–44.
40. Mary Ann Glendon, *Rights Talk: The Impoverishment of Political Discourse* (New York: Free Press, 1991).
41. Suzanne Pharr, "Multi-Issue Politics," *Transformation* 9 (January/February 1994): 3.
42. Ibid.
43. Jane S. Schacter, "The Gay Civil Rights Debate in the States: Decoding the Discourse of Equivalents," *Harvard Civil Rights/Civil Liberties Review* 29 (summer, 1994): 283–317.

CHAPTER 7

Gay Rights and American Politics

Without doubt, the group identities that have lasted longest and cut deepest are the ones that persecution has engraved. Once engraved, they stay engraved—that has been the reality.
— Todd Gitlin, "Where We're Coming From: Blinded Identities," *The Good Society*

O nce hidden in the shadows of American politics, the gay rights movement has now claimed a place on the national agenda. Before 1992, if the phrase *gay politics* meant anything at all to most Americans, it probably connoted only the struggle over funding AIDS research. In the tumultuous years since then, the political concerns of gay and lesbian Americans have often become front-page news. At the 1992 Republican National Convention in Houston, speaker after speaker warned in animated language about a gay threat to the traditional American family. Almost from the moment he assumed the presidency in 1993, President Bill Clinton was engulfed in controversy about his pledge to repeal the ban on gays and lesbians in the U.S. armed forces. In 1996 the U.S. Supreme Court decided that the voters of Colorado had violated the Constitution when they passed a referendum prohibiting protected legal status for gays, lesbians, and bisexuals. That same year, the prospect that the Hawaiian Supreme Court would mandate legal recognition of gay unions prompted social conservatives to raise national alarms about the specter of gay marriage. In response, the federal government passed the Defense of Marriage Act, designed to prevent same-sex marriages. The prominence of these issues suggests that the gay political movement, like its constituency, has begun to emerge from the closet.

Clearly, the issues raised by the lesbian and gay community have become the subject of much national debate. Prior to the early 1990s, however, the focus of gay politics was primarily at the local level and, indeed, much significant activity continues at the grass roots. The struggle to win protection against discrimination and thereby gain greater equality, one of the most basic goals for lesbians and gay men, has been concentrated in American cities and counties because there are no federal (and few state) antidiscrimination codes. Gays have met with considerable opposition and hostility in this quest, and a firestorm of political conflict has been the result in many communities. In this book, we have charted the contours of the battle over gay rights at the grass roots. This exploration has encompassed a close look at the political forces that promote local gay rights movements, the precise nature of legal protection achieved, the implementation and effect of such laws and policies, the conflict over sexual orientation in public schools, and the nature of the opposition movement.

As we note in the first chapter, the struggle over gay rights offers instructive insights about the politics of identity, the process of policy innovation, and the role of law in fostering social change. What have we learned about gay rights using these themes, and conversely, how might the findings of this study encourage us to think differently about American politics?

Identity Politics

When his fellow justices voted 6 to 3 to negate Colorado's ban on gay rights protection, Supreme Court Justice Antonin Scalia began his angry dissent with the declaration, "The Court has mistaken a *Kulturkampf* for a fit of spite."[1] With these words, Scalia gave official recognition to the "culture war" thesis that has been a staple of conservative political commentary for a decade or more.[2] According to this perspective, contemporary political battles represent fundamental differences over core American values. Unlike more typical debates, which stem from divergent political interests, cultural conflicts touch on deeply held worldviews about the nature of humankind and the source of moral authority in human society.[3]

In our view, the struggle over gay rights represents another frontier in the realm of identity politics. As we describe it in Chapter 1, this style of politics differs from more conventional conflicts in three ways: identity politics is rooted in new lines of political cleavage, aims to achieve a broad set of goals, and incorporates a wide variety of political strategies. In our investigation of local conflicts over gay rights ordinances and policies, we found all three characteristics in abundance.

The struggle over gay rights clearly represents a new dimension in local politics, a debate that centers on the fundamental question of who we are as a people, a community, a nation.[4] As is typical of identity politics, the issue brought new groups into the political arena and encouraged people to define their political interests in new ways. For gays and lesbians, organizing to secure legal protection is a way, among other things, of declaring that sexual orientation is a legitimate basis of social identity. As the lesbian activist Urvashi Vaid has asserted, "the gay rights movement has long strived to define gayness as an identity at once rooted in, but more significant than, our sexual behavior alone."[5] If sexual orientation is what makes gays a group or community in the eyes of the heterosexual world, then sexual orientation is precisely what gays must defend with legal means.

Many gays do not see the struggle for legal protection as an assertion of gay pride but rather as a defensive posture imposed upon them by the hostility of the straight world. Many opponents of gay rights clearly do not understand this aspect of the conflict, the almost reluctant decision by gays to organize politically on the basis of sexual orientation. Believing that antigay discrimination is trivial or nonexistent, they therefore deny the political relevance of sexual identity. We recall in this context our interview with a Republican leader in Cincinnati. He seemed genuinely bewildered, almost sorrowful, that gays would choose to bring controversy upon themselves when they could avoid all the fuss simply by keeping quiet about "private" preferences that were nobody else's business. What this perspective misses, according to gays and their allies, is that sexual orientation is inescapably "public" because it carries with it a whole package of social stereotypes that have been used to justify discrimination and ill treatment. Telling gays to keep their sexuality in the closet, which seems eminently reasonable to many heterosexuals, effectively forces gays to deny who they are in public. Unless these issues are addressed by a mobilized constituency, gay advocates contend, the abuse of gays and lesbians will continue or even intensify.

Because identity politics stimulates new groups to enter the political process, we were not surprised to find that many opponents of gay rights reported that they too were somewhat reluctantly dragged into the fight against local legislation. Many indicated that they had not previously taken a public stand on local issues but felt themselves compelled to do so because of the moral dimension of the gay rights issue.[6] This strong opposition was precisely what many professional educators feared, and it helps to explain why so many school districts have avoided the whole topic of sexual orientation. As we show in Chapter 6, the religious opponents saw the local legislation as threatening something they held dear. Accordingly, many people who had not previously seen any political relevance to their religious identities or sexual orientation later discovered that the defense of those qualities made it necessary to enter the political arena. They found themselves testifying at public hearings, writing letters to the editor, leafletting in neighborhoods and on street corners, holding prayer vigils at public meetings—all as self-described representatives of morality, decency, and the traditional family. That same impulse has produced sporadic political mobilization against abortion, "indecent" school reading materials, the Equal Rights Amendment, and similar morality issues. Such behavior is still less common in urban politics, however, than that associated with neighborhood, income, or employment interests.

Participants in conflicts over social identity also tend to have a broad set of goals. Identity-based political movements typically seek both tangible objectives involving the well-being of a constituency and more general goals pertaining to social respect. We found that to be true of the gay rights coalition. In the communities we studied, the usual impetus behind gay rights legislation was a sense of tangible grievance involving antigay discrimination. The passage of ordinances often followed public hearings at which gays reported in some detail about incidents of gay bashing, verbal harassment, the denial of housing, and threats to employment security.[7] Even if they were primarily aimed at combating such treatment, the campaigns often broadened into more general efforts to acquire social respect. By classifying gays as a minority entitled to legal protection, gay advocates hoped, the legislation would help lessen the stigma associated with homosexuality. Such laws might also build a climate of tolerance that was open and affirming to gays and lesbians, making them full citizens of their communities. In the eyes of many government officials and gay activists whom we interviewed, the hope was realized—in part. The passage of ordinances, especially where implementation was taken seriously, did seem to send a signal that was taken to heart by many who were otherwise disposed to sanction antigay feelings and behavior.

This larger aspect of the conflict was not lost on gay rights opponents. The movement for gay rights often excited an intense, even feverish, reaction "as if every act of homosexual sex were an act of terrorism against heterosexuality."[8] In the campaign against local legislation, the specifics of the proposals at issue were often lost or overlooked in much broader crusades to "save our children" or "take back our community" or "defend marriage and the family." These slogans may resonate with the broader public because many citizens also see the conflict as much more than a civil rights issue. The critics of gay rights asserted that gays wanted to go beyond formal legal protection, saying, in effect, "I demand that you acknowledge my sexual choices as the exact equivalent of yours."[9] In doing so, it was argued by the opponents, the gay rights movement was challenging American culture.[10] To critics, asserting the moral equivalence of heterosexual and homosexual relationships both undermined the religious basis of the law and threatened the entire system of traditional sex roles and patriarchy in American society. If gays saw antidiscrimination laws as a way to promote their full integration into American life, many religious traditionalists perceived the same laws as impugning their legitimacy by rejecting the social values that sustained their worldview.[11] The opponents, no less than the supporters, saw much higher stakes than protection from discrimination.

We are tempted to describe this aspect of identity politics—the broadening of goals to encompass things like social respect—as "symbolic." After all, both sides argued that the conflict over gay rights transcended mere tangible interests, touching instead on such abstract values as tolerance, citizenship, culture, and morality. Depending on which side was speaking, the battle for gay rights was either a struggle by a beleaguered minority to obtain the rights of full citizenship or a determined effort to confer legitimacy upon a perverse lifestyle. Unfortunately, as we have learned from previous efforts to use this terminology, some readers will insist on inserting the modifier *only* before the word *symbolic*, as if symbols were luxuries, abstractions that do not matter much. If gay rights legislation is *only* symbolic, one might conclude, then it is hardly worth the effort and controversy to pass it.

Those who would dismiss symbolic concerns as inconsequential need to be reminded that people are often willing to fight and die for symbols. Shooting wars are fought in the name of symbols—democracy, for example—and fought by soldiers who willingly risk life and limb to defend the flag, which is *only* a symbol of the nation it represents. By calling gay rights legislation symbolic, we most emphatically do not intend to diminish either its impact or its significance. Rather, the label acknowledges that such legislation has both narrow and broad ends, not all of which are tangible. The controversy is no less real or significant because of that.

The final characteristic of identity politics is the use of diverse tactics and strategies. The proponents and opponents of gay rights in our five communities did not shrink from using conventional political strategies—influencing election outcomes by endorsing candidates, providing financial contributions and free labor, lobbying public officials, and building coalitions with supportive groups. Nor did they refrain from what have been called "outsider" tactics—holding large public demonstrations, packing public hearings, threatening boycotts, sponsoring prayer vigils, spreading the word via radio talk shows, and the like.

These findings have a two-fold implication. Identity-based politics have long been the academic province of sociologists who tend to focus primarily on movements using social protest and unconventional methods to achieve change. Political scientists, more interested in conventional political processes such as elections and lobbying, have generally looked elsewhere for theoretical guidance. We hope this book will encourage sociologists and political scientists to learn from one another. A full appreciation of the gay rights movement requires paying attention both to its character as a social movement, the aspect that sociologists have studied, and to its explicitly political dimension—the quest for protective legislation. Within the discipline of political science, studies of this type of social movement show that identity politics and cultural theory are valuable theoretical tools for understanding contemporary political movements.

Models of Policy Innovation

Throughout this book, we analyze local gay rights movements through the lenses of four different models of policy innovation. Each of these perspectives—urbanism/social diversity, political opportunity structure, resource mobilization, communal protest—identifies social forces that encourage or inhibit the adoption of new public policies. These four frameworks are not mutually exclusive, and all seem to contribute substantially to our understanding of the complex process by which gay rights legislation is promoted, adopted, and resisted. In Chapter 3 we use the four perspectives to account for the adoption of gay rights legislation, distinguishing between the communities with legal protected status based on sexual orientation and those without such policies. Chapter 4 contains an exploration of the relevance of these models to different enforcement practices among the communities with ordinances or policies. When we look at school district policies concerning sexual orientation in Chapter 5, we once again find the perspectives useful in accounting for variations in the level of effort across communities. Finally, in Chapter 6 we discuss the opposition to gay rights largely in the framework of one of the four perspectives, the communal protest model.

At one level, we can say that all four models of policy innovation have proved useful in explaining some of the patterns we observed. The enactment of municipal laws and policies, their enforcement, and the parallel practices of local school districts all depended in greater or lesser degree upon community size and social diversity, a favorable political opportunity structure, the organizational and political resources commanded by the gay and lesbian community, and the balance of progressive and traditional religious groups. Generally speaking, the extent of gay rights protection increased (a) the larger and more diverse the community, (b) the greater the presence of supportive groups, (c) the better organized the local gay and lesbian community, and (d) the smaller the proportion of religious traditionalists. Not all the political patterns we observed fit this pattern, but most did.

Although our research techniques do not permit us to say so with certainty, we believe that the four major forces associated with various theories of policy innovation work together in a particular sequence. It is widely accepted that social movements such as the gay rights campaign require a degree of common identity among participants that grows out of a palpable sense of grievance. If the grievances of gays and lesbians are relatively constant from one place to another, the ability to develop a common social identity probably depends on the immediate social environment. For reasons we have already discussed, the most promising conditions for the development of a politicized gay identity (which we measure by indicators of resource mobilization) occur in large cities and college communities. Our measures of urbanism/diversity and political opportunity structure capture precisely these types of environments. The environments that promote political mobilization among gays and lesbians probably inhibit the development of a parallel social movement among religious traditionalists, the most likely opponents of gay rights legislation according to communal protest theory. Conversely, the types of communities that incubate religious traditionalism—smaller population centers that are not dominated by institutions of higher learning—also prove much less hospitable to the generation of a strong political identity among gays and lesbians. These generalizations are plausible conclusions that explain most of our findings, not iron laws that perform with absolute regularity.

How do these findings compare to the conventional wisdom of political science? We found a pair of anomalies, one fairly narrow and one quite broad. As mentioned above, the urbanism/social diversity perspective has identified demography as an important influence on public policy. Cities offer the anonymity, freedom, and social diversity that encourage the development of gay enclaves and ultimately facilitate the emergence of gay political organizations and activity. An important component of this model, the percentage of African Americans, has usually correlated with a high level of government spending and active efforts to combat discrimination. The pattern is explained by the propensity of the black community to regard government as an important ally and to believe that it should take the lead in protecting minorities against discrimination. In the case of gay rights, as in other questions of social morality, like abortion, the pattern is decidedly different. In our national survey of communities, the presence of African Americans did not correlate—positively or negatively—with adoption of gay rights policies or active efforts by school districts to provide education about sexual orientation and service to gays and lesbians.[12] The case studies showed African Americans to be ambivalent toward the prospect of gay rights policies. The strong belief in law as a means to combat discrimination was seemingly counterbalanced both by concern about possible competition with newly empowered gays and a strong vein of social conservatism. Sometimes the former impulse ruled, as when black officials in Philadelphia helped to pass protective legislation, but blacks were sometimes indifferent or, as in Cincinnati, the core element of the opposition coalition. Thus the findings suggest we need to qualify our assertions about the political tendencies of African Americans, depending on the policy area under study.

What also strikes us about these patterns is how much politics matters. This seemingly obvious conclusion stands in stark contrast to the conventional wisdom that still reigns among many students of public policy. When scholars first began systematic analysis of policy differences across cities and states, they often found that economics, not politics, was the key. The level of public services—measured by spending, taxation, employment, and innovation—was primarily determined by the economic resources and social traits of the population. As a rule, richer communities and states spent more per person, taxed at higher rates, employed more workers proportionately, and embraced new policies more quickly than less affluent jurisdictions. The things that political scientists study—political parties, elections, interest groups—did not seem to matter very much once economic and demographic differences were taken into account.[13]

This orthodoxy has come under attack as scholars have examined a wider array of policies with more sophisticated research methods. Economic resources and social composition matter but so do the local political culture and various aspects of the political system.[14] In line with these findings, we detected powerful political influences on the progress of gay rights in local communities. For most aspects of gay rights, the political opportunity structure was an important determinant. Gay rights movements were most likely to succeed where they could draw on the support of powerful allies—particularly college students (and, more recently, high school students for school programs)—local traditions of progressive politics (sympathetic elites), and accessible government agencies and infrastructures.

Passage of the policies—both city or county and school—followed a three-step process that included important political opportunity components. First, supporters documented a history of systematic discrimination to convince political elites and the public of the need for legal protection. Second, a reservoir of citizen support was reinforced through discussing needs in terms of justice ("discrimination is wrong") and safety issues, increasing the visibility of gay men and lesbians so more people personally knew someone with a homosexual orientation, and then capitalizing on public support for equal opportunity for all citizens. Third, the gay rights movement was compared to social movements in behalf of other minorities, especially African Americans, that are based on justice ("all Americans are guaranteed basic rights") as a moral principle, thereby also engaging supportive allies. Thus, extending civil rights statutes—taking advantage of existing political structures already in place—was the strategy used most frequently. In addition, the media often played a decisive role in creating a supportive environment for policy innovation through its role in educating the public about the need for a law and how to access systems for its enforcement. In contrast, when conservatives mobilized to fight enactment of a gay rights policy, they successfully deployed the negative attitudes of the public against homosexuality to convince political elites that support for gays and lesbians was lacking or that discrimination did not exist.

The geographical concentration and organizational strength of the gay community—known as the resource mobilization model—were extremely important as well for many kinds of sexual orientation policies. In Philadelphia and Cincinnati, for example, lesbians and gay men mobilized to help elect city officials who were supportive of gay rights legislation. Dynamic and skilled gay officials and leaders, such as Rita Addessa (Philadelphia) and John

Laird (Santa Cruz), proved instrumental in political organizing and lobbying on behalf of gay interests. As the case studies of school districts demonstrated with particular clarity, an energized gay leadership substantially increased the prospect that the educational establishment would address sexual orientation and the specific needs of gay and lesbian students. These findings suggest that gay rights policies in local governments and school districts do not just happen but are the result of political mobilization by policy entrepreneurs. These mobilized supporters worked to establish or utilize political institutions and actors open to innovation—the political opportunity structure—to affect how the gay rights law or policy was implemented. Our case studies showed that human rights commissions and equity offices, infrastructures dedicated to justice and equal opportunity, were best able to institute and enforce the policy, both in the cities and in schools.

By the same token, the path to gay rights laws and policies can be blocked by a determined constituency. This was most likely to happen where religious groups with socially traditionalist views were most heavily concentrated. Such concentration provided an organizational basis for mobilizing opposition in the name of "pro-family" values. This, too, is a profoundly political phenomenon. Economics and demography may set the broad outlines of public policy toward gays and lesbians, but the possibilities are realized or forestalled by the disposition of local political forces.

Reconsidering Law as an Instrument of Social Change

Antigay feelings in the United States are pervasive and deep-seated. According to the gay author Bruce Bawer, "there is no other prejudice in which people feel more morally justified; no other prejudice that reaches so high into the ranks of the intelligent, the powerful, the otherwise quite virtuous." Bawer quotes Peter Gomes, a Harvard professor, who says that homophobia is "the last respectable prejudice of the century." [15] Much of the debate surrounding gay rights legislation focuses on whether public laws and policies are able to change such entrenched societal patterns and beliefs. Citing earlier civil rights laws as precedents, gay rights advocates contend that all but the most virulently racist southerners changed their attitudes toward African Americans because of federal legislation and that antigay attitudes can be similarly altered. Opponents of this view argue that antidiscrimination legislation covering sexual orientation is simply unacceptable to many citizens, and even when adopted it is too limited in nature, scope, and enforcement to affect deep-seated beliefs.

We have found that gay rights measures are often helpful in altering behavior, attitudes, and institutions and thereby influencing social change. In a society in which law is valued and typically adhered to, civil rights legislation protecting gays has been one of the major goals of the post-Stonewall gay movement. Lesbians and gay men viewed such legislation as an important step toward reducing blatant forms of discrimination and achieving first-class citizenship. By likening their status to that of African Americans before the civil rights movement, gays successfully portrayed themselves as an oppressed minority deserving of legal protection by the state. The analogy to discrimination against blacks and civil rights proved to be politically astute. Although most Americans question the morality of homosexuality, they also believe that many gays face discrimination not unlike that confronted by African Americans and other minorities, and they think that prejudicial treatment is wrong. As a result, despite continuing antipathy to homosexual behavior, there is broad and growing public support for basic civil rights protections for gays and lesbians.

The civil rights analogy, moreover, enabled gay rights advocates to amend local, already-established civil rights laws rather than create new legislation. This incremental step was easier to achieve politically and stamped gays with the official imprimatur of minority status. By mid-1996, such protection had spread to approximately 159 communities and 17 states. According to the National Gay and Lesbian Task Force, these figures include 36 cities and counties that have adopted protections since May 1993, and thus the high rate of adoptions of the early 1990s has continued. Following the trend also apparent in the first years of the 1990s, gay rights measures have been spreading to places where political support is least apparent, such as the South, the Midwest, and smaller communities.[16]

Once enacted, these civil rights measures have had a decided effect in many communities. Evidence for this is abundant in both our nationwide survey and our case studies, as pointed out in Chapter 4. Most important, gay rights legislation has reduced discrimination based on sexual orientation. This is especially the case in employment, the most commonly covered institution. In the words of a high-level Philadelphia official, "It [the law] prevents gays from being openly harassed in the workplace and in public accommodations. They have a place to come for support and redress." In this sense, civil rights laws "define what is right and proper," and to the extent that such laws are obeyed, they change the behavior and ultimately the attitudes of those who discriminate.[17]

Perhaps of equal importance is our finding that protective legislation has enabled many lesbians and gay men to feel more safe and secure in general, and therefore more willing to come out. If the closet is a characteristic form of gay oppression, then allowing gays to stop hiding their sexual identity is a powerful form of liberation.[18] Moreover, as more Americans have come to know someone who is openly lesbian or gay, they have generally become more accepting of homosexuals. In addition, the adoption of gay rights legislation has often increased the political mobilization of gays and lesbians and prompted greater acceptance of other public policies supportive of homosexuals, such as domestic partner benefits, gay pride celebrations, and AIDS programs. For example, the number of cities and counties with some form of domestic partner benefits has more than doubled since 1993, totaling approximately forty-nine in April 1996.[19] At least thirty-seven (76 percent) of these communities with benefits for homosexual employees had previously adopted gay rights legislation.

The process of incorporation of sexual orientation into civil rights codes often provided important educational and symbolic functions as well. Although difficult to measure, these intangible effects are nonetheless significant. "Political acts," as Murray Edelman states, "are both instrumental and expressive."[20] The expressive, more abstract aspects of law are often overlooked, yet in the long run they are crucial in understanding the full impact of legislation. For example, public hearings and media attention surrounding the debate over gay rights created a greater awareness generally of the persecution that many gays face. Furthermore, actual adoption of legal sanctions protecting lesbians and gay men signaled that discrimination on the basis of sexual orientation was morally wrong and that government would play a role in redressing these wrongs. The passage of legislation, in this sense, increased the legitimacy and status of gays, a psychological and symbolic benefit of immense value.

Still, the ultimate success of law "is seen when its goals become institutionalized, that is, they are incorporated within the norms and activities of the institution."[21] We have seen that gay rights legislation and the gay movement generally have affected even the most resistant institutions. The business world, where many entrepreneurs originally opposed civil rights for gays, has shown increased acceptance of antidiscrimination policies, domestic partner benefits, employee associations, and other programs deemed helpful to gays. Public schools, often the scene of intense conflict over issues related to sexual orientation, have also begun to change. Education about sexual orientation and school support services for lesbian and gay youth are more likely to be offered in communities with protective legislation and an active gay constituency. Even the local police, traditionally one of the most virulently antigay organizations, have generally become not only less abusive but also more sensitive to the needs of gays. Although these organizations have only recently begun to shift priorities regarding lesbians and gays, such institutional changes are a vivid indicator of the extent of the cultural transformation that is taking place.

Clearly, civil rights law inclusive of sexual orientation has had a decided effect on attitudes and institutions in many communities. This legalistic approach, however, does have limitations. Gay rights legislation is rarely easy to enact or maintain; most cities and counties in the United States have yet to adopt legislation, and some locales have repealed the measures they previously adopted. The absence of federal law (as well as greater state law) has, of course, always been a liability. Even where local legislation is in place, it is often constrained by its narrow scope, numerous exemptions, or lack of enforcement. In addition, the most important effects of law on society typically take form as a slow, incremental development, a process of gradualism that is not readily noted in many communities.

Despite these limitations, gay rights laws have been a force of social change at the grass roots. As a minister in Cincinnati put it, "It [the law] is a stepping stone on the road to social acceptability of gays." Legislation alone, however, has not been sufficient to create major changes in society. Other political, economic, and social factors have also been instrumental in this complex process. Yet law itself has certainly been an important force in the cultural transformation that is occurring. Such legislation has served to regulate discriminatory behavior as well as articulate a vision of a more egalitarian society. Antigay attitudes and actions have not disappeared by any means, but civil rights codes have helped to grant to lesbians and gay men a degree of safety, legitimacy, and acceptance that they have never known previously.

Future Outlook

It is interesting and important to look at the current status of the lesbian and gay political movement and to speculate on its future. To tap these issues, we asked respondents that we interviewed in our case study communities to mention and explain what they perceived were the most pressing needs in the gay community. Their responses are summarized in Table 7-1.

The most commonly cited need concerned fair treatment and protection from discrimination. Respondents mentioned the need for federal legislation in order to guarantee widespread protection. Without it, lesbians and gay men are faced with the daunting challenge of attempting to gain antidiscrimination policies in every community, workplace, and school district in the country. Several of the other most frequently cited needs were in the area of education. A Cincinnati business representative (who was neither gay or lesbian nor a proponent of Issue 3) neatly summarized the assorted responses to gay and lesbian needs as follows:

We need education—for both gay and non-gay people—about what sexual orientation means. Youth need more support systems for coping—they are isolated . . . and ostracized by family and friends. Youth are very important—that's where attention must be directed! Gays and lesbians need legal protection against discrimination. They should be able to keep their children, live where they choose, spend time where they choose. Finally, we all need to become more sensitive to each other.

TABLE 7-1   CURRENT NEEDS OF GAYS AND LESBIANS (N=65)

Perceived need	Number of respondents	Percentage of respondents
Fair treatment and greater protection from discrimination, harassment	21	32
Support groups, services for gay youth	17	26
Domestic partner benefits, legalized marriage	15	23
More education about sexual orientation	12	18
AIDS education and services	12	18
Greater visibility, more role models, greater willingness to come out	7	11
Don't know, or no needs	8	12

Source: Data are from authors' national survey.

Note: Question asked of survey respondents: "What do you think are the current needs, if any, of gays and lesbians, including youths, in this community?" Needs mentioned by seven or more respondents are listed. Some respondents listed more than one need.

Given the function of schools as one of the most important influences of social norms in American society, it is not surprising that respondents predict the continuation and even intensification of conflict concerning the schools' role in adopting and implementing policies supportive of gays, including education about sexual orientation. As supporters argued in the civil rights movement for African Americans, schools, more so than any other institution, can facilitate the changes in attitudes that proponents for gay rights desire. As we have pointed out, this institutional potential has not been lost on opponents of gay rights. On the national front, advocates of traditional values, headed by Sen. Jesse Helms (R-N.C.), have sponsored bills that seek to withhold federal funds from schools that discuss homosexuality without condemnation.[22] Similarly, recent state initiatives have mostly been efforts to prohibit schools from addressing sexual orientation issues.[23]

Our respondents also mentioned, somewhat less frequently, the need for policies related to domestic partner benefits, encouragement to escape the closet and be more visible, and other legal rights, including same-sex marriage. These policies have been adopted less readily than antidiscrimination protection. Some communities and businesses now recognize domestic partners of homosexual employees and provide at least a few health, pension, or other benefits for them. Indeed this number has increased greatly in the mid-1990s. Still, Hawaii's anticipated recognition of gay marriages prompted passage of a federal Defense of Marriage Act and consideration of similar legislation in thirty-two states. Gay rights legislation may have paved the way for consideration of other policies, but it never was a guarantee that such policies would be endorsed, especially if they were perceived as threatening to the most basic institutions of society.

Local legislation and school programs will continue to grow to the degree that proponents of gay rights mobilize to build support among local citizens and political elites based on principles of justice and equality. The long-term trend is toward greater tolerance of homosexuality and especially for legal safeguards against discrimination based on sexual orientation. The recent Supreme Court decision in the Colorado case favoring gay rights may well encourage greater local efforts by lesbians and gay men to adopt legislation. At the same time, the high court's decision will likely mobilize the opposition as well to more fervent attempts to block such legislation. In regard to schools, programs addressing sexual orientation will depend on student support. Gay and lesbian youths (and gay and lesbian parents) are increasingly coming out while in school, which is putting greater pressure on the educational institution to respond. Moreover, younger cohorts are more likely to support gay and lesbian issues. Recent media coverage, including gay and lesbian characters on popular television programs such as *Ellen, Roseanne,* and *Melrose Place,* has, in the words of a Raleigh business owner, "created greater awareness and understanding," particularly among youth.

Ultimately the debate over extending gay rights and policies focuses on the more basic issue of whose identity warrants legal protection and public recognition. For many citizens in the middle, who want neither to condone discrimination nor to confer group rights, the debate may appear to be a kind of culture war. The outcome of these local conflicts is likely to depend on whether gay rights initiatives are seen to prohibit pernicious discrimination or to confer advantages on unpopular groups.

NOTES

Because of the controversial nature of this study, we promised the persons we interviewed that they would not be identified by name. Unless otherwise noted, all interviews pertaining to Cincinnati took place in Cincinnati in November 1994; all those pertaining to Philadelphia took place in Philadelphia in July 1994; all those pertaining to Raleigh took place either in Raleigh or Chapel Hill, N.C., in May 1994. All quotations and information not otherwise documented are from these interviews.

1. For the full text of the decision in *Romer v. Evans,* see the *Wall Street Journal,* May 20, 1996 (electronic edition at http://interactive2.wsj.com).
2. See James Davison Hunter, *Culture Wars: The Struggle to Define America* (New York: Basic Books, 1991).
3. We do not mean to suggest that this style of politics is altogether new in the United States. Kenneth Meier has identified something very similar in his "morality politics" model of such issues as abortion, regulation of alcohol and drugs, prostitution, and the like. Although we find considerable overlap between morality politics and identity politics, we think that the

identity politics framework fits a broader class of political conflicts. See Kenneth J. Meier, *The Politics of Sin: Drugs, Alcohol, and Public Policy* (Armonk, N.Y.: Sharpe, 1994), and Donald P. Haider-Markel and Kenneth J. Meier, "The Politics of Gay and Lesbian Rights: Expanding the Scope of the Conflict," *Journal of Politics* 58 (May 1996): 332–349.

4. Aaron Wildavsky, "Choosing Preferences by Constructing Institutions: A Cultural Theory of Preference Formation," *American Political Science Review* 81 (March 1987): 3–21.

5. Urvashi Vaid, *Virtual Equality: The Mainstreaming of Gay and Lesbian Liberation* (New York: Doubleday, Anchor, 1995), 192.

6. This conclusion applies to the local, grass-roots leadership of the anti–gay rights crusade, people who were mostly amateurs in the sense that they did not make their living from political mobilizing. If one examines some of the national organizations in the forefront of the antigay movement, it is clear that they have seized on this issue as a powerful recruiting tool.

7. As we noted in the previous chapter, the usual response of gay rights opponents was both to minimize the extent of the discrimination and to justify it as the legitimate exercise of discretion by citizens who had moral objections to homosexuality.

8. Vaid, *Virtual Equality*, 193.

9. William Raspberry, "Gay Ban Issue a Cultural Dilemma?" *Gainesville Sun*, February 6, 1993.

10. Calling this a "homophobic" reaction does not help us much to understand it. Rather, we see this posture as a kind of identity politics pursued by the opponents of gay rights, the flip side of the coin, so to speak.

11. Kenneth D. Wald, Dennis E. Owen, and Samuel S. Hill Jr., "Evangelical Politics and Status Issues," *Journal for the Scientific Study of Religion* 28 (March 1989): 1–16.

12. Even when it did correlate with some aspect of local gay rights protection, the African-American percentage of the population was usually found to disappear when we introduced controls for other variables like city size and income.

13. For a good summary of this topic, see the introduction and concluding essay in *The Determinants of Public Policy*, ed. Thomas R. Dye and Virginia Gray (Lexington, Mass.: Lexington, 1980).

14. Hwang Sung-Don and Virginia Gray, "External Limits and Internal Determinants of State Public Policy," *Western Political Quarterly* 44 (June 1991): 277–298; Charles J. Barrilleaux and Mark E. Miller, "The Political Economy of State Medicaid Policy," *American Political Science Review* 82 (December 1988): 1089–2009.

15. Bruce Bawer, *A Place at the Table: The Gay Individual in American Society* (New York: Simon and Schuster, 1994), 81.

16. National Gay and Lesbian Task Force, "Lesbian, Gay, and Bisexual Civil Rights Laws in the U.S.," report, National Gay and Lesbian Task Force, Washington, D.C., 1996.

17. Harrell R. Rodgers Jr. and Charles S. Bullock III, *Law and Social Change: Civil Rights Laws and Their Consequences* (New York: McGraw-Hill, 1972), 204.

18. See Andrew Koppelman, *Antidiscrimination Law and Social Equality* (New Haven: Yale University Press, 1996), 149–150.

19. National Gay and Lesbian Task Force, *A Sampling of Domestic Partner Benefits* (Washington, D.C.: National Gay and Lesbian Task Force, 1996).

20. Murray Edelman, *The Symbolic Uses of Politics* (Urbana: University of Illinois Press, 1967), 12; Edelman paraphrases the sociologist Ulf Himmelstrand here.

21. Frederick M. Wirt, *"I Ain't What I Was": Civil Rights in the New South* (Durham, N.C.: Duke University Press, forthcoming), chap. 10.

22. People for the American Way, *Hostile Climate: A State by State Report on Anti-Gay Activity, 1994* (Washington, D.C.: People for the American Way, 1994), 11.

23. National Gay and Lesbian Task Force, *Beyond the Beltway: State of the States 1995* (Washington, D.C.: National Gay and Lesbian Task Force, 1996).

APPENDIX

Survey Methodology

W e began our survey by consulting *Lesbian and Gay Civil Rights in the U.S.*, a comprehensive list of counties and cities with gay rights laws or policies. The list is compiled annually by the National Gay and Lesbian Task Force from newspaper accounts and activist reports. The 1993 edition of this publication identified 98 cities and 25 counties that provided some form of legal protection to gay men and lesbians. To validate this list, we asked officials of those cities and counties to list other, nearby jurisdictions that they believed had gay rights laws. Of the 63 localities identified by this snowball technique, all but 8 appeared on the list compiled by the task force, and those additional communities were duly included in our survey. Officials of 5 cities and 1 county on the task force's list reported that their communities did *not* have such an ordinance or policy in effect. Some of those communities, like Houston, had repealed ordinances, whereas others had discussed such legislation but had not actually adopted it. These communities were removed from the sample of ordinance localities, leaving 126 valid cases (101 cities and 25 counties). The population of most of the additional communities discovered by referral is under 50,000, suggesting a possible underrepresentation of small cities.

To examine gay rights legislation in these communities, we first needed to determine the appropriate public official to receive our mail questionnaire. An initial telephone inquiry of the city or county clerk was essential to acquire the name of the enforcement agency for the ordinance. If there was no enforcement organization, we asked the clerk to provide the name of the local official who was perceived to be most knowledgeable about the ordinance or policy and its effect. Thus we surveyed either the director of the enforcement agency or the public official judged to be knowledgeable about this local legislation.[1]

We compiled the list of school district officials within these 126 cities and counties in a similar manner. We telephoned each city or county school district office to obtain the name of the official in charge of health education or health services. In those cities and counties with more than one school district, we surveyed up to five districts. In cases in which there were more than five school districts in a community, we chose five at random. The total number of surveys mailed to school districts was 170.

Using Dillman's Total Design Method, we mailed our questionnaires to officials in July 1993.[2] Two follow-up mailings were made to all nonrespondents within the next three weeks. Over the next several months, by virtue of telephone calls urging nonrespondents to complete the survey or actual telephone interviews, we achieved a 100 percent return from city and county officials. Given our methodology and extremely high return rate, we are confident that this sample represents the vast majority of U.S. communities that included gays and lesbians in their antidiscrimination legislation as of mid-1993. Using a similar strategy in our survey of school districts, we received 123 returns, a response rate of 72 percent. Some communities with multiple districts had more than one response, and only 17 cities or counties produced no school district response. Thus, we received at least one district response from 81 percent, or 102, of these communities.

The comparison sample of communities without legal protection based on sexual orientation was randomly selected from the database of cities (7,175) and counties (3,034) maintained by the International City-County Management Association. We drew a sample of 177 cities and counties, matching the distribution of our ordinance sample. Forty localities in the comparison sample proved ineligible because they were too small, had an ordinance or policy, or were duplicates. These communities were removed, leaving 137. Brief questionnaires were sent to the clerks of the eligible communities in the summer of 1994. Following essentially the same strategy we used for the ordinance sample, we achieved a 91 percent response rate, obtaining information from 125 communities, which comprised 100 cities and 25 counties.[3] The same method was employed to obtain a list of school officials from this comparison sample of 125 communities without ordinances. A total of 121 of these school districts responded, yielding a 94 percent response rate.[4]

A listing of cities and counties with antidiscrimination ordinances or policies inclusive of sexual orientation as of mid-1993 follows:

CITIES

Albany, N.Y.	Baltimore, Md.
Alexandria, Va..	Berkeley, Calif.
Alfred, N.Y.	Birmingham, Mich.
Ames, Iowa	Boston, Mass.
Amherst, Mass.	Boulder, Colo.
Anchorage, Alaska	Brighton, N.Y..
Ann Arbor, Mich.	Brisbane, Calif.
Aspen, Colo.	Burlington, Vt.
Atlanta, Ga.	Cambridge, Mass.
Austin, Texas	Cathedral City, Calif.

Champaign, Ill.
Chapel Hill, N.C.
Chicago, Ill.
Cincinnati, Ohio
Columbus, Ohio
Corvallis, Ore.
Crested Butte, Colo.
Cupertino, Calif.
Daly City, Calif.
Davis, Calif.
Denver, Colo.
Detroit, Mich.
Durham, N.C.
East Hampton, N.Y.
East Lansing, Mich.
Evanston, Ill.
Flint, Mich.
Harrisburg, Pa.
Hartford, Conn.
Hayward, Calif.
Honolulu, Hawaii
Iowa City, Iowa
Ithaca, N.Y.
Kansas City, Mo.
Key West, Fla.
Laguna Beach, Calif.
Lancaster, Pa.
Long Beach, Calif.
Los Angeles, Calif.
Madison, Wis.
Malden, Mass.
Miami Beach, Fla.
Milwaukee, Wis.
Minneapolis, Minn.
Mountain View, Calif.
New Haven, Conn.
New Orleans, La.
New York, N.Y.
Oak Park, Ill.
Oakland, Calif.
Olympia, Wash.
Pacifica, Calif.

Palo Alto, Calif.
Pasadena, Calif.
Philadelphia, Pa.
Phoenix, Ariz.
Pittsburgh, Pa.
Portland, Me.
Portland, Ore.
Pullman, Wash.
Raleigh, N.C.
Riverside, Calif.
Rochester, N.Y.
Rockville, Md.
Sacramento, Calif.
Saginaw, Mich.
San Diego, Calif.
San Francisco, Calif.
San Jose, Calif.
Santa Barbara, Calif.
Santa Cruz, Calif.
Santa Monica, Calif.
Seattle, Wash.
St. Louis, Mo.
St. Paul, Minn.
Stamford, Conn.
State College, Pa.
Syracuse, N.Y.
Tampa, Fla.
Telluride, Colo.
Troy, N.Y.
Tucson, Ariz.
Tumwater, Wash.
Urbana, Ill.
Washington, D.C.
Watertown, N.Y.
West Hollywood, Calif.
West Palm Beach, Fla.
Worcester, Mass.
Yellow Springs, Ohio
York, Pa.

COUNTIES

Alachua County, Fla.

Alameda County, Calif.

Arlington County, Va.

Boulder County, Colo.

Clallam County, Wash.

Cook County, Ill.

Cuyahoga County, Ohio

Dane County, Wis.

Essex County, N.J.

Hennepin County, Minn.

Hillsborough County, Fla.

Howard County, Md.

Ingham County, Mich.

King County, Wash.

Minnehaha County, S.D.

Montgomery County, Md.

Northampton County, Pa.

Palm Beach County, Fla.

Prince George's County, Md.

Salt Lake County, Utah

San Mateo County, Calif.

Santa Barbara County, Calif.

Santa Cruz County, Calif.

Suffolk County, N.Y.

Tompkins County, N.Y.

NOTES

1. The information about each community was provided by an official in the human rights or human relations organization (38 communities), an official in personnel or a related department (55 communities), or an official with general authority, such as a city or county clerk, manager, or city attorney (33 communities).
2. Donald Dillman, *Mail and Telephone Surveys: The Total Design Method* (New York: Wiley, 1978).
3. Kenneth D. Wald, James Button, and Barbara A. Rienzo, "The Politics of Gay Rights in American Communities: Explaining Antidiscrimination Ordinances and Policies," *American Journal of Political Science* 40 (November 1996), app.
4. Our survey data are available through the Inter-University Consortium for Political and Social Research at the University of Michigan, Ann Arbor.

Index

ABOUT THE AUTHORS

James W. Button, Barbara A.
Rienzo, and Kenneth D. Wald

James W. Button (Ph.D., University of Texas) is professor of political science at the University of Florida, Gainesville. He has written widely on minority group and urban politics, and the processes of social change. Professor Button is the author of *Black Violence: Political Impact of the 1960s Riots* (1978). His book *Blacks and Social Change: The Impact of the Civil Rights Movement in Southern Communities* (1989) won the V.O. Key Book Award.

Barbara A. Rienzo (Ph.D., Southern Illinois University) is professor of health science education at the University of Florida, Gainesville. She has published numerous scholarly articles and book chapters and has consulted extensively on human sexuality education and implementation of school health programs. She is the coauthor with Roberta Ogletree, Joyce Fetro, and Judy Drolet of *Sexuality Education Curricula: The Consumer's Guide* (1994).

Kenneth D. Wald (Ph.D., Washington University in St. Louis) is professor of political science at the University of Florida, Gainesville. Professor Wald has written extensively about religion and politics. He is the author of *Religion and Politics in the United States*, Third Edition (CQ Press, 1997), *Crosses on the Ballot: Patterns of British Voter Alignment Since 1885* (1983), and numerous book chapters and scholarly articles. Wald has been a Fulbright senior lecturer and the recipient of research grants from the National Science Foundation and the National Endowment for the Humanities.